Business Leases: Termination and Renewal

Fourmat Publishing

Business Leases: Termination and Renewal
by Michael Haley, LL.M., Solicitor,
Lecturer at the University of Keele

London
Fourmat Publishing
1991

ISBN 1 85190 136 1

First published 1991

All rights reserved

© 1991 Michael Haley
Published by Fourmat Publishing, 133 Upper Street, London N1 1QP

Printed and bound in Great Britain by
Billing & Sons Ltd, Worcester

This book is dedicated
with much love to
Margaret, Stephanie and Julian Halliwell

Preface

Over the current century the law of landlord and tenant has developed haphazardly by virtue of a vast number of judicial decisions and fragmentary statutory intervention. Seemingly like Topsy, it keeps growing and growing. It is no surprise, therefore, that lawyers can feel overwhelmed by the extent and the ever-increasing complexity of the subject.

This book is concerned only with the law as it affects business tenancies. Part II Landlord and Tenant Act 1954 is of central importance in this analysis. The Act gives a business tenant security of tenure in offering the general rights to remain in occupation, following on from the original lease, and to obtain a new lease. Meanwhile, the landlord is entitled to a market rental income and, in certain prescribed circumstances, can override the tenant's claim for possession. The tenant who fails to obtain a new tenancy may be able to claim compensation for disturbance. Compensation for improvements, on quitting the premises, is available under Part I Landlord and Tenant Act 1927.

Albeit of a highly technical nature, the 1954 Act attempts to strike a balance between the interests of both parties and to offer some equality of bargaining strength. This it appears to have achieved. Diplock LJ paid tribute to the way the Act "... integrated into the familiar legal concepts about leasehold interest the policy of Parliament" (*Scholl Manufacturing Co* v *Clifton* (1967)). Apart from a number of amendments made by the Law of Property Act 1969, the statute remains largely unchanged. Unlike other areas of landlord and tenant law, the regulation of business tenancies has proved immune to shifts of policy and maintained a stability that is to be welcomed.

Although the Act will remain in force for the foreseeable future, there is, however, still room for reform. Such was made clear in the Law Commission's Working Paper No 111 (1988) on Part II Landlord and Tenant Act 1954. The major criticisms levied against the existing statutory structure are discussed within the present text. A Law Commission Report is expected during 1992, but its recommendations are likely to relate only to matters of detail and technicality. The basic operation and structure will, without doubt, remain extant and no major reform is envisaged.

My primary aim in writing this book is to provide a clear, accessible and practical guide to the workings of the 1954 Act, as it applies to commercial leases, and to offer a detailed and up-to-date analysis of the relevant case law. Although principally aimed at the practitioner, it is hoped that the book will have some value for those who teach and study commercial conveyancing.

I am grateful to Irene Kaplan of Fourmat Publishing for her courtesy and efficiency and for allowing this author the rare opportunity to write a modern text on a statute that is over thirty-six years old. I am also indebted to Fourmat for the use of the variety of precedent law forms which are reproduced in Appendix B.

My thanks extend to Karen Harrison for again typing a manuscript on my behalf, and to my friends and colleagues Margaret Halliwell and Jan Bell for their encouragement and support.

The law is stated as at 1 June 1991 and any errors, omissions and failings are my own responsibility.

Michael Haley
University of Keele
1 August 1991

Contents

		page
Chapter 1:	**Statutory intervention**	1
	1. The Landlord and Tenant Act 1927	2
	2. The momentum continued	3
	3. The Landlord and Tenant Act 1954	4
	4. The Law of Property Act 1969	5
	5. The present position	6
	6. Prospective reform	7
Chapter 2:	**Security of tenure: the statutory framework**	9
	1. The 1954 Act in operation	10
	2. Interplay of statutory provisions	12
	3. Landlords immediate and competent	14
	4. Information gathering	17
	5. Sub-tenancies: some complex issues	18
	6. Notices and their service	20
	7. Partnerships and joint tenancies	22
	8. The Crown and government departments	23
	9. Public interest and national security	24
	10. Contracting out: special provisions	27
	11. Ecclesiastical property	28
Chapter 3:	**Tenancies within the Act**	30
	1. Lease or licence	30
	2. Occupation of premises	35
	3. For the purposes of a business	39
	4. Excluded tenancies	44
	5. Contracting out: general provisions	49

Chapter 4:	**Continuation and termination**	55
	1. Contractual ties and the continuation tenancy	55
	2. Termination by the tenant	57
	3. Termination by the landlord	59
	4. Termination by agreement	61
Chapter 5:	**The landlord's statutory notice**	63
	1. The server	63
	2. Person to be served	64
	3. Timing of service	65
	4. Form and content	65
	5. Defects and omissions	68
	6. Split reversions	71
	7. Tenant's counternotice	73
Chapter 6:	**The tenant's initiative**	76
	1. The "pre-emptive strike"	76
	2. Availability of the right	78
	3. Form and content	79
	4. Effect of the request	80
	5. Landlord's response	81
	6. The need to go to court	82
	7. Jurisdiction and some procedural matters	82
	8. Statutory time limits	87
	9. Withdrawal of application	89
Chapter 7:	**The interim rent**	91
	1. Application for an interim rent	92
	2. Commencement and quantum	94
Chapter 8:	**Grounds of opposition**	98
	Ground A: Breach of repair	99
	Ground B: Rent arrears	99
	Ground C: Breaches of other obligations	100
	Ground D: Alternative accommodation	102
	Ground E: Uneconomic subletting	103
	Ground F: Demolition and reconstruction	104
	Ground G: Own occupation	113

Chapter 9:	**Rejection of the tenant's application**		119
	1. Final disposal (s 64)		120
	2. Compensation for disturbance		121
	3. Special provisions		123
	4. Amount of compensation		124
	5. The higher rate valuation		126
	6. Contracting out		128
	7. Misrepresentation		129
Chapter 10:	**The new lease**		131
	1. Property		132
	2. Duration		133
	3. Rent		137
	4. Other terms		141
Chapter 11:	**Compensation for tenant's improvements**		144
	Stage 1: Tenancies within the Act		146
	1. Premises		147
	2. Lease		148
	3. Exclusions		148
	4. Used wholly or partly for a trade or business		150
	5. Comparison with the 1954 Act		151
	Stage 2: What is an improvement?		152
	1. Qualifying conditions		154
	Stage 3: Procedures for obtaining compensation		156
	1. Preliminary notice of intention		157
	2. Landlord's objection		158
	3. Application to the court		159
	4. Certificate of execution		160
	5. Claiming compensation		161
	6. Time limits		162
	7. Quantum		163
	8. Reclaiming compensation from a superior landlord		164
	9. Landlord's tactics		165
	10. Recommendations for abolition		166
Appendix A:	Statutory sources		171
Appendix B:	Forms		213
Index			233

Table of cases

page

AG Securities v Vaughan [1990] 1 AC 417, [1988] 3 All ER 1058,
[1988] 3 WLR 1205 .... 32, 34
Abernethie v A M & J Kleiman [1970] 1 QB 10, [1969] 2 All ER 790,
[1969] 2 WLR 1364 .... 39, 40
Accountancy Personnel Ltd v Worshipful Company of Salters
(1972) 116 SJ 240 119
Adams v JR Glibbery & Sons Ltd (1991) CAT 22 January ... 107, 114
Adams v Green (1978) 247 EG 49 .... 135, 142
Addiscombe Garden Estates Ltd v Crabbe [1958] 1 QB 513, [1957]
3 All ER 563, [1957] 3 WLR 980 40
Ahern (PF) & Sons Ltd v Hunt (1988) 21 EG 69 .... 107, 109
Airport Restaurants v Southend-on-Sea Corporation [1960]
2 All ER 888, [1960] 1 WLR 880 74
Albermarle St, No 1, Re [1959] Ch 531, [1959] 1 All ER 250, [1959]
2 WLR 171 133
Aldwych Club Ltd v Copthall Property Co Ltd (1962) 185 EG 219 138
Ali v Knight (1983) 128 SJ 64, (1984) 272 EG 1165 84
Allnatt London Properties Ltd v Newton (1984) 45 P & CR 94,
[1984] 1 All ER 423 53
Amika Motors Ltd v Colebrook Holdings Ltd (1981) 259 EG 243 . 134
Appleton v Abrahamson (1956) 167 EG 633 140
Artemiou v Procopiou [1966] 1 QB 878, [1965] 3 All ER 539,
[1965] 3 WLR 1011 117
Artoc Bank & Trust Ltd v Prudential Assurance Co [1984]
1 WLR 1181, [1984] 3 All ER 538 94
Ashburn Anstalt v Arnold [1989] Ch 1, [1988] 2 All ER 147,
[1988] 2 WLR 706 .... 30, 32
Aslan v Murphy (Nos 1 & 2) [1989] 3 All ER 130, [1990]
1 WLR 766 33
Aspinall Finance Ltd v Viscount Chelsea [1989] 1 EGLR 103,
(1989) 09 EG 77 .... 37, 39
Atkinson v Bettison [1955] 3 All ER 340, [1955] 1 WLR 1127   109, 110
Austin Reed Ltd v Royal Insurance Co Ltd (No 1) [1956] EGD 174,
[1956] 1 WLR 765 106
Austin Reed Ltd v Royal Insurance Co Ltd (No 2) [1956] 3 All ER
490, [1956] 1 WLR 1339 120

Balls Brothers Ltd v Sinclair [1931] 2 Ch 325 153
Barclays Bank Ltd v Ascott [1961] 1 All ER 782, [1961] 1 WLR
717 .... 68, 69, 81
Barth v Pritchard (1990) 20 EG 65 110

Barton (WJ) Ltd v Long Acre Securities Ltd [1982] 1 All ER 465, [1982] 1 WLR 398 138
Baxendale (Robert) Ltd v Davstone (Holdings) Ltd [1982] 3 All ER 496, [1982] 1 WLR 1385 84
Beard v Williams [1986] 1 EGLR 148 101
Becker v Hill St Properties (1990) 38 EG 107 142
Bell v Alfred Franks & Bartlett & Co [1980] 1 All ER 356, [1980] 1 WLR 340 .... 37, 40, 41, 42, 43
Betty's Cafes Ltd v Phillips Furnishing Stores Ltd [1959] AC 20, [1958] 1 All ER 607, [1958] 2 WLR 513 .... 81, 98, 102, 105, 108, 109, 134
Bewlay (Tobacconists) Ltd v British Bata Shoe Co [1958] 3 All ER 652, [1959] 1 WLR 45 109
Bhattacharya v Raising (1987) CAT 25 March 32, 35
Biles v Caesar [1957] 1 All ER 151, [1957] 1 WLR 156 .... 68, 106
Billson and others v Residential Apartments Ltd [1991] The Times 26 February 154
Birch (A & W) Ltd v P B (Sloane) Ltd (1956) 167 EG 283 ..... 84, 108
Blackburn v Hussain (1988) 22 EG 78 .... 111, 112
Blake (Victor) (Menswear) Ltd v Westminster City Council (1978) 38 P&CR 448, (1978) 249 EG 543 95
Bloomfield v Ashwright Ltd (1984) 47 P&CR 78, (1983) 266 EG 1095   94
Bolsom (Sidney) Investment Trust Ltd v E Karmios & Co (London) Ltd [1956] 1 QB 529, [1956] 1 All ER 536, [1956] 2 WLR 625 80
Bolton (HL) Engineering Co Ltd v TJ Graham & Sons Ltd [1957] 1 QB 159, [1956] 3 All ER 624, [1956] 3 WLR 804 108
Bolton's (House Furnishers) Ltd v Oppenheim [1959] 3 All ER 90, [1959] 1 WLR 913 .... 68, 85
Bostock v Bryant (1990) 39 EG 64, [1990] 2 EGLR 101 32
Botterill & Cheshire v Bedfordshire C C [1985] 1 EGLR 82, 273 EG 1217 110
Bowes-Lyon v Green [1963] AC 420, [1961] 3 All ER 843, [1961] 3 WLR 1044 56
Boyer (William) & Sons Ltd v Adams (1975) 32 P&CR 89 36
Bracey v Read [1963] Ch 88, [1962] 3 All ER 472, [1962] 3 WLR 1194 .... 35, 147
Bradshaw v Pawley [1979] 3 All ER 273, [1980] 1 WLR 10 136
Branhills Ltd v Town Tailors Ltd (1956) 168 EG 642 108
Bresgall & Sons v London Borough of Hackney (1976) 32 P&CR 442 153
Bridgers v Stanford [1991] The Times 30 April 66, 67
Brighton College v Marriott [1926] AC 192 41
Bristol Cars v RKH Hotels (1979) 38 P&CR 411, (1979) 251 EG 1279 79
British & Colonial Furniture Co Ltd v William McIlroy Ltd [1952] 1 KB 107, [1952] 1 All ER 12 161

Table of cases

Broadmead v Corben-Brown (1966) 201 EG 111 131
Brooker Settled Estates v Ayres (1987) 282 EG 325, [1987] 1 EGLR 50 33
Burgess v Stafford Hotels Ltd [1990] 3 All ER 222, [1990] 1 WLR 1215 121

C & P Haulage v Middleton [1983] 3 All ER 94, [1983] 1 WLR 1461 154
Cadle (Percy E) & Co Ltd v Jacmarch Properties Ltd [1957] 1 QB 323, [1957] 1 All ER 148, [1957] 2 WLR 80 .... 109, 110
Cafeteria (Keighley) Ltd v Harrison (1956) 168 EG 668 37
Cairnplace Ltd v CBL (Property Investment) Co Ltd [1984] 1 All ER 315, [1984] 1 WLR 696 .... 142, 143
Cam Gears Ltd v Cunningham [1981] 2 All ER 560, [1981] 1 WLR 1011 115
Caplan (I & H) Ltd v Caplan (No 2) [1963] 2 All ER 930, [1963] 1 WLR 1247 .... 37, 60, 120
Capocci v Goble (1987) 284 EG 230, [1987] 2 EGLR 102 .... 105, 108
Cardiothoracic Institute Ltd v Shrewdcrest Ltd [1986] 3 All ER 633, [1986] 1 WLR 368 .... 49, 51
Cardshops Ltd v Davies [1971] 2 All ER 721, [1971] 1 WLR 591 137, 142
Cardshops Ltd v John Lewis Properties Ltd [1983] QB 161, [1982] 3 All ER 746, [1982] 3 WLR 803 125
Castle Laundry (London) v Read [1955] 1 QB 586, [1955] 2 All ER 154, [1955] 2 WLR 943 56
Cerex Jewels Ltd v Peachey Property Corporation (1986) 52 P&CR 127 (1986) 279 EG 971 112
Chapman v Freeman [1978] 3 All ER 878, [1978] 1 WLR 1298, (1978) 36 P&CR 323 42
Cheryl Investments Ltd v Saldanha [1979] 1 All ER 5, [1978] 1 WLR 1329, (1978) 37 P&CR 349 .... 42, 43
Chez Gerard Ltd v Greene Ltd (1983) 268 EG 575 ...... 108, 114, 116
Chipperfield (Michael) v Shell (UK) Ltd (1981) 42 P&CR 136, (1980) 257 EG 1042 136
Chiswell v Griffon Land & Estates Ltd [1975] 2 All ER 665, [1975] 1 WLR 1181 74
City Offices (Regent St) Ltd v Europa Acceptance Group plc (1990) 05 EG 71, [1990] 1 EGLR 63 110
Clark v Kirby-Smith [1964] Ch 506, [1964] 2 All ER 835, [1964] 3 WLR 239 130
Colchester BC v Smith [1991] 2 All ER 29, [1991] 2 WLR 540 34
Commissioners of Inland Revenue v Muller & Co [1901] AC 217 .. 139
Connaught Fur Trimmings Ltd v Cramas Properties Ltd [1965] 1 All ER 148, [1965] 1 WLR 46 (CA) 5, 9
Conway v Arthur [1988] 2 EGLR 113 97
Cook v Mott (1961) 178 EG 637 .... 109, 110

Corsini v Montague Burton Ltd [1953] 2 QB 126, [1953] 1 All ER 8, [1953] 2 WLR 1092 155
Craddock v Fieldman (1960) 175 EG 1149 70
Cramas Properties Ltd v Connaught Fur Trimmings Ltd [1965] 2 All ER 382, [1965] 1 WLR 892 (HL) 121, 122
Cristina v Seear [1985] 2 EGLR 128, (1985) 275 EG 595 .... 37, 39
Crowhurst Park, Re [1974] 1 All ER 991, [1974] 1 WLR 583 .. 83, 114
Cunliffe v Goodman [1950] 2 KB 237, [1950] 1 All ER 720 104
Curtis v Calgary Investments Ltd (1984) 47 P&CR 13 84

DAF Motoring Centre (Gosport) Ltd v Hutfield & Wheeler Ltd (1982) 263 EG 976 .... 105, 107
Davies v Brighton Corporation (1956) CLY 4863 139
Decca Navigator Co Ltd v GLC [1974] 1 All ER 1178, [1974] 1 WLR 748 .... 86, 113
Deerfield Travel Services Ltd v Leathersellers' Company (1983) 46 P&CR 132 158
Dellenty v Pellow [1951] 2 KB 858, [1951] 2 All ER 716 100
Dellneed v Chin (1987) 281 EG 531, [1987] 1 EGLR 75 34
Demag Industrial Equipment Ltd v Canada Dry (UK) Ltd [1969] 2 All ER 936, [1969] 1 WLR 985 86
Demetriou v Poolaction Ltd [1990] CAT 24 October 36, 38
Denny Thorn & Co Ltd v George Harker & Co Ltd (1957) 108 LJ 348 117
Department of Environment v Royal Insurance plc (1987) 54 P&CR 26, [1987] 1 EGLR 83 126
Diploma Laundry v Surrey Timber Co Ltd [1955] 2 QB 604, [1955] 2 All ER 922, [1955] 3 WLR 404 64
Dodds v Walker [1981] 2 All ER 609, [1981] 1 WLR 1027 ..... 65, 88
Dodson Bull Carpet Co Ltd v City of London Corporation [1975] 2 All ER 497, [1975] 1 WLR 781 71
Domer v Gulf Oil (GB) Ltd (1975) 119 SJ 392 36
Donegal Tweed Co Ltd v Stephenson (1928) 98 LJ (KB) 657 162
Dresden Estates v Collinson (1987) 281 EG 1321, [1987] 1 EGLR 45 .... 33, 34
D'Silva v Lister House Developments Ltd [1971] Ch 17, [1970] 1 All ER 858, [1970] 2 WLR 563 .... 31, 148
Duke v Wynne [1989] 3 All ER 130, [1990] 1 WLR 766 33
Dunnel (BJ) Properties v Thorpe (1989) 33 EG 36 33
Dutch Oven Ltd v Egham Estate & Investment Co Ltd [1968] 3 All ER 100, [1968] 1 WLR 1483 .... 86, 106

Edicron v William Whitely [1984] 1 All ER 219, [1984] 1 WLR 59 . 127
Edwards v Thompson (1990) 60 P&CR 222, [1990] 29 EG 41 108
Edwards (JH) & Sons Ltd v Central London Commercial Estates Ltd (1984) 271 EG 697 135

Table of cases

Eichner v Midland Bank Executor & Trustee Co [1970]
2 All ER 597, [1970] 1 WLR 1120 101
Engleheart v Catford [1926] EGD 192, 352 130
English Exporters (London) Ltd v Eldonwall Ltd [1973] Ch 415,
[1973] 1 All ER 726, [1973] 2 WLR 435 .... 94, 95, 96, 97, 138, 159
Espresso Coffee Machine Co Ltd v Guardian Assurance Co Ltd
[1959] 1 All ER 458, [1959] 1 WLR 250 .... 91, 108, 114
Essexcrest Ltd v Evenlex Ltd (1988) 01 EG 56, [1988] 1 EGLR 69 .. 51
Essex Plan Ltd v Broadminster (1988) 43 EG 34, [1988]
2 EGLR 73 .... 32, 33, 35
Europark (Midlands) Ltd v Town Centre Securities [1985]
1 EGLR 88, (1985) 274 EG 289 114
Euston Centre Properties Ltd v H & J Wilson Ltd (1982)
262 EG 1079 .... 140, 148
Evans Construction Co Ltd v Charrington & Co Ltd [1983] QB 810,
[1983] 1 All ER 310, [1983] 2 WLR 117 83
Evans (FR) (Leeds) Ltd v English Electric Co (1977) 36 P&CR 185,
(1977) 245 EG 657 137

Falcon Pipes Ltd v Stanhope Gate Property Co Ltd [1967] EGD 804 . 69
Family Housing Association v Jones [1990] 1 All ER 385, [1990]
1 WLR 779 .... 32, 33
Family Management v Gray (1979) 253 EG 369 .... 137, 139
Fawke v Viscount Chelsea [1980] QB 441, [1979] 3 All ER 568,
[1979] 3 WLR 508 .... 96, 97, 137
Fernandez v Walding [1968] 2 QB 606, [1968] 1 All ER 994,
[1968] 2 WLR 583 133
Fisher v Taylor's Furnishing Stores Ltd [1956] 2 QB 78, [1956]
2 All ER 78, [1956] 2 WLR 985 115
Follett (Charles) Ltd v Cabtell Investments Ltd (1988) 55 P&CR 36,
(1987) 283 EG 195, [1986] 2 EGLR 76 .... 96, 134
France v Shaftward Investments [1981] CAT 25 June 114
French v Lowen [1925] EGD 150 129
Fribourg & Treyer v Northdale Investments (1982) 44 P&CR 284,
(1982) 263 EG 660 123

GMS Syndicate Ltd v Gary Elliott Ltd [1982] Ch 1, [1981]
1 All ER 619, [1981] 2 WLR 478 57
Galinski v McHugh (1988) 21 HLR 47, (1989) 05 EG 89, [1989]
1 EGLR 109 22
Giannoukakis Ltd v Saltfleet Ltd [1988] 1 EGLR 73 137
Gilmour Caterers Ltd v St Bartholomew's Hospital [1956] 1 QB 387,
[1956] 1 All ER 314, [1956] 2 WLR 419 .... 105, 107
Gladstone v Bower [1960] 2 QB 384, [1960] 3 All ER 353, [1960]
3 WLR 575 46
Gloucester City Council v Williams [1990] The Times 15 May 34
Godbold v Martin The Newsagents Ltd (1983) 268 EG 1202 .. 140, 156

xvii

Gold v Brighton Corporation [1956] 3 All ER 442, [1956]
1 WLR 1291 .... 103, 142
Gorleston Golf Club v Links Estate (1959) CLY 1830 138
Grafton St London W1, No 14, Re [1971] Ch 935, [1971] 2 All ER 1,
[1971] 2 WLR 159 .... 74, 122
Grant v Gresham (1979) 252 EG 55 47
Gregson v Cyril Lord Ltd [1962] 3 All ER 907, [1963] 1 WLR
41 .... 105, 107
Gurton v Parrot [1990] CAT 11 December 42

Hadjiloucas v Crean [1987] 3 All ER 1008, [1988] 1 WLR 1006 . 33, 34
Hagee (London) Ltd v A B Erikson & Larson [1976] 1 QB 209,
[1975] 3 All ER 234, [1975] 3 WLR 272 .... 49, 50, 148
Haines v Florenson (1990) 09 EG 70 .... 143, 153, 154
Halberstam v Tandalco Corporation NV [1985] 1 EGLR 90, (1985)
274 EG 393 .... 96, 97
Hancock & Willis v GMS Syndicate Ltd (1983) 265 EG 473 . 36, 37, 61
Harewood Hotels Ltd v Harris [1958] 1 All ER 104, [1958]
1 WLR 108 138
Harley Queen v Forsyte Kerman (1983) 6 CLY 2077 35
Harris v Amery (1865) LRI CP 148 40
Harris v Black (1983) 127 SJ 224, (1983) 46 P&CR 366 83
Heath v Drown (1973) AC 498, [1972] 2 All ER 561, [1972]
2 WLR 1306 111
Herongrove Ltd v Wates City of London Properties plc [1988]
1 EGLR 82, (1988) 24 EG 108 .... 69, 72
High Road, Kilburn, No 88, Re [1959] 1 All ER 527, [1959]
1 WLR 279 .... 86, 91
Hillil Property & Investment Co v Naraine Pharmacy (1979) 39
P&CR 67, (1979) 252 EG 1013 .... 40, 42
Hills (Patents) Ltd v University College Hospital Board of
Governors [1956] 1 QB 90, [1955] 3 All ER 365, [1955]
3 WLR 523 .... 36, 40, 41
Hodge v Clifford Cowling & Co (1990) 46 EG 116 88
Hodgson v Armstrong [1967] 2 QB 299, [1967] 1 All ER 307, [1967]
2 WLR 311 .... 65, 87
Hogarth Health Club Ltd v Westbourne Investments Ltd (1990)
02 EG 69 .... 146, 160
Hogg Bullimore & Co v Co-operative Insurance Society (1984)
49 P&CR 105 65
Hopcutt v Carver (1969) 209 EG 1069 .... 99, 100
Horowitz v Ferrand (1956) 5 CL 207, [1956] CLY 4843 .... 99, 100
Housleys Ltd v Bloomer-Holt Ltd [1966] 2 All ER 966, [1966]
1 WLR 1244 .... 98, 109, 110
Hurstfell Ltd v Leicester Square Property Co [1988] 2 EGLR 105,
(1988) 37 EG 109 100
Hutchinson v Lambeth (1983) 270 EG 545 98

Table of cases

Huxford v Stoy Hayward & Co [1989] The Times 11 January, (1989) 5 BCC 421 88
Hyams v Titan Properties Ltd (1972) 224 EG 2017, (1972) 24 P&CR 359 142

Incorporated Council of Law Reporting for England and Wales, Re (1888) 22 QBD 279 40
Inland Revenue Commissioners v Maxse [1919] 1 KB 647 41
Interoven Stove Co Ltd v Hibbard & Painter & Shepherd [1936] 1 All ER 263 49
Ireland v Taylor [1949] 1 KB 300, [1948] 2 All ER 450 40

J T Development Ltd v Quinn [1990] CAT 6 December 74
Jacobs v Chaudhuri [1968] 2 QB 470, [1968] 2 All ER 124, [1968] 2 WLR 1098 .... 23, 83
Janes (Gowns) Ltd v Harlow Development Corporation (1979) 253 EG 799 .... 96, 133, 141
Javad v Aqil (1990) 41 EG 61, [1991] 1 All ER 243 .... 35, 49
Joel v Swaddle [1957] 3 All ER 325, [1957] 1 WLR 1094 110
Jones v Jenkins [1986] 1 EGLR 113, (1985) 277 EG 644 ..... 115, 116
Joss v Bennett (1956) 167 EG 207 107
Junction Estates v Cope (1974) 27 P&CR 482 57

Kammins Ballrooms Co Ltd v Zenith Investments (Torquay) Ltd [1971] AC 850, [1970] 2 All ER 871, [1970] 3 WLR 287 ... 2, 74, 87
Keith, Bayley, Rogers & Co v Cubes Ltd (1975) 31 P&CR 412 .... 56, 64
Kent Coast Properties v Ward (1990) 45 EG 107 42
Kirkwood v Johnson (1979) 38 P&CR 392, (1979) 250 EG 239 .... 133, 142

Lambert v F W Woolworth & Co Ltd [1938] Ch 883, [1938] 2 All ER 664 .... 145, 153
Land & Premises at Liss Hants, Re [1971] Ch 986, [1971] 3 All ER 380, [1971] 3 WLR 77 50
Land Reclamation Co Ltd v Basildon DC [1979] 2 All ER 993, [1979] 1 WLR 767 .... 35, 36, 148, 150, 154
Land Securities v Receiver for Metropolitan Police District [1983] 2 All ER 254, [1983] 1 WLR 439 153
Lansley v Adda Properties Ltd (1982) CLY 284 46
Lawrence v Carter (1956) 167 EG 222, (1956) 106 LJ 269 102
Lawrence (Frederick) Ltd v Freeman Hardy & Willis Ltd [1959] Ch 731, [1959] 3 All ER 77, [1959] 3 WLR 275 117
Leal v Dunlop Bio-Processes International Ltd [1984] 2 All ER 207, [1984] 1 WLR 874 84
Leathwoods Ltd v Total Oil (GB) Ltd (1986) 51 P&CR 20, [1985] 2 EGLR 237 .... 111, 115, 153

Leckhampton Dairies Ltd v Artus Whitfield Ltd (1986) 130 SJ
   225 63
Lecture League Ltd v LCC (1913) 108 LT 924, (1913) 29 TLR
   426 41
Lee-Verhulst (Investments) Ltd v Harwood Trust [1973] 1 QB 204,
   [1972] 3 All ER 619, [1972] 3 WLR 772 .... 37, 40
Leek and Moorlands Building Society v Clark [1952] 2 QB 788, [1952]
   2 All ER 492 48
Lennox v Bell (1957) 169 EG 753 108
Leslie & Godwin Investments Ltd v Prudential Assurance Co Ltd
   [1987] 2 EGLR 95, (1987) 283 EG 1565 135
Levy (AJ) & Son Ltd v Martin Brent Developments (1987) 283
   EG 646 .... 105, 107, 108, 113
Lewington v Trustees of the Society for the Protection of Ancient
   Buildings (1983) 266 EG 997, (1983) 45 P&CR 336 .... 73, 74
Lewis v MTC Cars Ltd [1975] 1 All ER 874, [1975] 1 WLR 457 67
Lewis v Weldcrest Ltd [1978] 3 All ER 1226, [1978] 1 WLR 1107 .. 42
Lex Service plc v Johns (1990) 10 EG 67 21
Linden v DHSS [1986] 1 All ER 691, [1986] 1 WLR 164 24
Livestock Underwriting Agency v Corbett & Newton (1955) 165
   EG 469 106
Lloyd's Bank v City of London Corporation [1983] Ch 192, [1983]
   1 All ER 92, [1982] 3 WLR 1138 .... 90, 123
London & Provincial Millinery Stores v Barclays Bank [1962]
   2 All ER 163, [1962] 1 WLR 510 134
London Hilton Jewellers Ltd v Hilton International Hotels Ltd
   (1990) 20 EG 69 .... 106, 108
Long Acre Securities Ltd v Electro Acoustic Industries (1990)
   06 EG 103, [1990] 1 EGLR 91 59
Long (Nevill) & Co (Boards) Ltd v Firmenich & Co (1984) 47
   P&CR 59, (1983) 268 EG 572 .... 35, 57, 72
Lonsdale (Earl) v A-G [1982] 3 All ER 579, [1982] 1 WLR 887 46
Lovely & Orchard Services Ltd v Daejan Investments (Grove Hall)
   Ltd (1977) 121 SJ 711, (1977) 246 EG 651 .... 131, 137
Lyons v Central Commercial Properties Ltd [1958] 2 All ER 767,
   [1958] 1 WLR 869 99

Maison Kaye Fashions v Horton's Estate Ltd (1967) 202 EG 23 ... 100
Manchester Garages Ltd v Petrofina (UK) Ltd (1974) 233 EG 509 . 106
Manfield & Sons Ltd v Botchin [1970] 2 QB 612, [1970]
   3 All ER 143, [1970] 3 WLR 120 49
Marks v British Waterways Board [1963] 3 All ER 28, [1963]
   1 WLR 1008 104
McCarthy v Bence [1990] 1 EGLR 1 32
Meadows v Clerical Medical & General Life Assurance Co [1981]
   Ch 70, [1980] 1 All ER 454, [1980] 2 WLR 639 60

Table of cases

Meah v Mouskos [1964] 2 QB 23, [1963] 3 All ER 908, [1964]
2 WLR 27 84
Meah v Sector Properties [1974] 1 All ER 1074, [1974]
1 WLR 547 87
Method Developments Ltd v Jones [1971] 1 All ER 1027, [1971]
1 WLR 168 116
Meyer v Riddick (1990) 60 P&CR 42, [1990] 1 EGLR 107, (1990)
18 EG 97 114
Mikeover Ltd v Brady (1989) 21 HLR 513, [1989] 2 EGLR 61,
(1989) 59 P&CR 218 33
Miller (John) (Shipping) Ltd v Port of London Authority
(Practice Note) [1959] 2 All ER 713, [1959] 1 WLR 910 86
Minimet Enterprises v Mayor and Burgesses of Croydon [1989]
CAT 24 August 34
Mirza v Nicola (1990) 30 EG 92 .... 107, 108
Monson (Lord) v Bound [1954] 3 All ER 228, [1954] 1 WLR 1321 .. 45
Moody v Godstone RDC [1966] 2 All ER 696, [1966] 1 WLR 1085 ... 21
Morar v Chauhan [1985] 3 All ER 493, [1985]
1 WLR 1263 .... 114, 117, 119
Morcom v Campbell-Johnson [1956] 1 QB 106, [1955] 3 All
ER 264, [1955] 3 WLR 497 153
Morgan v Jones [1960] 3 All ER 583, [1960] 1 WLR 1220 85
Morris v Patel (1987) 281 EG 419, [1987] 1 EGLR 75 69
Morris Marks v British Waterways Board [1963] 1 WLR 1008 68
Morrison Holdings Ltd v Manders Property [1976] 2 All ER 205,
[1976] 1 WLR 533 38
Morrow v Nadeem [1987] 1 All ER 237, [1986] 1 WLR 1381 ... 69, 70
Moss v Mobil Oil (1988) 06 EG 109, [1988] 1 EGLR 71 72
Murray v Lloyd [1990] 2 All ER 92, [1989] 1 WLR 1060 88

NCP Ltd v Colebrook Estates Ltd (1983) 266 EG 810 138
NCP Ltd v Paternoster Consortium Ltd (1990) 15 EG 53 135
National Electric Theatres Ltd v Hudgell [1939] Ch 553, [1939]
1 All ER 567 .... 145, 147, 153, 155, 165
New Zealand Government Property Corporation v H M & S Ltd
[1982] 1 QB 1145, [1982] 1 All ER 624, [1982] 2 WLR 837 .. 57, 144, 154
Nicolaou v Pitt (1989) 21 EG 71, [1989] 1 EGLR 84 .... 32, 33
Northcote Laundry Ltd v Frederick Donnelly Ltd [1968] 2 All
ER 50, [1968] 1 WLR 562 .... 116, 117
Nuflats & Properties Ltd v Sheckman (1959) 174 EG 39 35
Nursey v Currie (P) (Dartford) Ltd [1959] 1 All ER 497, [1959]
1 WLR 273 .... 67, 115

Oakley v Wilson [1927] 2 KB 279 31
O'Callaghan v Elliott [1966] 1 QB 601, [1965] 3 All ER 111, [1965]
3 WLR 746 46
Ogwr BC v Dykes [1989] 2 All ER 880, [1989] 1 WLR 295 32

xxi

O'May v City of London Real Property Co Ltd [1983] 2 AC 726,
  [1982] 1 All ER 660, [1982] 2 WLR 407 ..... 93, 137, 139, 141, 142
Orenstein v Donn [1983] CAT 5 May 135
Orlik (G) (Meat Products) v Hastings & Thanet Building Society
  (1974) 118 SJ 811, (1974) 29 P&CR 126 .... 132, 133
Oscroft v Benabo [1967] 2 All ER 548, [1967] 1 WLR 1087 139
Osnaburgh Street, Nos 52, 54, 56, Re [1957] CLY 1947 138
Owen Owen Estate Ltd v Livett [1956] Ch 1, [1955] 2 All ER 513,
  [1955] 3 WLR 1 .... 144, 145, 156

Page v Sole [1991] CAT 24 January 100, 114, 116
Panton Street (No 5), Haymarket, Re (1959) 175 EG 49 ..... 137, 142
Parkes v Westminster Roman Catholic Diocese Trustee (1978)
  36 P&CR 22, (1978) 247 EG 555 .... 40, 116
Partridge v Mallandine (1886) 18 LCD 276 41
Pasmore v Whitbread & Co Ltd [1953] 2 QB 226, [1953] 1 All
  ER 361, [1953] 2 WLR 359 155
Pearson v Alyo (1990) 60 P&CR 50, [1990] 1 EGLR 114 ... 14, 63, 69
Pelosi v Newcastle Arms Brewery (Nottingham) Ltd (1981) 259
  EG 247, (1982) 43 P&CR 18 .... 144, 156, 161
Philipson-Stow v Trevor Square Ltd (1980) 257 EG 1262 68
Photo Centre Ltd v Grantham Court Properties (Mayfair) Ltd
  (1964) 191 EG 505 121
Piper v Muggleton [1956] 2 QB 569, [1956] 2 All ER 249, [1956]
  2 WLR 1093 .... 15, 84
Plessey Co plc v Eagle Pension Funds (1990) 35 EG 75 125
Polyviou v Seeley [1979] 3 All ER 853, [1980] 1 WLR 55 ... 74, 80, 87
Poster v Slough Estates [1969] 1 Ch 495, [1968] 3 All ER 257,
  [1968] 1 WLR 1515 57
Price v Esso Petroleum Co Ltd (1980) 255 EG 243 153
Price v West London Investment Building Society [1964] 2 All
  ER 318, [1964] 1 WLR 616 21
Pritam Kaur v S. Russell & Sons Ltd [1973] 1 QB 336, [1973]
  1 All ER 617, [1973] 2 WLR 147 87
Pulleng v Curran (1982) 44 P&CR 58 .... 36, 38, 42

R v Secretary of State for the Environment ex parte Powis [1981]
  1 All ER 788, [1981] 1 WLR 584 25
Ratners (Jewellers) Ltd v Lemnoll (1980) 255 EG 987 96
Rawasdeh v Lane [1988] 2 EGLR 109, (1988) 40 EG 109 100
Real & Leasehold Estates Investment Society v Medina Shipping Ltd
  (1968) 112 SJ 862, (1968) 208 EG 733 43
Redfern v Reeves (1978) 247 EG 991, (1978) 37 P&CR 364 112
Regis Property Co Ltd v Lewis & Peat Ltd [1970] Ch 695, [1970]
  3 All ER 227, [1970] 3 WLR 361 .... 94, 96
Rene Claro (Haute Coiffure) Ltd v Hallé Concerts Society [1969]
  2 All ER 842, [1969] 1 WLR 909 16

Table of cases

Reohorn v Barry Corporation [1956] 2 All ER 742, [1956]
1 WLR 845 .... 104, 105, 107, 134
Rhyl UDC v Rhyl Amusements Ltd [1959] 1 All ER 257, [1959]
1 WLR 465 70
Riley (EJ) Investments Ltd v Eurostile Holdings Ltd [1985]
3 All ER 181, [1985] 1 WLR 1139 .... 65, 88
Rolls v Miller (1884) 27 Ch D 71 40
Rom Tyre & Accessories Ltd v Crawford St Properties Ltd (1966)
197 EG 565 132
Romulus Trading Co Ltd v Trustees of Henry Smith's Charity
(1990) 32 EG 41 113
Ross Auto Wash Ltd v Herbert (1978) 250 EG 971 37
Rossi, ex parte [1956] 1 QB 682 .... 21, 22
Rous v Mitchell [1991] 1 All ER 609 81
Royal Life Saving Society v Page [1979] 1 All ER 5, [1978]
1 WLR 1329, (1978) 37 P&CR 349 42
Russell v Booker (1982) 5 HLR 10, (1982) 263 EG 513 45

Safeway Food Stores v Morris (1980) 254 EG 1091 67
St Martin's Theatre, Re [1959] 3 All ER 298, [1959] 1 WLR 872 ... 86
Sainty v Minister of Housing & Local Government [1964]
EGD 368, (1964) 15 P&CR 432, (1964) 189 EG 341 153
Sardinia Sulcis v Al Taiwwab [1990] The Times 21 November 84
Scholl Manufacturing Co Ltd v Clifton (Slimline) Ltd [1967]
1 Ch 41, [1966] 3 All ER 16, [1966] 3 WLR 575 ...... vii, 9, 11, 50, 56
Scottish & Newcastle Breweries Ltd, Re [1985] 2 EGLR 130, (1985)
276 EG 77 153
Sector Properties Ltd v Meah (1974) 229 EG 1097 22
Selim Ltd v Bickenhall Engineering Ltd [1981] 3 All ER 210, [1981]
1 WLR 1318 87
Sharma v Knight [1986] 1 WLR 757 83
Shell-Mex & BP Ltd v Manchester Garages [1971] 1 All ER 841,
[1971] 1 WLR 612 30
Shelley v United Artists (1990) 16 EG 69 .... 14, 15
Short v Greeves (1988) 8 EG 109 45
Singh v Malayan Theatres [1953] AC 632, [1953] 3 WLR 491 102
Skeet v Powell-Sheddon [1988] 2 EGLR 112, (1988) 40 EG 116 ... 114
Smith v Anderson (1880) 15 Ch D 247 40
Smith v Draper (1990) 60 P&CR 252, [1990] 2 EGLR
69 .... 59, 68, 70, 71, 80, 81
Smith v Metropolitan Properties Co Ltd [1932] 1 KB 314 161
Smith v Northside Developments Ltd (1987) 283 EG 1211, [1987]
2 EGLR 151 .... 32, 33, 34
Smith (AJA) Transport Ltd v British Railways Board (1980)
257 EG 1257 .... 69, 70, 107, 121
Southport Old Links Ltd v Naylor (1985) 273 EG 767, [1985]
1 EGLR 66 72

Spalding v Shotley Point Marina (1986) Ltd [1989] CAT
  24 January 112, 113
Spook Erection Ltd v British Railways Board (1988) 21 EG 73,
  [1988] 1 EGLR 76 107
Stevens & Cutting Ltd v Anderson [1990] 11 EG 70 .... 70, 87
Stevenson & Rush (Holdings) Ltd v Langdon (1978) 38 P&CR 208,
  (1978) 249 EG 743 52
Stidolph v The American School in London Educational Trust Ltd
  (1969) 211 EG 925, (1969) 20 P&CR 802 69
Stratton (RJ) Ltd v Wallis Tomlin & Co Ltd (1986) 277 EG 409,
  [1986] 1 EGLR 104 .... 61, 82
Stream Properties Ltd v Davis [1972] 2 All ER 746, [1972] 1 WLR 645 .. 95
Street v Mountford [1985] AC 809, [1985] 2 All ER 289, [1985]
  2 WLR 877 .... 31, 32, 33, 34, 35
Stribling v Wickham (1989) 27 EG 81 33
Stuchbery & Son v General Accident Fire & Life Assurance Corporation
  Ltd [1949] 2 KB 256, [1949] 1 All ER 1026 .. 2, 3, 31, 144, 150, 151
Stylo Shoes Ltd v Prices Tailors Ltd [1960] Ch 396, [1959] 3 All ER
  901, [1960] 2 WLR 8 22
Sun Alliance & London Assurance Co Ltd v Hayman [1975]
  1 All ER 248, [1975] 1 WLR 177 66
Sunlight House, Quay St, Manchester, Re (1959) 173 EG 311 134
Sunrose Ltd v Gould [1961] 3 All ER 1142, [1962] 1 WLR 20 69
Swales (JG) & Co v HS Mosley [1968] CLY 2187 47

Tarjomani v Panther Securities Ltd (1983) 46 P&CR 32 .... 52, 62
Teasdale v Walker [1958] 3 All ER 307, [1958] 1 WLR 1076 .. 36, 37, 48
Teesside Indoor Bowls Ltd v Borough Council of Stockton on Tees
  (1990) 46 EG 120 88
Tegerdine v Brooks (1977) 245 EG 51, (1977) 36 P&CR 261 69
Tennant v LCC (1957) 121 JP 428, (1957) 55 LGR 421 70
Texaco Ltd v Benton & Bowles (Holdings) Ltd (1983) 127 SJ 307,
  (1983) 267 EG 355 94
Thomas v Hammond-Lawrence [1986] 2 All ER 214, [1986]
  1 WLR 456 .... 93, 95
Thomas v Sorrell (1673) Vaugh 330 30
Thorne (Sandown Lodge) v New Sherwood School (1962) 181 EG 859 . 57
Thorne v Smith [1947] KB 307, [1947] 1 All ER 39 130
Thornton (JW) Ltd v Blacks Leisure Group (1987) 53 P&CR 223,
  (1986) 279 EG 588, [1986] 2 EGLR 61 .... 115, 116
Tottenham Hotspur Football & Athletic Co Ltd v Princegrove
  Publishers Ltd [1974] 1 All ER 17, [1974] 1 WLR 113 51
Trans-Britannia Properties Ltd v Darby Properties Ltd [1986]
  1 EGLR 151, (1986) 278 EG 1254 36
Trustees of Henry Smith's Charity v Hemmings (1983) 265 EG 383 .. 155
Trustees of Henry Smith's Charity, Kensington v Wagle & Tippet
  [1990] 1 QB 42, [1989] 2 WLR 669 43

Table of cases

Turner & Bell v Searles Ltd (1977) 33 P&CR 208, (1977) 244
  EG 1023 .... 98, 101
Upsons Ltd v E Robins Ltd [1956] 1 QB 131, [1955] 3 All ER 348,
  [1955] 3 WLR 584 .... 118, 134, 135
Wandsworth London Borough Council v Singh [1991] The Times
  6 March 35, 37
Ward v Warnke (1990) 22 HLR 497 32
Wates Estate Agency Services Ltd v Bartleys Ltd (1989) 47 EG 51 ... 114
Wates v Rowland [1952] 2 QB 12, [1952] 1 All ER 470 153
Watkins v Emslie (1981) 132 NLJ 295, (1982) 261 EG 1192 .... 70, 78
Watney v Boardley [1975] 2 All ER 644, [1975] 1 WLR 857 62
Webb v London Borough of Barnet (1989) 11 EG 80 .... 42, 43
Weinbergs Weatherproofs v Radcliffe Paper Mill Co [1958]
  Ch 437, [1957] 3 All ER 663, [1958] 2 WLR 1 55
Westerbury Property & Investment Co Ltd v Carpenter [1961]
  1 All ER 481, [1961] 1 WLR 272 67
Westminster City Council v British Waterways Board [1985]
  AC 676, [1984] 3 All ER 737, [1984] 3 WLR 1047 107
Wetherall, Doe d v Bird (1834) 2 AD & EL 161, (1833) 6 C & P
  195 40
Wheeler v Mercer [1957] AC 416, [1956] 3 All ER 631, [1956]
  3 WLR 841 49
Whitley v Stumbles [1930] AC 544 147
Williams v Hillcroft Garage Ltd (1971) 115 SJ 127, (1971) 22 P&CR
  402 84
Willis v Association of Universities of the British Commonwealth
  [1965] 1 QB 140, [1964] 2 All ER 39, [1964] 2 WLR 946 115
Wimbush (AD) & Sons Ltd v Franmills Properties Ltd [1961]
  Ch 419, [1961] 2 All ER 197, [1961] 2 WLR 498 .... 116, 117
Wine Shippers (London) Ltd v Bath House Syndicate Ltd [1960]
  3 All ER 283, [1960] 1 WLR 989 86
Wirral Estates Ltd v Shaw [1932] 2 KB 247 23
Wolfe v Hogan [1949] 2 KB 194, [1949] 1 All ER 570 43
"Wonderland", Cleethorpes, Re [1965] AC 58, [1963] 2 All ER 775,
  [1963] 2 WLR 1426 .... 7, 145
Woodbridge v Westminster Press Ltd [1987] 2 EGLR 97, (1987) 284
  EG 60 96
Woodruff v Hambro [1990] CAT 14 November 53
XL Fisheries v Leeds Corporation [1955] 2 QB 636, [1955] 2 All
  ER 875, [1955] 3 WLR 393 .... 15, 26, 81
Ye Olde Cheshire Cheese Ltd v The Daily Telegraph [1988] 3 All
  ER 217, [1988] 1 WLR 1173 .... 40, 47
Young, Austen & Young v BMA [1977] 2 All ER 884, [1977]
  1 WLR 881 90

Chapter 1

Statutory intervention

Business tenancies are subject to the provisions of the Landlord and Tenant Acts 1927 and 1954. Before 1927, there was an absence of legislation which applied exclusively to commercial leases. The relationship of business landlord and business tenant was governed by the common law, as adapted and applied by the courts, with some piecemeal statutory modification of general application (for example, the Distress for Rent Acts 1689 and 1737 and the Law of Property Act 1925). For the tenant there existed well recognised dangers which the common law proved unable to eradicate. Apart from a pervasive inequality of bargaining power, the tenant at the end of the contractual term could be faced with certain unenviable options: business closure or a new lease at an inflated rent; and potential loss arising from improvements carried out on the premises.

As early as 1889, the Select Committee on Town Holdings advocated a partial solution to the tenant's dilemma. Although it was not suggested that business tenants should be given security of tenure, the Select Committee believed that on quitting the premises, tenants should be able to claim compensation for the loss of goodwill or for the value of improvements made. Despite legislation being enacted in Ireland, attempts to introduce similar statutory regulation in England and Wales proved ineffective. Such Parliamentary intervention had to wait until well into the twentieth century.

When legislation eventually came into being, it was as a result of the deliberations (but not the recommendations) of the Select Committee on Business Premises (which reported in 1920). This committee stressed the need for legislative controls so as to protect business tenants from unconscionable treatment by their landlords. It took a further seven years before the legislature responded to this call to limit the freedom to contract and to protect business tenants against their lack of bargaining strength.

1. The Landlord and Tenant Act 1927

The first step towards the statutory regulation of business tenancies was taken in Part I Landlord and Tenant Act 1927. The Act entitled a tenant, required to vacate business premises at the expiry of a lease, to compensation for improvements and goodwill or, in limited circumstances, to a new tenancy. The purpose of the Act was explained by Lord Greene MR in *Stuchbery & Son* v *General Accident Fire & Life Assurance Corporation Ltd* (1949): "It was obviously thought by the legislature to be unjust that the landlord should obtain that type of unearned increment on the termination of a lease ...".

The effect of the Act can be summarised as follows:

(a) the tenant was allowed compensation for improvements carried out by that tenant or predecessors in title, the preconditions for a successful claim being that the improvement added to the letting value of the holding and that notice had been served on the landlord before the improvement was made. Albeit in an amended form, these are the only provisions of Part I Landlord and Tenant Act 1927 which remain in force today;

(b) the tenant could claim compensation for loss of goodwill on quitting the premises. To recover, the tenant had to prove that the premises had been occupied, either by him or a predecessor in title, for the purposes of a trade or business for a minimum period of five years. In addition, it had to be shown that the goodwill increased the rental value of the premises following the departure of that tenant;

(c) no security of tenure was offered except in the limited situation where the business tenant was entitled to compensation for loss of goodwill, but the sum to be awarded would be insufficient to cover the loss associated with moving to, and setting up business in, new premises. In such circumstances the tenant could claim a new lease in lieu of compensation. As Viscount Dilhorne, in *Kammins Ballrooms Co Ltd* v *Zenith Investments (Torquay) Ltd* (1971), concluded: "The court was thus for the first time

Statutory intervention

given the jurisdiction to order the grant of a new tenancy of business premises".

There were serious draw-backs and defects with the statutory scheme. Although compensation for improvements was available to business and professional tenants of not less than five years' standing, the goodwill provisions (and, thereby, renewal rights) extended only to those who had carried on a trade or business for that requisite period. Professional tenants could not, therefore, take advantage of these protective measures: *Stuchbery* v *General Accident* (1949). Compensation for goodwill, moreover, was based upon the notion of "adherent goodwill" (ie the goodwill had to be attached to the premises so as to increase subsequent rental values and did not follow the tenant). This was something that many tenants found difficult to prove. The tenant's claim for a new tenancy was also defeated if the landlord showed that suitable alternative accommodation was available; the premises were required for the landlord's occupation (or occupation by an adult son or daughter of the landlord); the premises were to be demolished or redeveloped; or the grant of a new lease would be inconsistent with good estate management. Due to the many limitations imposed, the Act worked badly and, consequently, the protection afforded to business tenants was scant. This was the conclusion drawn in 1949 by the *Interim Report of the Leasehold Committee* (Cmd 7706). It is hardly surprising, therefore, that the goodwill and new lease provisions were subsequently repealed and are of no modern significance.

2. The momentum continued

In 1948, a Leasehold Committee (initially named the Uthwatt Committee) was set up to examine, amongst other things, the position of business tenants. The committee considered whether a system of rent control and security of tenure should apply to commercial leases. An interim report (Cmd 7706, 1949) and, then under the chairmanship of Jenkins LJ, a final report (Cmd 7982, 1950) were published. At both stages minority reports were appended to the majority reports. Both majority reports concentrated upon the defects of the 1927 legislation and contained, with differences of emphasis, extensive recommendations through which the defects could be remedied. There was no evidence of widespread tenant abuse, but the committee did believe that there existed individual landlords who exploited unfairly their position of advantage. Although the committee believed that there should be no all-round system of rent control, it did advocate a radical movement which would offer business tenants security of tenure. This is what the business community primarily desired.

The emphasis was placed upon the tenant being given a statutory right to a new lease (regardless of any adherent goodwill) for a term not exceeding fourteen years, at an open market rent and on other terms as agreed or set by the court. The landlord was to be given the right to oppose the tenant's claim on prescribed grounds which were fewer in number than under the 1927 Act. Compensation for disturbance was to be an alternative in such cases where the landlord could establish a special reason for not continuing the lease. The renewal scheme was designed, moreover, to offer protection to professional tenants as well as those who were involved in a trade or business.

Although some of the committee's recommendations were never followed, within the two reports can be found the framework of what was eventually to become the Landlord and Tenant Act 1954. The movement from compensation towards security of tenure was to become the indelible hallmark of subsequent legislation.

An immediate consequence of the final report was the Leasehold Property (Temporary Provisions) Act 1951. The Act followed the recommendations of the interim and final reports in general terms only. It was destined to have a life span of three years and gave tenants (of retail shop premises only) the ability to apply to the court for a new tenancy not exceeding one year. Further applications could later be made and, in theory, a series of extensions built up. The scheme represented a stop-gap measure until a permanent system could be devised.

Meanwhile a government White Paper was being compiled and was published in January 1953 (Cmd 8713). In principle, the White Paper agreed with the general recommendations of the Leasehold Committee, but differed as regards the detailed mechanics of the scheme.

3. The Landlord and Tenant Act 1954

On 1 October 1954, Part II Landlord and Tenant Act 1954 came into being. This Act brought with it additional and extensive benefits for the business tenant. Its contents were based on the White Paper proposals of the previous year. Part II deals

Statutory intervention

with business premises and replaces those parts of the 1927 Act which dealt with compensation for goodwill and the grant of new tenancies. The Leasehold Property (Temporary Provisions) Act 1951 was repealed.

Part II of the Act sets up a somewhat revolutionary procedure for the renewal of business leases. It gives business tenants within its scope (including professional persons and non-profit making organisations), comprehensive security of tenure by facilitating, subject to certain conditions, the continuation and renewal of their tenancies. Although an emphasis is placed upon agreement by the parties, the Act offers the tenant the valuable right to apply to the court for a new lease when agreement cannot be achieved. In such a case, the landlord can successfully oppose the tenant's application only on limited grounds. Flat rate compensation is available to a tenant who is forced to quit the premises, but only where the landlord's opposition is based upon particular grounds (for example, the landlord's intention to redevelop or occupy the premises). In *Connaught Fur Trimmings Ltd* v *Cramas Properties Ltd* (1965), Harman LJ contended that this compensation for disturbance reintroduced the notion of compensation for goodwill by a side-wind.

Subject to agreement between the parties, when a new tenancy is ordered by the court it will follow the terms of the original lease and be at an open market rent. The court is unable, however, to grant a lease exceeding fourteen years.

The law as to compensation for improvements remains within the ambit of the Landlord and Tenant Act 1927. Part III of the 1954 Act, however, modifies some of the original restrictions on the right to compensation.

4. The Law of Property Act 1969

The legislative objective of the 1954 Act proved to work quite successfully. Traders could retain their business premises, while landlords received a full market rent and maintained the right to recover possession if the tenant was in default under the lease or the premises were needed for redevelopment or for that landlord's own occupation. The Act had gone some way to equalising the bargaining strength of the parties and had proved beneficial both to the tenant and the landlord.

Nevertheless anomalies and uncertainties emerged. A variety

were identified by the Law Commission in 1969 (*Report on the Landlord and Tenant Act 1954 Part II*, Law Com No 17) and, as a result, a number of significant reforms were introduced by the Law of Property Act 1969. The principle of the 1954 Act remained intact, but some fine tuning of the mechanics of the system occurred. The major alterations made by the Law of Property Act 1969 were:

   (a) the introduction of an interim rent procedure while the terms of the new tenancy were being determined;
   (b) the allowance of greater flexibility in permitting temporary lettings to fall outside the 1954 Act and in the court's power to sanction "contracting out" of the security of tenure provisions;
   (c) the extension of the court's power to grant a new tenancy and to order the terms on which it is granted;
   (d) the facilitation of compensation payable to the tenant for disturbance;
   (e) the correction of anomalies which had arisen in connection with partnerships and associated companies.

5. The present position

The relationship of the Landlord and Tenant Acts of 1927 and 1954 has to be appreciated. The most effective way of achieving this is not to look for common factors (of which, essentially, there are few), but rather to segregate the provisions of the respective Acts. There emerge two broad divisions: first, compensation for improvements which is still governed by the 1927 legislation; and, second, security of tenure which is regulated by the 1954 Act. The appropriate provisions of both statutes are reproduced in Appendix A.

The provisions relating to compensation for improvements remain in force very much as originally enacted in Part I Landlord and Tenant Act 1927. As mentioned earlier, certain minor amendments were made in Part III of the 1954 Act. Due to the security of tenure provisions, compensation for improvements is considered fairly unimportant in contemporary times. Nevertheless, in a limited number of cases it can still prove to be of real value. Although both statutes apply to business tenancies, because of different definition provisions it is possible that the 1927 Act will extend to some tenancies to which the 1954 Act does not apply (and

Statutory intervention

vice versa). Failure to secure renewal does not of itself deprive the tenant of any claim for compensation for improvements.

The law on security of tenure for business tenants is governed by Parts II and IV Landlord and Tenant Act 1954. These provisions are in practice extensively used and operated and the Act, as was made clear in *Re "Wonderland", Cleethorpes* (1965), "... in important respects derogates from the common law rights of the landlord: he is no longer master of the situation to grant or deny a new lease to his tenant ...". Unfortunately, the legislation is in parts poorly drafted and the statutory machinery established is highly technical and complex.

6. Prospective reform

Although responsible for the amendments contained in the Law of Property Act 1969, there were areas of concern, about the operation of the Landlord and Tenant Act 1954, which the Law Commission declined to investigate. Such problem areas included the definition of the term "business"; the complexity, timing and service of the statutory notices and counter-notices; the predicaments of small companies and of partnerships; and the lack of sanctions for the failure by landlords and tenants to provide information as required by the Act.

Little further development occurred until 1984, when the Department of the Environment undertook a review of the workings on the 1954 Act and its effect on business tenants. In 1985, this review concluded that no legislative changes were required. The Act was said to operate satisfactorily and to draw an even balance between the rights of the commercial landlord and the commercial tenant.

Nevertheless there remained areas of detail, within the statutory scheme, which were widely held to be in need of reform. The matter was championed once again by the Law Commission and, in 1988, a Working Paper was published (No 111). This Working Paper concentrated attention upon certain technical defects present in the statutory scheme and suggested provisionally the means by which they could be overcome. It was stressed, however, that no major changes were necessary.

The areas in need of finer tuning identified in the Working Paper were:

    (a) concept of occupation for the purposes of a business;

(b) service of notices and counter-notices;
(c) lack of penalties for the refusal to supply information as required by the Act;
(d) time limits concerning court applications;
(e) applications for an interim rent;
(f) contracting out of the Act;
(g) surrender and offer-back clauses;
(h) compensation for the refusal of a new tenancy and for misrepresentation.

The proposals put forward in the Working Paper are examined at the appropriate places in this book. Although a Law Commission Report is awaited in 1992, it is highly probable that the conclusions of the Working Paper will be followed. It may be that legislative changes will be introduced in due course, but they are certain to be of only minor consequence. In any event, the regulation of business tenancies has never enjoyed a high political profile and, in sharp contrast to the residential sector, is likely to remain a matter of low priority for Parliament.

As regards compensation for tenants' improvements, more drastic reform has been recommended by the Law Commission. In a 1989 report (*Landlord and Tenant Law Compensation for Tenants' Improvements*, Law Com No 178), the Law Commission advocated the abolition (subject to transitional provisions) of the statutory machinery. The Commission adopted the view that the compensation scheme was seldom used and therefore of no practical value. This conclusion is not unassailable and it remains to be seen whether the recommendation will be acted upon.

There is, however, most certainly a need for reform of the existing compensation provisions. The procedural formalities, in particular, need to be simplified, and the ability of a landlord to contract indirectly out of the scheme needs to be reduced. A series of improving reforms were recommended in the Law Commission Working Paper 1987 (No 102). The existing compensation scheme and its defects are considered fully in Chapter 11.

Chapter 2

Security of tenure: the statutory framework

The Landlord and Tenant Act 1954 provides for the continuation and renewal of business tenancies or, where the landlord successfully establishes certain grounds of opposition, for compensation payable to the tenant for disturbance. The statutory provisions concerning security of tenure are to be found in Parts II and IV of the Act, as amended. It is unfortunate that the provisions are fraught with difficulty and sometimes suffer the consequences of being imperfectly drafted. The skills of the draftsman came under vitriolic attack, for example, by the Court of Appeal in *Connaught Fur Trimmings Ltd* v *Cramas Properties Ltd* (1965). Salmon LJ lamented that the draftsman suffered from "... a most slovenly mode of expression ..." and voiced the wish " ... that it were possible to order the costs here and below to be paid out of the pocket of the draftsman who created the maze in which we now find oùrselves". Danckwerts LJ was more restrained in his criticism, but commented that the legislation was " ... a most confusing and tantalising statute". Although much-needed changes were introduced by the Law of Property Act 1969, there is still room for improvement.

The scheme of the Act needs to be viewed as a whole. Security of tenure, in contrast to its applicability to residential tenants, is not available by reason of any general principle, but rather its existence is the culmination of a number of procedural steps taken by the parties. It must be appreciated therefore, that : "The Act like much modern legislation is a statutory interference with freedom of contract and like many such interferences is apt to produce complications" (*per* Harman LJ in *Scholl Manufacturing Co* v *Clifton* (1967)).

In recognition of such difficulties, this chapter has a dual purpose: first, to introduce by way of a summary the operation of the statutory scheme; second, to serve as a convenient means through which to group together a miscellany of matters that either need to be appreciated at the outset or constitute special (and, in the main, complex and detailed) provisions outside the mainstream application of the Act.

1. The 1954 Act in operation

By way of an outline, the Act can be seen to operate, in relation to business leases, on a variety of levels. These are:

(a) by the device of a continuation tenancy, the Act prevents leases, to which it applies, coming to an end (whether by effluxion of time or the landlord's common law notice to quit) on the expiry of the original contractual term: s 24. This means that the tenant can remain in possession, and is still responsible for performing the leasehold covenants, while the landlord remains liable on the covenants and cannot regain possession, except under the provisions of Part II. The existing tenancy is, therefore, automatically and indefinitely extended;

(b) at common law there exist various methods by which a lease can be terminated: for example, expiry of a fixed term, merger, notice to quit, forfeiture and surrender. As regards tenancies within its ambit, the Act overrides the common law rules concerning termination and provides that such a tenancy can be ended only by certain prescribed methods: s 24(2). There are five means of termination available in substitution for the common law rules:

  (i) forfeiture—the Act ensures that the forfeiture of the lease (including the forfeiture of a superior lease) remains unaffected. Forfeiture, therefore, precludes a tenant from claiming security of tenure;

  (ii) surrender—although this common law method is retained, the Act adds the requirement that the tenant must have been in occupation in right of the tenancy for at least one month before the instrument of surrender was executed: s 24(2)(b). This is to prevent avoidance of the statutory provisions by the simple expedient of having the lease and the document of surrender executed at the same time;

  (iii) tenant's notice to quit—this is also subject to the

Security of tenure: the statutory framework

qualification that the tenant had been in occupation in right of the tenancy for one month: s 24(2)(a). As regards a periodic tenancy, the notice will be an ordinary notice to quit: s 24(2). In the case of a lease of fixed duration, the notice must be in writing and served on the immediate landlord not less than three months before the contractual date of expiry: s 27(1);

(iv) statutory notice by the landlord—this type of notice is governed by s 25. The interrelationship between the common law rules and the statutory provisions is illustrated in *Scholl Manufacturing Co* v *Clifton* where the exercise of a break-clause in the lease ended the contractual tenancy, but the landlord still needed to serve a statutory notice so as to regain possession. Until that time, the tenant was able to enjoy the benefits of a s 24 continuation tenancy;

(v) rejection of a new tenancy by the court—if agreement for a renewal is not achieved by the parties, the matter must be resolved by the court. The court is empowered to reject the tenant's application on specified grounds: s 30.

Although merger (ie, the tenant buying out the landlord's interest) is not specified in s 24(2), it is logical to conclude that there can be no statutory continuation of a lease which is no longer in existence;

(c) as regards the notices and counternotices which may arise in the course of an application for, or resistance of, a new tenancy (ss 25–27), the Act imposes a series of procedures and formalities which must be strictly adhered to;

(d) during a continuation tenancy, the Act allows the landlord to apply to the court for an interim rent to be set: s 24A(1);

(e) the Act entitles the tenant to a new tenancy not exceeding fourteen years, at a full market rent and upon such other terms as are decided by the court or agreed with the landlord (ss 32–35). The procedures laid down by the Act must, however, be followed;

(f) the Act allows the landlord to oppose the new tenancy arising on one or more of the seven grounds listed in s 30(1). If any such ground is established, the court must reject the tenant's application;

(g) the Act enables a tenant who, without fault, is denied a new lease to claim compensation for disturbance: s 37. Whether compensation will be awarded depends upon which of the s 30 ground(s) the landlord successfully relies.

2. Interplay of statutory provisions

For greater appreciation of the workings of Part II Landlord and Tenant Act 1954, it is of some use to consider initially how the statutory provisions may be employed and to demonstrate the possible permutations by presenting them in diagrammatic form on the opposite page.

In practice, the following alternatives may arise:

(a) the tenant may not desire a new lease and may wish to quit the premises at the end of the contractual term. To ensure that a continuation tenancy does not arise, the tenant must serve the landlord with a notice to quit. As mentioned in relation to a fixed term lease, this will be a s 27 notice and, as regards a periodic tenancy, the notice will be governed by the common law: s 24;

(b) the landlord may seek to terminate the lease and thereby prevent a new lease being granted. The landlord must serve a s 25 notice not earlier than twelve months, and no later than six months, before the date of termination specified in the notice. The notice must state one or more of the statutory grounds of opposition. The tenant has two months in which to serve a counternotice on the landlord and a further two months in which to apply to the court for a new tenancy;

(c) the tenant may initiate the renewal procedure and serve a s 26 request on the landlord. This will set out the tenant's proposals and must be served not earlier than twelve months, and no later than six months, before the date of termination specified in the s 26 request. The landlord has two months in which to serve a counternotice stating opposition and the ground(s) upon which the opposition is based;

(d) either party may have failed to follow the prescribed termination procedures. An invalid notice is of no effect. Accordingly, the party must draft a new notice or request and serve that in compliance with the requirements of Part II;

Security of tenure: the statutory framework

Charting the renewal provisions

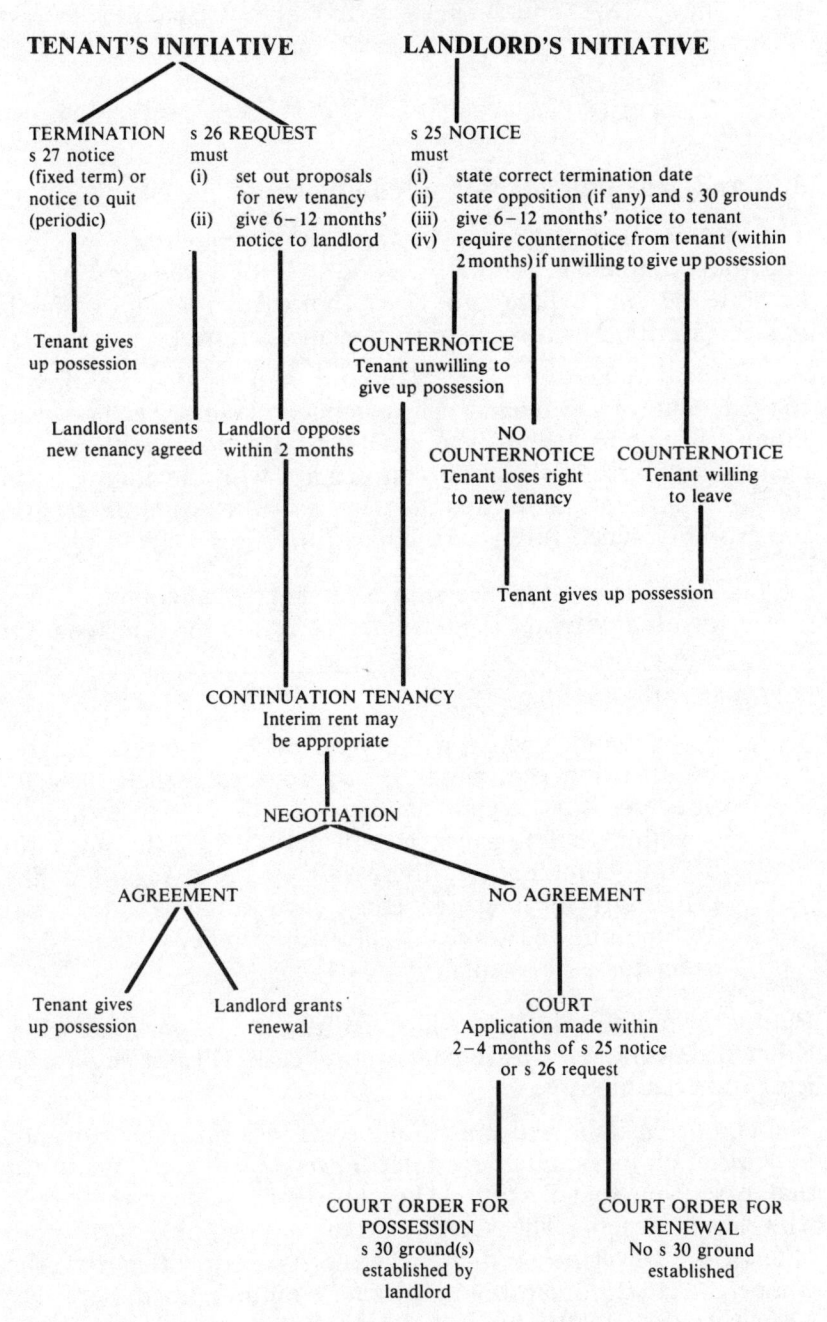

TENANT'S INITIATIVE

TERMINATION
s 27 notice
(fixed term) or
notice to quit
(periodic)

↓

Tenant gives
up possession

s 26 REQUEST
must
(i) set out proposals for new tenancy
(ii) give 6–12 months' notice to landlord

↓

- Landlord consents new tenancy agreed
- Landlord opposes within 2 months

LANDLORD'S INITIATIVE

s 25 NOTICE
must
(i) state correct termination date
(ii) state opposition (if any) and s 30 grounds
(iii) give 6–12 months' notice to tenant
(iv) require counternotice from tenant (within 2 months) if unwilling to give up possession

↓

COUNTERNOTICE
Tenant unwilling to give up possession

- **NO COUNTERNOTICE** Tenant loses right to new tenancy
- **COUNTERNOTICE** Tenant willing to leave

Tenant gives up possession

CONTINUATION TENANCY
Interim rent may be appropriate

↓

NEGOTIATION

- **AGREEMENT**
  - Tenant gives up possession
  - Landlord grants renewal
- **NO AGREEMENT**
  - **COURT**
    Application made within 2–4 months of s 25 notice or s 26 request
    - **COURT ORDER FOR POSSESSION** s 30 ground(s) established by landlord
    - **COURT ORDER FOR RENEWAL** No s 30 ground established

(e) the parties may agree to the grant and terms of a new lease and thereby avoid the need both to use the statutory machinery and to go to court.

3. Landlords immediate and competent

The Act draws a distinction between the "immediate" landlord and the "competent" landlord. Although the same person may be both the "immediate" and the "competent" landlord, this is not necessarily the case where sub-tenancies have been created.

The immediate landlord is the landlord who granted the interest to the tenant (or sub-tenant). The competent landlord is, however, more difficult to identify because it is a concept with a time element. By virtue of s 44 (in conjunction with the complex Sch 6), the competent landlord is the person who owns an interest in the property which fulfils certain conditions, namely:

(a) it is an interest in reversion expectant (whether immediately or otherwise) on the termination of the relevant tenancy; *and either*

(b) it is the fee simple; *or*

(c) it is a tenancy which will not end within fourteen months by effluxion of time and, in respect of which, no s 25 notice or s 26 request has been given so as to terminate it within that fourteen month period. For the purposes of this computation, there fall to be disregarded any extensions to cater for court proceedings (under s 64) or time allowed (under s 36(2)) on the revocation of an order for a new tenancy: s 44(1).

Put more simply, s 44(1) provides that the competent landlord is either the freeholder or a tenant whose lease will not end for at least fourteen months.

The competent landlord must hold under a legal estate and not by virtue of an equitable estate: *Pearson* v *Alyo* (1990). In that case Nourse LJ said: "The subsection is concerned only with legal owners. The Act would be unworkable if it were otherwise". Nevertheless, there is authority to the effect that the competent landlord can hold under an equitable lease: *Shelley* v *United Artists* (1990). This case should, however, be limited to its own facts, that is, a specifically enforceable agreement to grant a new lease to the inferior landlord (albeit at that stage equitable) can be added to the end of the original term so as to maintain that landlord's status as the competent landlord. The Court of Appeal also accepted that a failure to correct the tenant's mistaken belief as to the identity of the competent landlord, and to disclose the identity of the new competent landlord, gives rise to an estoppel. This is so even though the tenant could have made further enquiries (for example, the service of a s 40 notice – see page 17).

Accordingly, where there is a fixed term head lease and a sublease (which is within the scope of the Act), the competent landlord will be the head lessee until the last fourteen months of the head lease. If this lease has less than fourteen months to run, the competent landlord will be the freeholder and not the sub-tenant's immediate landlord: *Shelley* v *United Artists*.

Differences emerge, however, according to whether the sub-tenancy is of the whole or of part only of the property comprised in the head lease. If the whole of the property is sublet, the head lessee will no longer occupy any part of the demised premises and, therefore, will not be protected by the provisions of Part II. The head lease will expire by effluxion of time or pursuant to an ordinary notice to quit. As soon as the head lease enters its last (contractual) fourteen months, the head lessor will become the competent landlord of the sub-tenant.

Where the head lessee sublets only part of the premises and continues to occupy the remainder for the purposes of a business, the head lease remains within the protection of the Act. It cannot be ended by effluxion of time or the landlord's common law notice to quit. The statutory procedures must be used and, unless and until a statutory notice is served to bring the head lease to an end within fourteen months, the immediate landlord continues to be the competent landlord of the sub-tenant.

It can be seen, therefore, that where sub-tenancies are involved and the immediate landlord fails to satisfy the conditions of s 44, the landlord next in the chain, whose interest does comply, is the competent landlord. Although there can be only one competent landlord at any given time, changes can occur during the period when renewal or termination is being sought: *XL Fisheries* v *Leeds Corporation* (1955). As the new competent landlord steps into the shoes of the predecessor, it is necessary that the new party be joined to any proceedings under Part II: *Piper* v *Muggleton*

(1956). Accordingly, if the tenant requests a new tenancy, and does not make the new competent landlord a party to the action, those proceedings will fail: *Rene Claro (Haute Coiffure) Ltd* v *Hallé Concerts Society* (1969).

Where the interest of a competent landlord is subject to a mortgage, under which the mortgagee is in possession or a receiver has been appointed, the mortgagee is deemed to act in the capacity of the competent landlord: s 67. The mortgagee or receiver must, accordingly, be joined to the new tenancy proceedings.

The distinction between these types of landlord is vital because in some sections of Part II "landlord" means the immediate landlord, whereas in others the reference is to the competent landlord. It is useful to segregate these statutory provisions:

(a) the *immediate landlord* plays a role in the following, but limited, termination procedures:
  (i) the notice to quit given by a periodic tenant, who does not seek a new tenancy, is served on the immediate landlord (s 24(2));
  (ii) the written notice given by a tenant to end a fixed term lease is served on the immediate landlord (s 27(1) and (2));
  (iii) any agreement as to surrender is between the tenant and the immediate landlord (s 24(2));
  (iv) forfeiture can occur only at the instigation of the immediate landlord (s 24(2));
(b) except for the above procedures, a tenancy to which Part II extends can be terminated or renewed only with the participation of the *competent landlord*. Therefore a s 25 notice can be served only by a competent landlord, and a tenant's s 26 request served only on a competent landlord. The rationale is that the freeholder or the leaseholder with a term of fourteen months or more will act with more care and responsibility than a tenant approaching the end of his lease.

The involvement of the competent landlord in the interim rent procedure is also necessary. The weakness of this provision lies in the fact that, where sub-tenancies exist, the competent landlord will have nothing to gain by activating the interim rent machinery. In such a case the benefit will be that of the immediate landlord only. Therefore an interim rent might not be applied for.

Security of tenure: the statutory framework

4. Information gathering

As shown above, the procedures contained within Part II require that certain steps be taken by the correct person and at the correct time. Central to the statutory machinery is that both parties be able to identify each other and to ascertain the nature and extent of their respective interests. This is of paramount importance where subletting has occurred. The tenant will need to know who the competent landlord is and the landlord will need to be aware of the details of any sub-tenancy. Accordingly, a facility exists within s 40 whereby both parties can acquire the requisite information.

By virtue of s 40(2), a tenant can serve a notice (in the prescribed form) provided that his tenancy is within the scope of Part II and is either for a term certain exceeding one year or for any term certain and thereafter from year to year. The notice may be served on any person having a superior interest, including any mortgagee in possession of such an interest: s 40(3). Following service, it is the duty of the recipient to respond in writing within one month and state whether he is either the freeholder or a mortgagee in possession of the freehold: s 40(2). If he is neither of these, the recipient must provide the best information he can give concerning the name and address of his (or his mortgagor's) immediate landlord, the term of the lease and the earliest date (if any) on which the tenancy can be terminated by notice to quit: s 40(2). A reversioner served with such a notice must also disclose the fact of any mortgagee in possession of his interest in the premises and, where this is so, provide that mortgagee's name and address: s 40(3).

Similarly, the immediate or a superior landlord can serve a notice (in the prescribed form) on the tenant requiring the tenant to respond in writing and within one month. The information to be given concerns whether he occupies the premises or part of them wholly or partly for the purposes of a business carried on by him and the details of any sub-tenancy granted: s 40(1). These details must identify the premises comprised in the sub-tenancy, its term (including the provisions for termination by notice to quit), the rent, the name of the sub-tenant, whether the sub-tenant is (to the best knowledge and belief of the respondent) in occupation of the premises and, if not, the sub-tenant's address: s 40(1)(b).

One qualification exists: a s 40 notice cannot be served by or on a tenant more than two years before the date on which (discounting the statutory renewal provisions) the lease (a) is due to expire or (b) can be brought to an end by the landlord's notice to quit: s 40(4). This provision is intended to avoid purposeless and vexatious notices being served by either party.

Although s 40 imposes duties, it provides no redress for their non-observance. The absence of any specified penalty can be seen to undermine the effectiveness of what would otherwise be an important safeguard for those who wish to exercise their statutory rights. The Law Commission's Working Paper (No 111) considered this issue and proposed that an express sanction be incorporated into the Act (para 3.2.37). The Working Paper was unsure whether the sanction should be a criminal one and/or one to prevent the defaulter taking other statutory steps (para 3.2.38). It did, however, propose in broad terms that there should be an express right of damages against the defaulter (*ibid*). Short of fraud, the only possible current redress for a party suffering loss is for breach of a statutory duty. This is, as yet, both an untried and an untested avenue.

5. Sub-tenancies: some complex issues

The protection of the Act extends to a sub-tenant as to any other tenant: s 69(1). The statutory machinery has been adapted, therefore, so as to operate where there is a chain of tenancies. As shown above, the identification of the competent landlord is crucial because many of the functions ascribed by the Act to "the landlord" fall for the competent landlord to exercise. Accordingly, the Act contains a series of rules which regulate the relationship between the competent landlord and any mesne or superior landlord. These detailed provisions are located within Sch 6.

By way of clarification, it should be noted that persons with an interest superior to the competent landlord are called "superior landlords", and those with an interest between the competent landlord and the tenant in possession are referred to as "mesne landlords" (Sch 6 para 1).

The provisions of Sch 6 can be paraphrased as follows:

> (a) the power of the court to order reversionary leases (para 2). Under para 2, the court is able to grant a new tenancy (under the terms of Part II) which, whether by agreement or determination by the court, can extend beyond the date that the immediate landlord's interest comes to an

Security of tenure: the statutory framework

end. This is achieved by the creation of such reversionary tenancies as may be necessary to secure the grant of the new lease, and to ensure that what the Act refers to as the "inferior tenancy" may be prolonged beyond the end of a superior tenancy.

This is backed up by the provisions of s 65 which are designed to regulate the situation where a tenancy is extended to or beyond the expiry of a superior tenancy. By virtue of s 65:

(i) as long as it subsists, the superior tenancy is deemed to be an interest in reversion expectant (immediately expectant if no intermediate tenancy exists) upon the termination of the inferior tenancy, even though that inferior tenancy will continue beyond it: s 65(1);

(ii) when the immediate superior tenancy ends, the "continuing" tenancy emerges as a tenancy held directly under the superior landlord next in the chain: s 65(2); s 139(1) Law of Property Act 1925;

(iii) the existing tenancy may be continued under the Act, beyond the date when a reversionary lease has been granted to come into effect. If this occurs, the reversionary tenancy takes effect subject to the continuing tenancy: s 65(3). This prevents evasion of the Act by the granting of a reversionary tenancy to take effect when the original contractual tenancy ends. The reversionary tenancy, in this instance, takes effect subject to the renewal rights under the original tenancy. Similarly, the reversionary tenancy is the superior tenancy where the new tenancy, which is granted under Part II, runs into the period of the reversionary lease: s 65(4);

(b) the competent landlord can bind any mesne landlord (para 3(1)). This applies to any notice given to terminate the lease and to any agreement made with the tenant as to the grant and terms of a new tenancy. The competent landlord is empowered to execute a new lease, and this takes effect as if the mesne landlord was a party to it (para 3(2));

(c) if the competent landlord acts without the consent of the mesne landlord, he may be liable to pay compensation to the mesne landlord for any consequential loss (para 4(1)).

There is the proviso, however, that the mesne landlord's consent cannot be unreasonably withheld, but may be given subject to reasonable conditions (para 4(2)). Such conditions might include the payment of compensation or the modification of any notice to be served on, or agreement to be reached with, the tenant (para 4(2)). Questions of reasonableness are to be decided by the court (*ibid*). As shown earlier, because of the provisions of para 3 these matters do not directly concern the tenant;

(d) an agreement which the competent landlord proposes to enter may have an effect on the interest of a superior landlord. By virtue of para 5, the consent of every superior landlord, who will be the immediate landlord of the tenant during any part of the period covered by the agreement, is necessary before the agreement can be effective. Accordingly, the competent landlord cannot bind either a superior landlord or the freeholder where the agreement with the tenant is to run beyond the end of the competent landlord's lease;

(e) where a landlord's s 25 notice is served and a superior landlord becomes the competent landlord, that notice can be withdrawn by the new landlord (para 6). A prescribed form of withdrawal must be followed and it is without prejudice to any future notices given by the new landlord. It is necessary, however, that the withdrawal occurs within two months of the s 25 notice being served;

(f) if the competent landlord serves a s 25 notice or receives a s 26 request, and his tenancy is one which could be or will be brought to an end within sixteen months of the service of that notice, the competent landlord must forthwith send a copy of the notice to his immediate landlord (para 7(a)). The immediate landlord must then send a copy to his superior landlord (if any) and the process is to be continued up the chain until the notification reaches the freeholder (para 7(b)).

6. Notices and their service

The operation of the Part II machinery relies heavily upon the service of appropriate notices. Specimens of the most used documents are reproduced in Appendix B. Many are required to be

Security of tenure: the statutory framework

in the form (or substantially similar to the form) prescribed by the Secretary of State: s 66(1). It is particularly important to note that a new prescribed version of the s 25 notice came into effect on 29 September 1989.

It is crucial that the correct form is used; otherwise the notice may be rendered invalid. Printed forms, with suitable blanks to be completed, are published by law stationers; use of such forms is clearly advisable.

The provisions of s 23 Landlord and Tenant Act 1927 apply to the service of notices under both Part I of that Act and Part II of the 1954 Act: s 66(4). These provisions require that any notice, request, demand or other instrument under the 1927 and 1954 Acts must be in writing. By virtue of s 23(1), service may occur in any of the following ways:

(a) personal service. This is the most effective and certain means of service;

(b) by leaving it at the party's last known place of abode in England and Wales. "Abode" includes place of business for these purposes: *Price* v *West London Building Society* (1964);

(c) by sending it through the post in a registered (or recorded: s 1 Recorded Delivery Service Act 1962) letter to him there. Section 7 Interpretation Act 1978 states that, in the absence of contrary evidence, service is deemed to be effected by properly addressing, prepaying and posting a letter containing the document. The statutory presumption is that it has been delivered in the ordinary course of the post. Accordingly, where a registered letter was returned marked "undelivered. No response", there was clear evidence that it had not been delivered: *Ex parte Rossi* (1956). Nevertheless, in *Lex Service plc* v *Johns* (1990) the Court of Appeal held that the presumption of service was not rebutted where a recorded delivery letter was illegibly signed for by someone (identity unknown) and merely asserted not to have been received by the tenant. This re-affirmed the decision of the High Court in *Moody* v *Godstone RDC* (1966). If the law were otherwise, the service provisions would be rendered nugatory because it would be open to anyone to claim non-receipt as a triable issue. In *Lex Service*, Glidewell LJ hinted that the court may be influenced by whether time was or was not of the essence. *Rossi* was distinguished on the basis that time was there of the essence;

(d) in the case of a local or public authority or statutory or public utility, by service on the secretary or other proper officer. In the case of a local authority, service may occur at an office designated for receiving such notices: s 231(1) Local Government Act 1972. As regards the other bodies, service may be at their principal office;

(e) on a limited company by sending the notice to the company's registered office by ordinary post: s 725(1) Companies Act 1985;

(f) on the landlord's duly authorised agent (see *Sector Properties Ltd* v *Meah* (1974)). Due to the limited nature of the notice to be served under the 1927 legislation, there is no correlative provision for the service of notices by landlords. Although this anomaly has never been rectified by Parliament, the ordinary rules of agency will apply and the tenant's solicitor (or other agent) will be able to accept service: *Galinski* v *McHugh* (1988).

These modes of service are not exhaustive and exist to assist the serving party: *Galinski* v *McHugh*. Actual receipt of the notice is, therefore, good service even though the specified methods of service are not followed: *Stylo Shoes* v *Prices Tailors* (1960). The purpose of s 23(1) is to ensure that the notice is received and that there is (actual or deemed) proof of service.

The tenant is further assisted by s 23(2) which provides that, unless and until the tenant of a holding is notified that there has been a change of landlord, service on the original landlord will be deemed to be sufficient. This must be read in conjunction with the competent landlord provisions considered above.

Special provisions apply to premises held by joint tenants and used for the purposes of a partnership.

7. Partnerships and joint tenancies

A problem, experienced before the enactment of s 9 Law of Property Act 1969, concerned a tenancy held by a partnership where not all of the partners were active in the business. Until the creation of the new s 41A of the 1954 Act, it was necessary that all of the joint tenants joined in the renewal and termination

Security of tenure: the statutory framework

procedures: *Jacobs* v *Chaudhuri* (1968). The modifications made by s 41A remedy this situation, subject to certain conditions, by allowing the tenants who carry on the business to act on behalf of any other partners.

Before this provision applies, the following conditions must be satisfied:

(a) at some time during the subsistence of the current tenancy a business was carried on upon the premises in partnership with all the joint tenants, with or without others, and the tenancy was held as partnership property (s 41A(1)(b) and (c));

(b) the tenancy is currently held by two or more joint tenants (ie where the property is vested in one person his partners receive no benefit from the new provision), not all of whom carry on a business there, and the other tenants do not occupy any part of the premises as tenants for the purposes of some other business (s 41A(1)(a) and (d)).

Where these conditions are met, the tenants carrying on the business at a given time are called "business tenants"; it is they who derive benefit from the provision. The remaining partners are termed "the other joint tenants": s 41A(2).

The benefit afforded by s 41A is that it permits certain notices and applications, within the Part II machinery, to be served by or on the "business tenants" only. These include a s 26 request or a s 27 notice (s 41A(3)) and a s 24(1) application for a new tenancy (s 41A(5)). "Business tenants" are also qualified to accept service of a landlord's s 25 notice: s 41A(4). As regards an order for a new tenancy under s 29(1), the court may grant it to the "business tenants" exclusively (s 41A(6)) and it is they who will recover any s 37 compensation for disturbance (s 41A(7)).

8. The Crown and government departments

Subject to certain qualifications, the Crown is within the s 44 classification of a landlord for the purposes of Part II of the Act: s 56(1). Without this express inclusion, the Crown would not be bound by the security of tenure provisions: *Wirral Estates Ltd* v *Shaw* (1932). The Act provides that where the landlord's interest is held by Her Majesty in right of the Crown or the Duchy of Lancaster, or is held by the Duchy of Cornwall, the tenant (provided that he otherwise qualifies for protection) is entitled to the full benefits of Part II: s 56(1). Subject to some exceptions, the same general rule applies where the landlord's interest is held by a government department: s 56(1) (see below).

For the purposes of the Act, when an interest belongs to Her Majesty in right of the Duchy of Lancaster, the Chancellor of that Duchy represents Her Majesty and is deemed to own the interest (Sch 8 para 1). As regards the Duchy of Cornwall, such person as the Duke appoints to represent him is deemed to own the interest (Sch 8 para 2).

The Crown may also, in certain circumstances, take advantage of the protection of Part II in the capacity of a tenant: s 56(1). For such protection to exist, the premises must be occupied for the purposes of a business and within the catchment of s 23 (see Chapter 3). One modification of this rule exists exclusively in connection with tenancies held by, or on behalf of, a government department. Special provision is made whereby premises occupied for the purposes of a government department are deemed to be occupied for the purposes of a business: s 56(3) (see *Linden* v *DHSS* (1986)). This sidesteps the need to demonstrate whether occupation by a government department is occupation for the purposes of a business. Even if the premises are not occupied for the purposes of a government department, the department is protected by Part II provided that no rent is payable by any other occupier: s 56(4). The government department is, therefore, deemed to be still in occupation for its own purposes.

Furthermore, any provisions which require that the premises should have been occupied for the purposes of the tenant's business for a period of time (for example, s 37 relating to compensation for disturbance) or that, on a change of tenant, the new occupier should have succeeded to the business of his predecessor (for example s 37 or Sch 9), are negated. Therefore, where there is occupation for the purposes of a government department, any such period of time or succession requirement can be deemed to be satisfied: s 56(3).

9. Public interest and national security

Although the landlord's interest being held by a government department does not in itself prevent a tenant from claiming security of tenure, there are a series of provisions which, on the grounds of public interest or national security, can curtail the tenant's right to a new tenancy.

The public interest ground applies where the interest of the competent landlord (or any superior landlord) belongs to, or is held for the purposes of, either a government department or one of the bodies listed in ss 28 and 38(2) Leasehold Reform Act 1967. This list includes any local authority, regional or special area health authority, development corporation, statutory undertaker or the National Trust. For these purposes, however, Commissioners of Crown Lands are not a government department: s 57(8).

The Minister (or Board) in charge of the appropriate government department may issue a certificate to the effect that the use or occupation of the property (or any part of it) comprised in the tenancy will be changed from a specified date and that this is required for the purposes of the relevant public body: s 57(1). As regards the National Trust, the certificate is issued under the terms of s 57(7). This certification excludes the tenant's right to renew. There is, however, no need for the change to be essential. It is sufficient that it is required in the circumstances: *R v Secretary of State for the Environment ex parte Powis* (1981).

A further alternative is open to the landlord by virtue of s 57(5) which allows a different type of certificate to be issued where the tenant's application for a new tenancy is already under way and no order has yet been made. This certificate is to the effect that it is necessary, in the public interest, that the court must include as a term of the new tenancy that it shall be determinable by six months' notice to quit by the landlord (ie a break-clause will be inserted). The new tenancy will, however, be one to which Part II applies.

None of these certificates may be issued unless the tenant has been given preliminary notice (no form is prescribed) that the Minister (or Board) is contemplating the issue of the document: s 57(2). The tenant then has twenty-one days in which to make written representations to the Minister (or Board) concerning the matter (*ibid*). Account must be taken of the representations (if any) before the decision to issue the certificate is reached (*ibid*). There is no appeal against the giving of the certificate.

The legal consequences of the issue of the certificate depend upon whether the tenancy is terminated by a landlord's s 25 notice or a tenant's s 26 request for a new tenancy.

First, if a s 25 notice is served much turns on the date of termination specified in the notice. If the date specified therein is not earlier than the date set out in the certificate (and the s 25 notice contains a copy of the certificate), the tenant can make no application for a new tenancy: s 57(3). When the date of the termination is earlier than the date specified in the certificate (and, again, provided that a copy of the certificate is contained in the s 25 notice), the court can grant a renewal, but only for a term expiring not later than the date specified: s 57(3). The new tenancy will be outside the protection of Part II and there can be no further renewal: s 57(3)(b).

Second, where the tenant makes a s 26 request for a new tenancy, much depends upon whether the request is made before or after the issue of the certificate. If the s 26 request is served after the certificate, the landlord can serve a notice, within two months, containing a copy of the certificate. Where the date specified in the request, as the termination date of the existing tenancy, is not earlier than the date set out in the certificate, the tenant cannot make an application for a new tenancy: s 57(4). Where the date contained in the s 26 request is earlier than the date contained in the certificate, a new tenancy can be granted, but for a duration no longer than the certificate date: s 57(4). This tenancy is outside the Part II machinery (*ibid*). It should again be appreciated that the landlord must serve the preliminary notice before these restrictions on the tenant's rights apply.

When the tenant's s 26 request precedes the issue of the certificate, the request is invalid if the preliminary certification notice has been given by the Minister (or Board) or is given within two months of the tenant's request: s 57(4). The consequence is that the current tenancy continues with the proviso that, once the decision as to whether to issue a certificate has been taken, the tenant can make a fresh s 26 request.

These provisions apply even when the authority using them acquired the reversion after the tenant served a s 26 request: *XL Fisheries* v *Leeds Corporation* (1955). The requisite steps to be taken by the landlord within the two-month period, however, are still necessary.

Where the landlord's interest belongs to, or is held for the purposes of, a government department, s 58(1) enables the tenancy to be terminated on the grounds of national security. This special provision prevents the operation of the Part II machinery. The procedure requires a certificate from the Minister (or Board) of the government department to the effect that for reasons of national security it is necessary that the use or occupation of the premises leased shall be discontinued or changed: s 58(1).

Security of tenure: the statutory framework

Unlike the other type of certification discussed above, there is under s 58 no requirement for any preliminary notice to be given to the tenant. The issue of a certificate does, however, have implications with regard to the service of a s 25 notice or s 26 request.

Where the landlord, after the issue of the certificate, serves a s 25 notice (which contains a copy of the certificate) the tenant is unable to apply for a new tenancy: s 58(1)(a). Although the provisions of s 25(5) and (6) (detailing the opposition to a new tenancy) do not apply, the ordinary requirements of s 25 must be satisfied by the notice (see Chapter 5).

If the tenant makes a s 26 request for a new tenancy then, whether or not the certificate has been issued at that date, the landlord can within two months serve a notice (containing a copy of the certificate) so as to preclude the tenant's application: s 58(1)(b). The notice should set a date on which the tenancy is to come to an end. If that date is earlier than the date for termination specified in the s 26 request, and is at least six months from the giving of the counternotice – and not earlier than the date the tenancy could be terminated at common law – the current tenancy will end on the date set in the notice: s 58(1)(b). In all other cases, it will terminate on the date specified in the s 26 request.

Further provisions apply to the Department of Trade and Industry which may certify that a change of use or occupation is necessary or expedient, as regards premises located in a development area or an intermediate area, where the DTI or the English Industrial Estates Corporation is the landlord: s 60(1). For these purposes s 58(1) (a) and (b) apply in the same manner as they do to government departments (see above).

In addition, the Secretary of State for Wales may issue a similar certificate, concerning property leased by the Welsh Development Agency or the Development Board for Rural Wales, for the purpose of providing employment appropriate to the needs of the area: ss 60A(1) and 60B(1).

10. Contracting out: special provisions

The provisions discussed above concern the restriction of the tenant's right to a new tenancy, but they do not affect the existing lease of the tenant. There are, however, further procedures through which government departments and statutory undertakers can contract out of Part II.

Where the landlord's interest belongs to, or is held for the purposes of, a government department, the parties may agree that, upon the Minister (or Board) in charge of the department issuing a certificate to the effect that it is for reasons of national security, the use or occupation of the property should be discontinued or changed: s 58(2). This agreement enables the landlord to terminate the tenancy by the service of a notice to quit of such length as agreed (*ibid*). It may also be agreed that, after the service of the notice, the tenancy shall not be one to which Part II applies. Such agreements are valid notwithstanding the restrictions upon contracting out imposed by s 38(1) (see Chapter 3).

Where the landlord's interest is held by a statutory undertaker, the landlord can, by virtue of s 58(3), enter an agreement with the tenant that, upon the certification of the appropriate Minister (or Board), the landlord can terminate the tenancy by notice to quit of an agreed length. It may also be agreed that, after the giving of the notice, the tenancy will cease to be one to which Part II applies. The certification here is that the whole or a part of the premises demised is urgently required for carrying out repairs needed for the proper operation of the landlord's undertaking: s 58(3).

The tenant may be able to obtain compensation when he is disadvantaged by the operation of the special provisions described under this and the preceding sub-heading. It is established by s 59(1) that a tenant who is precluded from obtaining a new tenancy at all, or a new tenancy beyond a specified date, on account of a certification under ss 57 and 58, can claim compensation from the landlord. The amount of compensation is calculated according to the terms of s 37 (see Chapter 9).

There is, moreover, no contracting out of compensation, except as provided for in s 38(2) and (3): s 59(1) and (2). There are, however, further restrictions on the recoverability of compensation where the certificate was issued under either s 60A (*re* the Welsh Development Agency) or s 60(B) (*re* the Development Board for Rural Wales): s 59(1A) and (1B).

11. Ecclesiastical property

Section 61 contains a series of modifications in relation to tenancies of ecclesiastical property. These provisions are straight-

Security of tenure: the statutory framework

forward and designed to prevent the incumbent of a benefice from taking action, as a landlord, under Part II without the knowledge and approval of the Church Commissioners. These provisions apply also to benefices the patronage of which belongs to Her Majesty in right of the Crown or the Duchy of Lancaster or to the Duchy of Cornwall: s 61(2).

The modifications introduced by s 61 are as follows:

(a) the consent of the Church Commissioners (and no other person) is required to validate any agreement entered into, or action taken, by the incumbent under Part II: s 61(1)(a);

(b) any payment of compensation for disturbance (under s 37) may, at the discretion of the Commissioners, be paid on behalf of the incumbent from their funds: s 61(1)(b);

(c) when the Commissioners make such a compensation payment, the revenues and possessions of the benefice are to stand charged with the repayment of any sum so expended: s 61(1)(e);

(d) the Commissioners have the right to appear and be heard in any proceedings to which the incumbent is a party. Any order made in Part II proceedings is binding on the Commissioners: s 61(1)(c);

(e) for the purposes of the Act, during any vacancy of the benefice the incumbent's interest is deemed to vest in the Church Commissioners: s 61(1)(d).

Chapter 3

Tenancies within the Act

The protection of Part II Landlord and Tenant Act 1954, subject to certain common law and statutory exceptions, extends to "any tenancy where the property comprised in the tenancy is or includes premises which are occupied for the purposes of a business carried on by him or for those and other purposes" (s 23(1)). Accordingly, there must be a tenancy; the tenant must occupy the premises demised; that occupation must be wholly or partly for business purposes; and the tenancy must not be excluded from protection by any other statutory provisions. Each of these pre-requisites needs to be examined.

1. Lease or licence

As the Act applies only to tenancies, licences are excluded from its protection: *Shell-Mex & BP Ltd* v *Manchester Garages* (1971). It is unfortunate that the distinction between a lease and a licence is not always easy to draw; prompted by the extent of the litigation that this has provoked, the Law Commission regarded it as "a matter for consideration" whether occupation licences should be abolished or, if maintained, whether they should be treated any differently from tenancies within protective legislation such as the 1954 Act (*Landlord and Tenant: Reform of the Law* (1987) Law Com No 162). Parliament is not expected to act upon these particular deliberations.

A licence is regarded as being fundamentally different from a lease in that the licence does not create a legal estate and bestows only a personal privilege upon the licensee: *Ashburn Anstalt* v *Arnold* (1988). The classic exposition is that of Vaughan CJ in *Thomas* v *Sorrell* (1673): "... a dispensation or licence properly passeth

Tenancies within the Act

no interest, nor alters or transfers property in any thing, but only makes an action lawful which without it had been unlawful". Nevertheless, the rights of a licensee (albeit of a personal and not proprietary nature) may be enforced both at law and in equity.

A lease is recognised in s 1(1) Law of Property Act 1925 as being a legal estate in land. For a lease to exist at law, however, it must satisfy certain requirements. It must be created in the proper manner (see ss 52(1) and 54(2) Law of Property Act 1925) and certain conditions as to duration must be met, that is, the beginning and end of the term must be capable of being ascertained (*Oakley* v *Wilson* (1927)). A periodic tenancy can satisfy these conditions by retrospective calculation. Finally, exclusive possession must be granted (*Street* v *Mountford* (1985)).

The definition of a tenancy, for the purposes of Part II, expressly includes subleases and agreements for a lease, but excludes mortgage terms (s 69(1)). In *D'Silva* v *Lister House Developments Ltd* (1970), it was made apparent that the protection of Part II extends to a sub-tenant even when the under-lease was granted in breach of a covenant contained in the head lease. The prohibition was held not to affect the sub-tenant because he was not a party to that covenant. The provisions of s 23(4), which prevent the Act applying where the tenant is in breach of a user covenant, do not apply to this situation. Unauthorised business user is considered later in this chapter.

The problem which has perplexed the courts on numerous occasions is how to distinguish between a tenancy and a licence agreement. This is largely due to the fact that the similarities between the two are often striking. Both will, in general, embody contractual terms concerning consideration, repairs, exclusive occupation and termination procedures, for example. The danger, as recognised by the House of Lords in *Street* v *Mountford*, is of the demarcation between them becoming "wholly unidentifiable".

(a) Identifying a lease

The solution, as advocated by Lord Templeman in *Street*, appears straightforward: "... [where] accommodation is granted for a term at a rent with exclusive possession ... the grant is a tenancy ... No other test ... appears to be understandable or workable". Although in some subsequent decisions this principle has been applied slavishly (for example, see *Ward* v *Warnke* (1990)), it is not decisive. It has now been established that the payment of rent, albeit influential, is not a necessary feature of a tenancy and that a "no rent-no tenancy" rule does not exist: *Ashburn Anstalt* v *Arnold*. In addition, as recognised in *Street*, the grant of exclusive possession may, in exceptional circumstances, be consistent with a licence agreement (*Essex Plan* v *Broadminster* (1988); *Ogwr BC* v *Dykes* (1989)), for example where there is no intention to create legal relations; where a service occupancy exists; where the occupation is due to an act of friendship or generosity; or it arises as a result of a family arrangement. In these (or similar) circumstances it is open to the court to conclude that occupation is referable to a relationship other than a tenancy. Therefore, legal rules do not always provide an unequivocal answer in this area of the law.

There can be no doubt that exclusive possession is the key factor in making the distinction between a lease and a licence: *Ashburn Anstalt*. It is a pre-requisite of a tenancy, but (as mentioned) is no guarantee that a tenancy has been created: *Bostock* v *Bryant* (1990). Perhaps the sensible approach is to view the grant of exclusive possession as giving rise to a rebuttable presumption that a lease has been created (*Bostock*; *Nicolaou* v *Pitt* (1989)). There does, moreover, appear to be a marked reluctance on the part of the courts to include cases within the exceptional cateegories where, despite exclusive possession, a licence is entered (see *Family Housing Association* v *Jones* (1990); *Bhattacharya* v *Raising* (1987)).

Exclusive possession is primarily a matter of law and must be distinguished from exclusive occupation which is a question of fact: *Smith* v *Northside Developments Ltd* (1987). An occupier can, therefore, have exclusive use of the premises without having the right of exclusive possession: *AG Securities* v *Vaughan* (1988). It is singularly unhelpful that the courts do, on occasion, confuse this somewhat basic terminology (for example, see *McCarthy* v *Bence* (1990)).

Exclusive possession was explained by Lord Templeman in *Street* in the following manner:

> "The tenant possessing exclusive possession is able to exercise the rights of an owner of land, which is in the real sense his land albeit temporarily and subject

to certain restrictions. A tenant armed with exclusive possession can keep out strangers and keep out the landlord unless the landlord is exercising limited rights reserved to him by the tenancy agreement to enter and view and repair."

Accordingly, in *Smith* v *Northside Developments* the Court of Appeal admitted that, if in doubt, the court should look for exclusive possession with the particular emphasis upon whether the landlord can be excluded. This is often difficult to discern; it can be obscured when the agreement calls itself a licence and, moreover, expressly denies the occupier exclusive possession. Admittedly, such tactics alone are insufficient to guarantee the existence of a licence (*Family Housing Association* v *Jones*), but it is an inescapable conclusion that if exclusive possession is effectively denied, both at law and in fact, there can be no tenancy (*Essex Plan Ltd* v *Broadminster*).

It is for the court, and not for the parties, to determine whether a lease or licence has been created: *Nicolaou* v *Pitt*. It is the true bargain, as opposed to the apparent bargain, struck between the parties which must be examined (*Aslan* v *Murphy* (1989); *Duke* v *Wynne* (1989)). The objective intentions of the parties and the real rights under the agreement must be identified; therefore each case should normally turn upon its own facts and each transaction should be examined in the light of all the surrounding circumstances: *Stribling* v *Wickham* (1989).

As regards written agreements, the court must approach the documents in an evenhanded manner and apply the normal rules of construction: *Hadjiloucas* v *Crean* (1987). The label attached by the parties to the transaction is inconclusive (*BJ Dunnel Properties* v *Thorpe* (1989)), but it may constitute *prima facie* evidence of intention (*Dresden Estates* v *Collinson* (1987)). The court must, however, be astute to detect any sham (or pretence) agreements and misleading labels: *Street* v *Mountford*. Although unrealistic provisions in the contract can be disregarded (*Brooker Settled Estates* v *Ayres* (1987)), the court cannot simply re-write the agreement before it (*Mikeover* v *Brady* (1989)). If the defendant does not show that the agreement is a sham, then the agreement will be construed as it stands: *Essex Plan Ltd* v *Broadminster*.

Where there is no written agreement, there is of course nothing for the court to construe. A different approach is adopted and the decision of the court is based purely upon the surrounding circumstances: *Smith* v *Northside Developments*. The method of approach discussed above is, accordingly, inappropriate to oral agreements.

(b) Licences of business premises

The *ratio* of *Street* v *Mountford* is confined to residential premises in sole occupation where exclusive possession has been granted. To what extent the principles expounded by Lord Templeman will go beyond these boundaries is uncertain. Clearly, the test and approach applied by the House have been enthusiastically followed by many judges, but they are not of universal application. In *Hadjiloucas* v *Crean* (1987), the Court of Appeal saw a risk that judges might misinterpret and misapply the *Street* principles. They have been held to be inappropriate to oral agreements (see above) and shown not to work well in relation to shared occupancies (*AG Securities* v *Vaughan*). Nevertheless, the impact of *Street* is felt outside the residential market. The decision has been accepted in the context of transactions involving agricultural land (*Colchester BC* v *Smith* (1991)) and commercial property (*Dellneed Ltd* v *Chin* (1987)). As regards business premises, however, some refinement of the *Street* principles has been attempted. In *Dresden Estates* v *Collinson*, the Court of Appeal suggested that, as the attributes of residential and business premises are different, the indicia of a tenancy in one context may not be as relevant or as influential in the other. The conclusion seemingly to be drawn is that it may be easier to create a commercial licence than a residential licence of premises: *Minimet Enterprises* v *Mayor and Burgesses of Croydon* (1989).

Although it remains a risky adventure, it seems that there are several remaining uses for licences (or "management agreements") in the business sector. These are:

(i) where there is clearly and genuinely no exclusive possession granted: *Dresden Estates*. This would be so where there is a sharing of floor space, ie, a trade concession agreement (*Smith* v *Northside Developments*); where occupation is limited to only part of the day or week (*Minimet Enterprises*); or occupation of a market stall (*Gloucester City Council* v *Williams* (1990));

(ii) perhaps, where the licence is granted by a company which has no power to create a lease;
(iii) where the licence is to allow a prospective tenant into occupation pending the grant of a lease: *Essex Plan Ltd* v *Broadminster*. This was a possibility recognised in *Street*, but in order to work it has to be certain that the intended transaction will take place: *Bhattacharya* v *Raising* (1987). Even if the licence fails, it is likely that the parties will have created a tenancy at will which (as will be shown) is also outside the ambit of the 1954 Act: *Javad* v *Aqil* (1990).

2. Occupation of premises

(a) Premises

For the Act to apply there must be a tenancy of "premises". Usually, what is included within the scope of this term is self-evident. The expression is construed widely as including the land and any buildings on it. There is, however, no need for any building: *Wandsworth Borough Council* v *Singh* (1991). In *Bracey* v *Read* (1963) gallops used for the purpose of training and exercising racehorses were held to be premises. Open land used for a car-park was classified as premises in *Harley Queen* v *Forsyte Kerman* (1983).

Nevertheless, Part II of the Act does not extend to tenancies of incorporeal hereditaments such as a right of way (*Land Reclamation Co Ltd* v *Basildon DC* (1979)) or a lease of chattels (*Nuflats & Properties Ltd* v *Sheckman* (1959)). Such rights would, however, qualify for protection if they were granted as ancillary rights under the lease of corporeal premises: *Nevill Long & Co (Boards)* v *Firmenich & Co* (1984). The Law Commission in its Working Paper No 111 (1988) provisionally concluded that this distinction is illogical and that leases of incorporeal hereditaments should be classified as "premises" and that the qualifying conditions of s 23(1) be adapted accordingly (paras 3.1.21; 3.1.22). The Law Commission thought that this adaptation would entail a move away, in s 23, from the word "occupy" and its substitution by the word "use". It is thought, however, that this change of emphasis alone would not affect the treatment of incorporeal hereditaments (they are outside Part I Landlord and Tenant Act 1927 which requires the premises to be "used" for the purposes of a business: see Chapter 11).

(b) Occupation

The premises must be occupied by the tenant or his employee (s 23(3)) before the statutory provisions can apply. If not, the tenant has no protection under the Act: *Teasdale* v *Walker* (1958). Occupation must, moreover, persist throughout the lease and any proceedings for a new lease: *Domer* v *Gulf Oil (Great Britain) Ltd* (1975). Accordingly, if this condition ceases to be fulfilled at any time, the landlord can apply to have the tenant's application dismissed for a lack of *locus standi*: *Demetriou* v *Poolaction* (1990).

Occupation turns on an issue of fact and it must be real and genuine: *Pulleng* v *Curran* (1982). In *Land Reclamation Co*, the court held that a tenant could not occupy a right of way or other incorporeal right. Such rights could only be enjoyed. Other problems can arise, as will be shown, where the property is occupied by others or is not directly part of a business.

The decisive test is the degree of control and user exercised by the tenant: *Hancock & Willis* v *GMS Syndicate Ltd* (1983). In *William Boyer & Sons Ltd* v *Adams* (1975), for example, the tenant sublet part of the premises and provided various services for the sub-tenants. In the light of the degree of control retained and services provided, the tenant was still in occupation of the premises. As was made clear in *Hills (Patents) Ltd* v *University Hospital Board* (1956), although possession in law is single and exclusive, occupation can be shared. Nevertheless, in *Trans Britannia Properties Ltd* v *Darby Properties Ltd* (1986), a tenant who was in the business of subletting lock-up garages was held, by virtue of the lack of control, not to be in occupation of the holding. It should also be remembered that subletting of the whole of the premises will normally deprive the tenant of the protection of the Act (see Chapter 2). Nevertheless these cases demonstrate that, if subletting is the business of the tenant and sufficient control is retained by him, occupation can continue and the tenancy can remain within s 23(1). In *William Boyer & Sons Ltd* v *Adams* it was said that: "The activities of the defendant are sufficient to show that he is not so much acting as a landlord passively receiving rent, but as the manager of a business actively earning profits by providing accommodation, facilities and services by devoting time for this purpose." However, this test of "sufficiency" is only of relevance where sub-tenants have been let into occupation: *Wandsworth Borough Council* v *Singh* (1991).

Occupation through an agent, representative or employee will suffice: *Cafeteria (Keighley) Ltd* v *Harrison* (1956). In *Singh*, the Court of Appeal made it clear that "occupation" was to be given its popular meaning and stressed that physical presence (of the tenant, his servants or his agents) and control for the purpose of a business carried on by the tenant were the central factors. The manager/agent must, however, genuinely be acting on behalf of the tenant and this is indicated by the tenant's degree of control, financial interest in the business, and right to resort to the premises: *Teasdale*. Representative occupation is clearly essential when the tenant is a company: *Lee-Verhulst (Investments) Ltd* v *Harwood Trust* (1972). It has also been held that one company can manage another company's business: *Ross Auto Wash Ltd* v *Herbert* (1978). There are, however, restrictions upon this principle: problems arise where the premises are occupied and the business is run by a separate legal entity from the tenant. In *Cristina* v *Seear* (1985), the tenants ran a business through several companies; although the tenants were the controlling shareholders of the companies, the court held that it was the companies and not the tenants who were in occupation. The distinction between this case and *Ross Auto Wash* concerns the degree of control and management of the premises retained by the tenant. There would, of course, be no problem if the lease is assigned to the company.

The situation becomes complicated when the tenant moves out of occupation, but still intends to apply for a new tenancy. At first glance, s 23 will no longer be satisfied. Nevertheless, the mere fact that the tenant is not in *de facto* occupation at the time the contractual tenancy ends, or the application for a new tenancy is made, is not conclusive: *Aspinall* v *Viscount Chelsea* (1989). The issue is one of fact and degree: *Teasdale* v *Walker* (1958). Certainly, if the tenant abandons the premises the protection of the statutory provisions will cease: *Hancock and Willis* v *GMS Syndicate Ltd*. A tenant will not, however, necessarily fall outside the Act by moving out of occupation temporarily. A seven months' absence, for example, did not break the continuity of business occupation in *Caplan (I & H) Ltd* v *Caplan (No 2)* (1963). Occupation can also be intermittent. In *Bell* v *Alfred Franks & Bartlett & Co Ltd* (1980), for example, premises sometimes (but not always) used for storage purposes remained within Part II. A similar reasoning applies where the premises are temporarily unoccupied by virtue of illness, bankruptcy or economic recession: *Pulleng* v *Curran*. If the premises are rendered uninhabitable by reason of disrepair (the landlord being under no obligation to repair) and the tenant cannot afford to effect the repairs, it would be impracticable for the tenant to carry on his business there. Accordingly, regardless of the professed intentions of the tenant, he will no longer be in occupation: *Demetriou* v *Poolaction* (1990). Conversely, where fire destroys the premises and the tenant moves out until the premises are fit to occupy, the tenant has not ceased occupation for the purposes of s 23(1): *Morrison Holdings Ltd* v *Manders Property* (1976). As Lord Scarman explained: "In order to apply for a new tenancy under the 1954 Act a tenant must show either that he is continuing in occupation of the premises for purposes of a business carried on by him or, if events over which he has no control have led him to absent himself, that he continues to exert and claim his right to occupy". In this case the tenant continued to rely upon his right to occupy. It is prudent, in such a situation, to communicate the intention to return to the landlord.

It should not be overlooked that under s 40 the landlord can serve notice on the tenant, requiring the tenant to notify him whether the tenant is in occupation of the premises or any part thereof (see Chapter 2).

The Act contains special provisions relating to occupation by beneficiaries, partnerships and companies. These can be summarised as follows:

(i) business premises demised to trustees, but occupied by all (or any) of the beneficiaries under the trust are deemed to be occupied by the trustee tenants: s 41(1). Trustees normally have no power to trade;

(ii) where business premises are let to partners as joint tenants, it is not necessary that all occupy the premises: s 41A. In such a case, the right to renew may pass to those partners who actually carry on the business (see Chapter 2);

(iii) where the tenant is a company, the occupation of the demised premises by another company in the same group suffices: s 42(2). Accordingly, the tenant company is deemed still to be in occupation. A company is in the same group as another if one is a subsidiary of the other or they are both subsidiaries of a third company: s 42(1). As

Tenancies within the Act

to whether a company is a subsidiary of another, recourse must be had to s 736 Companies Act 1985 which requires that, for a company to be a subsidiary, the parent company must either hold over half the subsidiary's nominal share capital or be a shareholder of the subsidiary controlling the composition of its board of directors.

In cases not covered by the statutory exceptions, the rule persists that the tenant must be the occupier. It has already been shown that an individual tenant trading through the medium of a company has no occupation and, therefore, no renewal rights (*Cristina v Seear*). The company cannot be regarded as the *alter ego* of the tenant because the separate legal identity of the company is one of substance and not merely form. Although it might be possible to construct an argument that such a tenant could be brought within the trustee-beneficiary exception, the Law Commission's Working Paper concluded that there was a need for reform (para 3.1.13). By removing the corporate veil, and treating companies as identical to the individuals who control them, a more realistic and logical approach would be adopted (para 3.1.16).

3. For the purposes of a business

The tenant must not merely occupy the premises; the occupation must be for the purposes of a business carried on by him. The tenant is not, however, required to carry on the business on the premises; as will be demonstrated, ancillary use can suffice. It should also be appreciated that continuous day-to-day trading is unnecessary provided that the thread of business user is not broken: *Aspinall Finance Ltd v Viscount Chelsea* (1989).

The Act defines business as including "a trade, profession or employment and includes any activity carried on by a body of persons whether corporate or unincorporate" (s 23(2)). This definition applies throughout Part II of the Act (s 46).

The distinction is drawn in s 23(2) between tenants who are individuals and those who are bodies (for example, trade unions and friendly societies) or corporations (for example, local authorities, statutory undertakers and nationalised industries). It is only for bodies and corporations that the extension to "any activity" is made: *Abernethie v A M & J Kleiman* (1970). The activities of a government department are expressly included within this provision (s 56(3)).

"Activity" has been given a wide meaning by the courts. In *Addiscombe Garden Estates* v *Crabbe* (1958) it covered the "activity" of a members' tennis club. Other cases have extended the meaning to the governors' running of a National Health Service hospital (*Hills (Patents) Ltd* v *University College Hospital Board of Governors* (1956)); the provision of a community centre (*Parkes* v *Westminster Roman Catholic Diocese Trustee* (1978)); use as a garage (*Bell* v *Alfred Franks & Bartlett & Co* (1980)); the running of a restaurant and the use of storage areas for restaurant purposes (*Ye Olde Cheshire Cheese Ltd* v *The Daily Telegraph* (1988)); and the supply of residential accommodation (*Lee-Verhulst Ltd* v *Harwood* (1972)). A limitation was, however, imposed by the Court of Appeal decision in *Hillil Property & Investment* v *Naraine Pharmacy* (1979): the activity must, in order to qualify under s 23(2), be correlative and similar to the concepts of "trade", "profession" or "employment". In *Hillil* the casual dumping of waste, from other premises, on the demised premises at the expiration of the tenancy was held not to be an "activity". The same conclusion was drawn in *Abernethie* where the running of a Sunday school for one hour a week was not regarded as an "activity" for these purposes.

The understanding of the word "business" is broad based. Lindley LJ in *Rolls* v *Miller* (1884) said that it included "... almost anything which is an occupation, as distinguished from a pleasure — anything which is an occupation or a duty which requires attention is a business ...". It is well established that the term connotes commercial activity with the aim of making a gain or profit (*Re Incorporated Council of Law Reporting for England and Wales* (1888)). The actual making of a profit is not essential, nor does payment itself necessarily constitute a business (*Rolls* v *Miller*). In *Smith* v *Anderson* (1880), the court relied on the dictionary meaning and concluded that a business was "... anything which occupies the time and attention and labour of man for the purpose of profit".

The term "trade" is viewed as being of a narrower meaning than "business" (*Harris* v *Amery* (1865)). It connotes the activity of buying and selling (*Doe d Wetherall* v *Bird* (1834)) and will normally (but not necessarily) involve a profit making aspect (*Re Incorporated Council of Law Reporting for England and Wales*). A guest house run on a non-profit basis has been held to be a trade (*Ireland* v *Taylor* (1949)) and a college was held to be carrying on a trade even though it was a charitable institution (*Brighton College* v *Marriott* (1926)). An activity may be capable of being classed as both a business and a trade (*ibid*).

The concept of a "profession" enjoys a scope less certain than "business" or "trade". A working definition is that of Scrutton LJ who understood a profession to be an:

> "... occupation requiring either purely intellectual skill or manual skill controlled, as in painting, sculpture or surgery, by the intellectual skill of the operator, as distinguished from an occupation which is substantially the production or sale or arrangement for production and sale of commodities" (*IRC* v *Maxse* (1919)).

In holding that a solicitors' practice was a profession, Greene MR in *Stuchbery* v *General Accident* (1949) attempted to explain the distinction further: "A professional man is selected for employment by reason of his professional skill. His position is not like that of a keeper of a shop where a trade or business is carried on". These explanations, although general, do offer some guidance. It is clear that the category of professionals is wide and includes clergy, doctors, lawyers, accountants, surveyors and architects, for example. Beyond this, much reliance is placed upon the common-sense of the judge.

The word "employment" is used in the sense of meaning a calling and is broad enough to cover most occupations. In *Partridge* v *Mallandine* (1886) it was said by Denman J, "I do not think that employment means only where one man is set to work by others to earn money; a man may employ himself so as to earn profits in many ways". For example, it extends to the occupation of a lecturer (*Lecture League Ltd* v *LCC* (1913)) or the carrying on of a teaching hospital (*Hills (Patents)* v *University College Hospital* (1955)).

(a) Business use

Sometimes it may be difficult to distinguish between what is and what is not a business use. Particular problems can arise with ancillary user, where no actual business activity is carried on the premises. The general rule is that this use will suffice for the purposes of s 23(1): *Bell* v *Alfred Franks & Bartlett & Co*. There the passive storage of cartons in a lock-up garage was held to be occupation for business purposes. Conversely, the dumping of builder's spoil, on the conversion of two shops into one, was held not to be occupation for business purposes: *Hillil Property & Investment Co* v *Naraine Pharmacy*. Similarly, in *Chapman* v *Freeman* (1978) the owner of a hotel, who had the tenancy of a nearby cottage for the purpose of housing hotel staff, was held not to be protected by Part II because the cottage was not occupied for the purpose of the hotel business – it was merely convenient and not necessary for the staff to use the cottage. It seems, therefore, that ancillary use has to be necessary for the business.

A similar approach is adopted in the context of mixed user. In *Royal Life Saving Society* v *Page* (1978), the Court of Appeal held that the degree of business use is crucial and that the Act does not apply where such use was minimal and incidental. Difficult questions can arise, however, where the premises are used for a variety of purposes or where the use changes during the course of the tenancy. The following propositions emerge from judicial decisions:

(i) s 23(1) allows the possibility for the premises to be used partly for business and partly for other purposes: *Gurton* v *Parrot* (1990);

(ii) as regards premises used also partly for residential purposes, protection under Part II prevents any protection arising under the Rent Act 1977 or Housing Act 1988: *Webb* v *London Borough of Barnet* (1989);

(iii) where the premises are used in whole or part for business purposes, the *prima facie* presumption is that s 23 applies: *Cheryl Investments Ltd* v *Saldanha* (1979); *Kent Coast Properties* v *Ward* (1990);

(iv) if the lease totally prohibits business use of the premises, s 23(1) does not apply to that tenancy: s 23(4); *Bell* v *Alfred Franks & Bartlett*;

(v) if the premises are used mainly for residential purposes and the business use is incidental, s 23(1) does not extend to any part of the premises: *Lewis* v *Weldcrest* (1978); *Cheryl Investments* v *Saldanha*;

(vi) changes in use during the course of the lease might take the tenancy from one statutory code to another: *Pulleng* v *Curran*. None the less, it is well established that where there is a tenancy of mixed business and residential purposes, the cessation of business does take the premises outside the scope of the 1954 Act, but it does not automatically render it a regulated tenancy under the Rent Act 1977: *Webb* v *London Borough of Barnet*. Conversely, a wholly residential tenancy which later develops a substantial business user will, it seems, transfer more easily from the residential code to the business code: *Cheryl Investments Ltd* v *Saldanha*. This issue is returned to below, but it must be appreciated that a mere unilateral change or abandonment of user, unless embodied within a new contract between the parties, cannot operate to change codes: *Trustees of Henry Smith's Charity, Kensington* v *Wagle & Tippet* (1989); *Wolfe* v *Hogan* (1949).

(b) Unauthorised business use

There is no clear-cut rule stating whether a tenant who carries on a business without the approval of his landlord is entitled to the protection of Part II; instead there is a rather elaborate provision to deal with business user contrary to the terms of the lease. The view expressed by the Law Commission in its Working Paper (No 111) was that: "The way in which the position is at present expressed provides the opportunity for evading the Act" (para 3.1.26). A business carried on in breach of either a blanket prohibition against business use or a covenant prohibiting the general carrying on of trade, profession and/or employment does not qualify for the protection of Part II: s 23(4). This rule does not apply to a prohibition which relates only to part of the premises; is directed against use for the purposes of a specified business; or restricts use to a particular business: s 23(4).

The rule gives way, however, where the tenant's immediate landlord (or the landlord's predecessor in title) consented to the breach or the immediate landlord (but not a predecessor in title) acquiesced in it: s 23(4). The difference of approach concerning the predecessor in title reflects the fact that the current landlord could not be aware of a predecessor's state of mind. For these purposes, "consent" connotes a positive act of acceptance and demands more than a mere absence of objection: *Bell* v *Franks & Bartlett*. "Acquiescence" is the passive failure to take steps concerning a known breach (*ibid*). Knowledge is the key factor. The landlord's consent will, presumably, then be inferred: *Real & Leasehold Estates* v *Medina Shipping* (1968).

It should also be appreciated that a breach which does not take the tenancy outside the scope of the Act might still be a basis for forfeiture of the lease or a ground for opposing a new tenancy under s 30(1)(c).

As mentioned above, the Law Commission saw a potential for evasion by the manipulation of the present provisions. The example provided was where a landlord has acquiesced in the establishment of an unauthorised business, but now wishes to escape the security of tenure provisions. The landlord can easily achieve this by assigning the freehold to an associate who, having neither consented or acquiesced in the user, can terminate the tenancy without going through the statutory machinery (para 3.1.30). To avoid this arising, the Working Paper concluded provisionally that the same test for both the current and former landlords be used "... so that ownership of the reversion is not critical to whether the tenant enjoys renewal rights" (para 3.1.31; 32).

4. Excluded tenancies

There are a variety of exclusions from the scope of Part II. Many are listed in s 43, some arise under other statutory provisions and one is derived from the common law. These exceptions to the general availability of security of tenure are discussed below.

(a) Agricultural tenancies

The Act does not extend to agricultural holdings (s 43(1)(a)). Agricultural holdings are defined in s 1 Agricultural Holdings Act 1986 as:

> "the aggregate of the land (whether agricultural land or not) comprised in a contract of tenancy which is a contract for an agricultural tenancy, not being a contract under which the said land is let to the tenant during his continuance in any office, appointment or employment held under the landlord".

The vital ingredients of an agricultural holding are that the property is used for agriculture and is so used for the purpose of a trade or business: s 1 Agricultural Holdings Act.

Where the letting is for a business with an agricultural aspect, a

Tenancies within the Act

difficulty arises as to which statutory code is applicable. Whether such a holding falls under the Agricultural Holdings Act 1986 or the Landlord and Tenant Act 1954 appears to turn upon what is the substantial user (*Lord Monson* v *Bound* (1954)). If the tenancy *prima facie* satisfied both codes, then it will be excluded from the scope of the Landlord and Tenant Acts: *Short* v *Greeves* (1988). On a subsequent change of user, the test of dominant purpose will again apply and could result in a former agricultural holding being metamorphosed into a business tenancy, thus coming within the ambit of the Landlord and Tenant Acts.

In *Russell* v *Booker* (1982), the Court of Appeal laid down a five stage test:

(i) the purpose expressed in or contemplated by an agreement is the essential factor;

(ii) if the original agreement has been superseded by a new contract, the purpose may be considered in the light of that new contract;

(iii) such a new contract may be inferred by the court from user known to the landlord;

(iv) a mere unilateral change of user cannot of itself bring the tenancy within the protection of a different statutory code; and

(v) where no particular user has been provided for in, or contemplated by, the agreement, actual and subsequent user will determine the question of which code is to apply.

The Law Commission's Working Paper on the Landlord and Tenant Act 1927 (No 102) identified some anomalies that could arise in the categorisation process. The example was given where the use of the land is connected with horses, not normally classed as livestock (para 2.9). If the land is used for the grazing of horses and is for the purpose of a trade or business, it is an agricultural holding. Where there is no commercial aspect to the grazing, it is neither an agricultural holding nor a business tenancy. Land used for horses other than for grazing is not usually an agricultural holding, but if the use is part of a trade or business the Landlord and Tenant Acts can apply. The Working Paper also expressed doubt as to which code commercial farm letting for a fixed term of more than one, but fewer than two years, falls into (para 2.10). There is authority that such a letting is not within the Agricultural Holdings Act (*Gladstone* v *Bower* (1960)); if this is correct, it seems that the Landlord and Tenant Acts apply.

(b) Mining leases

Tenancies created by mining leases do not attract the right to renew under the Landlord and Tenant Act 1954: s 43(1)(b). A mining lease is one granted for mining or a related purpose; a definition is offered in s 25 Landlord and Tenant Act 1927 (see Chapter 11) which extends to mines and minerals and thereby includes all substances that can be obtained from beneath the surface of the earth for the purpose of profit. There is no right, therefore, to renew a tenancy for sand and gravel working: *O'Callaghan* v *Elliott* (1966). The definition does not, however, exclude a tenancy for the drilling of oil and gas: *Lonsdale (Earl)* v *A-G* (1982).

(c) Wholly residential use

As discussed above, the 1954 Act can apply to tenancies of premises which are let for both business and residential use. Provided that the business constitutes a reasonably substantial use of the premises, a separate residential use does not prevent the provisions of Part II applying to the whole premises. As mentioned previously, such a tenancy cannot also be a regulated tenancy within the Rent Act, nor can it be an assured tenancy within the Housing Act 1988.

(d) On-licensed premises

Part II of the Act does not apply, subject to some exceptions, to a tenancy (granted before 11 July 1989) of premises licensed for the sale of intoxicating liquor for consumption on the premises: s 43(1)(d). Off-licensed premises remain within the Act, as do registered (as opposed to licensed) clubs: *Lansley* v *Adda Properties Ltd* (1982). Legislation has recently been enacted to ensure that on-licensed tenancies granted after 11 July 1989 (unless in pursuance of a contract entered into before that date) are no longer excluded: s 1(1) Landlord and Tenant (Licensed Premises) Act 1990. See the provisions of s 1(2) and (3) of the 1990 Act

Tenancies within the Act

below for changes to take effect on 11 July 1992. The rule of non-protection has always been the subject of exceptions listed in s 43(1)(d)(i–ii). These can be categorised under two heads:

(i) premises which are structurally adapted to be used and are used *bona fide* for a business which is a hotel, inn and/or restaurant and where a substantial proportion of the business is not the sale of intoxicating liquor. A "substantial proportion" is decided with reference to all the facts: *Grant* v *Gresham* (1979). In that case the court refused to set down any mathematical formula, but did hold that 17–18 per cent was not substantial. Most guest houses and hotels will, therefore, be within the catchment of the Act. In *J G Swales & Co* v *H S Mosley* (1968) takings of a restaurant in a public house amounted to one-third of the total receipts and this was held not sufficiently substantial to bring the tenancy within the Act. In *Ye Olde Cheshire Cheese*, 44 per cent of sales being non-alcoholic was sufficiently substantial;

(ii) premises adapted to be used and *bona fide* used for either judicial or public administrative purposes; as a theatre or place of public or private entertainment; as a public garden or picture gallery; for exhibitions; or for any similar purpose to which the holding of a licence is merely ancillary. Refreshment rooms at a railway station are specifically included within Part II of the Act (as opposed to such facilities at bus stations and air terminals); the railway station refreshment room exception does not require the holding of the liquor licence to be ancillary to the purposes for which the premises are used.

The Landlord and Tenant (Licensed Premises) Act 1990 repeals s 43(1)(d) in relation to leases granted after 11 July 1989: s 1(1). Such on-licensed premises can therefore be fully protected by the 1954 Act. As mentioned above, tenancies created before this date continue to be excluded by s 43(1)(d). This exclusion is now, however, only on a transitional basis. Leases currently excluded under s 43(1)(d) will automatically be brought within the security of tenure provisions on 11 July 1992: s 1(2) of the 1990 Act. In the interim period, the landlord or tenant can terminate the lease in accordance with the contractual methods agreed. If the contract does not allow for termination before 11 July 1992, the

1990 Act allows a landlord's s 25 notice; a tenant's s 26 request; and a tenant's s 27(1) notice, as appropriate, to be served before 11 July 1992 and to be effective from that date: s 1(3). For this purpose it is deemed that s 43(1)(d) has already been repealed.

(e) Service tenancies

Part II does not apply to a tenancy granted to the tenant as a holder of an office, appointment or employment, which ends (or becomes liable to end) when that service or employment is terminated: s 43(2). If the tenancy was granted after 30 September 1954 (the commencement date of the Act) there is a proviso that, for this exclusion to apply, the tenancy must be in writing, and it must express the purpose of the grant: s 43(2). This purpose must be clear. The court can ascertain whether the alleged service agreement is genuine or is a sham: *Teasdale* v *Walker* (1958).

(f) Short tenancies

The Act does not apply to a lease for a term of years certain not exceeding six months, unless there is provision for renewal or extension beyond six months or the tenant (and/or predecessor in business) has been in occupation for more than twelve months: s 43(3). This provision allows for a maximum of two consecutive tenancies to be granted for a period totalling twelve months provided that there is no provision in the first tenancy relating to the grant of the second. Due to the "occupation" limitation, however, its usefulness is restricted to new tenants and new businesses. As noted in Chapter 2, occupation by different government departments in succession is regarded as continuing the same business (s 56(3)).

It should be appreciated that the exemption appears to extend only to fixed term leases. Although an argument may be put forward to support a periodic tenancy being a term of years certain (*Leek and Moorlands Building Society* v *Clark* (1952)), it is unsafe to rely on such a proposition.

(g) Statutory exceptions

There is no right to renew an extended tenancy granted under the Leasehold Reform Act 1967: s 16(1) of the 1967 Act. In addition, there can be no renewal under Part II, after the fifty year term granted under the 1967 Act expires, of any sub-tenancy derived out of it. There are a variety of other statutory exceptions; these include, for example, the Civil Aviation Act 1982, the Transport Act 1982, the Gas Act 1986, and the Dockyard Services Act 1986.

(h) Public bodies

As explained fully in Chapter 2, the tenant's rights may be considerably curtailed on the grounds of public interest or national security where the landlord is one of a number of specified public bodies (ss 57, 58, 60, 60A, 60B).

(i) Tenancies at will

A tenancy at will is outside the protection of Part II: *Wheeler* v *Mercer* (1957). It matters not whether the tenancy at will arises by implication of law or is created expressly: *Manfield & Sons Ltd* v *Botchin* (1970). The court, however, will be astute to ensure that the purported tenancy at will is not really a veiled periodic tenancy: *Hagee (London) Ltd* v *A B Erikson & Larson* (1976). It is imperative that the tenancy is made terminable at the will of either party and that there should be avoided any terms which are inconsistent with such a tenancy (for example provisions as to re-entry and forfeiture). The safest use of a tenancy at will is where the tenant is holding over at the end of a lease or has moved into possession pending negotiations of the terms of a lease: *Javad* v *Aqil* (1990). In *Cardiothoracic Institute* v *Shrewdcrest* (1986), for example, a tenant holding over at the expiry of a contracted out lease was held to be a tenant at will.

A landlord may prefer to create a tenancy at will instead of a licence agreement because the remedy of distress for rent cannot be used in respect of payments under a licence: *Interoven Stove* v *Hibbard & Painter & Shepherd* (1936).

5. Contracting out: general provisions

In its original form, the 1954 Act contained a blanket prohibition on contracting out: s 38(1). As a result of the Law of Property Act 1969, a radical facility was introduced by which the parties could make a joint application to the appropriate court requesting the approval for the grant of a fixed term lease to which the Act will not apply: s 38(4). This is the main method by which landlords avoid their tenants having security of tenure under the Act. Applications for the approval of such agreements are common (judicial statistics reveal more than 11,000 applications per year). The conditions of s 38(4) must, however, be satisfied before the parties can take advantage of this procedure:

(a) the tenancy must be granted for a term of years certain which includes a term certain of less than a year: *Re Land & Premises at Liss, Hants* (1971). The lease may include an option to surrender before its term ends (ie, a break clause): *Scholl Manufacturing Co v Clifton* (1967);

(b) before the tenancy is granted, both parties must apply to the appropriate court for approval. This joint application can be made either to the High Court (by *ex parte* originating summons and supporting affidavit to the Chancery Division) or to the county court (by originating application). Before the Courts and Legal Services Act 1990, in practice the parties usually agreed that, regardless of the rateable value exceeding £5,000, the matter would be within the jurisdiction of the county court specified in the application. The attraction of this election is that the county court procedure is simpler, speedier and cheaper. Normally, the proceedings will not require the attendance of the parties, but if one side is not legally represented both parties will be required to attend a hearing;

(c) the parties must set out in their joint application the reason why they wish the lease to be contracted out of the Act. There is no guidance as to when the court will refuse an application properly made. As the agreement is usually reached between business people who have received legal advice, there is little scope for the court to justify refusal on the merits of the application: *Hagee v Erikson & Larson*. It is not unknown, therefore, for a lease of twenty-five years' duration to be contracted out. None the less, refusals do occur. There must be no suggestion of coercion or oppression. In 1986, the county court had a refusal rate of 15 per cent but, as made clear by the Law Commission's Working Paper (No 111), there is no means of knowing whether these refusals were for lack of merit or on technical grounds;

(d) the agreement must be contained in (or endorsed on) the lease or any other document as specified by the court. In *Tottenham Hotspur* v *Princegrove Publishers Ltd* (1974), however, the sanctioned agreement took effect, although not contained in or endorsed on the lease, where the tenant continued in possession and paid an increased rent under the new tenancy.

The Working Paper took the view that, even if the court did not adopt an interventionist approach, the need for judicial approval maintained some importance. The Law Commission believed that the present system was useful because it ensured that the matter of exclusion was brought to the attention of the tenant (para 3.5.11). It did, however, consider whether the role could be shifted from the court and be adopted by the tenant and his solicitor (para 3.5.12). As a further alternative, it was mooted that the Act could prescribe the circumstances in which contracting out agreements were allowed (para 3.5.13). Both suggestions avoid what many perceive as a largely formal court application, and still offer some protection for the tenant.

Other than with the approval of the court, all agreements purporting to exclude or to modify the statutory rights of the business tenant are void (s 38(1)). This is, however, subject to the special provisions (as examined in Chapter 2) relating to government departments and statutory undertakings (ss 57(8), 58(2) and (3)).

The landlord should always be aware of the possibility that the court's approval could be withheld. It is, therefore, advisable for any agreement to be made conditional upon the court's approval. A tenancy unconditionally granted cannot retrospectively be brought within s 38(4) by a later application and approval: *Essexcrest Ltd* v *Evenlex Ltd* (1988). A condition that the tenancy is dependent on the obtaining of an order under s 38(4) will, however, prevent a legally binding tenancy coming into existence until the court order has been obtained: *Cardiothoracic Institute* v *Shrewdcrest Ltd*.

Surrenders, offers back and sundry devices

The prohibition against contracting out of the Act contained in s 38(1) is comprehensive. Any attempt to sidestep it (without the sanction of the court under s 38(4)) by imposing some penalty or disability on the tenant, if he exercises his rights under Part II, is void: *Stevenson & Rush (Holdings) Ltd* v *Langdon* (1978). It matters not whether the purported contracting out provision is in the lease or contained in an ancillary agreement.

Uncertainty arises in connection with surrenders and agreements to surrender; the so-called offer back clauses; and a variety of untried and untested avoidance measures which are thought to be effective. These aspects of "contracting out" need to be examined.

A tenancy terminated by surrender is not entitled to protection under the 1954 Act: s 24(2). It is not, however, possible for a tenant to execute a deed of surrender before he has taken up possession. In fact, s 24(2) requires the tenant to have been in occupation for one month before he can surrender his lease. The Act, moreover, draws a distinction between an agreement to surrender at a future date and an actual surrender. An agreement to surrender will be void by virtue of s 38(1), unless sanctioned by the court under the provisions of s 38(4)(b). By virtue of this section, the court is given the power to authorise such agreements, on the joint application of the parties, on such date or in such circumstances as it specifies. This may be viewed as both reasonable and justifiable. The Act prevents the easy avoidance of its protection by not allowing agreements to surrender to be entered into at the same time as the lease itself. None the less, it does not compel the tenant to retain the lease, having been in occupation for one month, if he does not wish to retain it. As the Law Commission's Working Paper (No 111) explained:

> "To prevent the tenant surrendering the property to his landlord would be an encroachment on his freedom which is not necessary to defend the statutory right of renewal. On the other hand, to obtain from a tenant an undertaking in advance that he will surrender the lease sometime later is to invite him to forgo those rights before he is in a position to judge how matters will stand at the date in question. The Act therefore limits the parties' freedom of contract when the tenant might be susceptible to undue persuasion by the landlord, without unnecessarily limiting their freedom to bargain" (para 3.5.18).

A problem identified in the Working Paper is that the differentiation between surrenders and agreements to surrender is not always clear. *Tarjomani* v *Panther Securities Ltd* (1983) was

Tenancies within the Act

invoked by way of illustration. In this case, the landlord and the tenant agreed in writing that the lease would be surrendered that day. As there was no deed executed (see s 52(1) Law of Property Act 1925), and despite the clear intention that surrender should be immediate, there was no effective surrender, but merely an agreement to surrender. The agreement was void under s 38(1). The Working Paper expressed the view that the Act should cease to invalidate agreements to surrender which are intended to take effect immediately (para 3.5.20).

An inconsistency between s 24(2)(b) (the "occupation for one month" qualification) and s 38(1) was seen by the Law Commission: the former section contemplates that agreements to surrender can be entered, and yet s 38(1) renders such agreements void unless authorised by the court. Although the Working Paper recommended that s 24(2)(b) be amended to exclude reference to agreements, the inconsistency alleged does not necessarily exist. It is possible for the sections to rest easily together by reading in a requirement that agreements sanctioned by the court can receive such authorisation only where the tenant has been in occupation for one month, with other non-authorised agreements thus remaining void under s 38(1). This interpretation appears to be consistent with the Court of Appeal decision in *Woodruff* v *Hambro* (1990).

Offer back clauses usually provide that when the tenant wishes to assign, he undertakes first to offer to surrender the lease to the landlord. The landlord has the option to accept the tenant's surrender and, if surrender occurs, it will terminate the tenant's lease. If the landlord declines the offer, the tenant can assign the lease with the landlord's consent (which cannot be unreasonably withheld). A problem arises where the landlord accepts the offer, but the tenant does not wish actually to surrender the lease. The agreement is void under s 38(1) (*Allnatt London Properties Ltd* v *Newton* (1984)) and cannot be enforced by the landlord. If the right to assign is dependent on the landlord rejecting the offer back clause, the tenant is unable to assign without being in breach of the assignment covenant; he thus faces the risk of forfeiture. An unsatisfactory stalemate is thereby achieved. The Working Paper recommended that this situation should be overcome by reform (retrospective in effect): para 3.5.27; 28. The means by which reform should be achieved are, however, uncertain. The Law Commission suggested several alternatives (para 3.5.33):

(i) to invalidate the offer back clause in whole or part;

(ii) to allow the landlord to apply to the court to validate a particular agreement on the ground of there being special circumstances justifying a surrender;

(iii) to allow the court to authorise the agreement on the grounds that the tenant would receive a full market value and would not be prejudiced by any subsequent disposal of the holding;

(iv) to validate a standard form of offer back clause, other forms to be invalid.

A series of potential avoidance measures have long been thought to be adequate to sidestep the provisions of Part II. All include the grant of a lease for a duration longer than the parties really intend with, in each instance, a tenant's option to surrender at the end of the true term. The danger exists that such agreements could be disregarded as shams. In addition, such measures are now unnecessary because of the ability to contract out under s 38(4), but do need to be considered briefly for the sake of completeness:

(i) the grant of a term intended to be for five years could be granted for eight years with a heavily inflated rent being reserved for the final three years. This guarantees surrender before the contractual period expires;

(ii) a lease could be granted for a term two years longer than intended and, at the same time, a sublease in favour of the landlord could be executed for that last two year period. This ensures that the tenant is not in occupation when the right to renew the head-lease arises;

(iii) the grant of a lease for two years longer than intended with a covenant prohibiting all business use for the last two years. Once again, the commercial tenant will have little option but to surrender the lease or face forfeiture.

Chapter 4

Continuation and termination

The basic aim of the Landlord and Tenant Act 1954 is to confer on business tenants security of tenure without otherwise interfering with market forces. The mechanism used to achieve this policy is contained in s 24(1) which provides that a tenancy, within Part II, can be terminated only by one of the methods set out in the Act. These methods of termination form an amalgam of novel statutory procedures and established common law modes. The majority depend upon the action or inaction of the tenant; the others can be activated only by the landlord or with the joint agreement of the parties. Until one of the recognised means of termination occurs, the tenancy continues automatically, essentially on the same terms as before.

1. Contractual ties and the continuation tenancy

Before examining the means, as prescribed by the Act, by which a tenancy protected by Part II can be terminated, it is helpful to explain the interaction of the common law rules and the superseding statutory provisions. The best (and technically correct) approach, by which this understanding can be attained, is to draw a distinction between the severance of the original contractual relationship and the termination of the Part II tenancy.

The continuation tenancy runs on from the time that the contractual relationship ends. Although the Act does not prevent the original lease being brought to an end by any method provided by the contract (for example, the exercise of a break-clause), it does provide that a continuation tenancy can be terminated only as permitted by statute: *Weinbergs Weatherproofs* v *Radcliffe Paper Mill Co* (1958). From this perspective the landlord's notice to quit may terminate the contractual relationship, but (as it is not one of the approved methods) it does not affect the tenant's estate in the land. However, the service of the notice does offer the competent landlord the right to serve a statutory notice (under s 25) for a date not earlier than that on which the contractual lease will end: *Castle Laundry (London)* v *Read* (1955). Similarly, the mere exercise of a break-clause by the landlord ends the original contract, but does not prevent a continuation tenancy arising: *Scholl Manufacturing Co* v *Clifton* (1967). In both situations the landlord must satisfy the requirements of the lease and the formalities demanded by s 25. This is possible, for example, by exercising a break-clause (or serving notice to quit) in a manner that operates for the purposes of both the contract and s 25: *Keith, Bayley, Rogers & Co* v *Cubes Ltd* (1975). A single notice could suffice, but it is generally recommended (so as to minimise the consequences of error) that the documentation be kept distinct in all cases. This may be inevitable where the immediate landlord and the competent landlord are not one and the same person. The severance of the contractual ties requires the involvement of the common law landlord, whereas the termination of a continuation tenancy is the responsibility of the competent landlord (see Chapter 2).

Where the tenant serves a notice to quit, the position is very different. The Act is not concerned with tying the tenant to a continuation tenancy; it exists to benefit and not to fetter the tenant. Accordingly, the Act allows a tenant's notice to sever the contractual relationship *and* to terminate the tenancy: s 24(2). The general rule is that the tenant's notice will be served on the immediate landlord.

As previously explained, where the contractual tenancy comes to an end (for example, by effluxion of time or landlord's notice to quit) it is not essential that a new tenancy should be granted immediately to take its place. A new lease may come into existence subsequently by virtue of a court order (s 29) or by agreement (s 28). In the intervening period (which may be measured in years if neither party is particularly interested in activating the renewal provisions), the old tenancy continues automatically without either party having to do anything: s 24. The terms of the lease remain unaffected, except that there is a statutory variation of the termination provisions (see above): *Bowes-Lyon* v *Green* (1963). Where the tenant holds over after the end of the contractual tenancy, the tenancy comes under the provisions of s 24; it is not deemed to be a common law,

Continuation and termination

implied periodic legal tenancy: *Thorne* v *New Sherwood School* (1962).

The tenant under a continuation tenancy retains an interest in the land which, subject to restrictions imposed in the original lease, is assignable and is, on breach of covenant, liable to forfeiture. Any assignment of the landlord's reversion leaves unaffected the statutory rights of the tenant. The continuation tenancy is of an uncertain duration and can be terminated only by one of the prescribed means discussed below. Until that time, the terms and conditions of the contractual lease govern the s 24 tenancy. Accordingly, it follows that:

(a) the tenant is entitled to the same premises as under the original tenancy: *Poster* v *Slough Estates* (1969);

(b) the liability of a guarantor may continue under the continuation tenancy, but this depends upon the wording of the guarantor's covenant: *Junction Estates* v *Cope* (1974);

(c) the old rent remains payable, unless an interim rent is applied for (and set) under s 24A (see Chapter 7);

(d) a right of the tenant to remove tenant's fixtures remains enforceable during the continuation period: *New Zealand Government Property Corp* v *H M & S Ltd* (1982);

(e) rights of way (and other incorporeal hereditaments) enjoyed under the original tenancy are enforceable during the continuation tenancy: *Nevill Long & Co* v *Firmenich & Co* (1983);

(f) a continuation of the head lease will support an underlease for a longer term than the original head lease: s 65;

(g) covenants which run with the land are fully enforceable during continuation: *GMS Syndicate Ltd* v *Gary Elliott Ltd* (1981).

2. Termination by the tenant

The tenant can end the existing tenancy in one of the following ways:

(a) the tenant can serve on the competent landlord a formal request for a new tenancy under s 26 (this is discussed in detail in Chapter 6);

(b) by notice to quit.

The tenant is not bound to submit to the continuance of his tenancy. The exact method of preventing this occurrence depends largely on whether the tenancy is periodic or fixed term. In the case of a periodic tenancy (or a fixed term lease determinable by notice), the tenant can serve on his immediate landlord a notice to quit, in accordance with the terms of the lease, to bring that tenancy to an end: s 24(2). A continuation tenancy under s 24 will not then arise. There is, however, a limitation imposed by s 24(2)(a) which requires the tenant to have been in occupation under the lease, before such notice is served, for at least one month. This is designed to defeat a device, previously employed, whereby the tenant was persuaded to give a notice to quit at the commencement of the tenancy thereby bringing the tenancy to an end on the expiry of the notice. Devices of this kind are, in any event, no longer necessary because of the ability to contract out of the Act and to grant short leases outside the ambit of the statutory protection (see Chapter 3). The one month requirement also ensures that the notice is given voluntarily by the tenant. A tenant who does not wish a fixed term tenancy to continue under Part II may prevent a continuation tenancy from arising by serving a s 27 notice. It is provided by s 27(1) that the tenant can serve on his immediate landlord, not less than three months before the contractual date of expiry of a fixed term, a notice in writing that he does not seek the continuation of that lease. This method is appropriate where the tenant wishes to quit the premises and the landlord does not accept the surrender and shows no sign of issuing a s 25 notice (see below). No special form of notice is required. The tenant must, however, have been in occupation as tenant for at least one month preceding the service of this notice: s 27(2). This reflects an anti-avoidance stance (see above).

Where a lease originally granted for a fixed term is being continued under s 24, the tenant can bring that continuation tenancy to a close by serving on his immediate landlord at least three months' written notice expiring on a quarter day: s 27(2). Provided that it is to expire after the continuation tenancy arises, the notice can be served either before or after the date that the contractual term lapses: s 27(2). Although not expressly stated, it is assumed that the reference in s 27(2) to quarter days means the usual quarter days (ie, 25 March/Lady Day; 24 June/Mid-Summer; 29 September/Michaelmas; and 25 December/Christmas). The Law Commission's Working Paper (No 111) identified an anomaly in that the period of notice differs according to the date when it is given. The example provided was that a notice on 24 September can expire on 25 December (92 days) whereas a notice given on 30 September cannot expire until 25 March (176 days). The Working Paper recommended the amendment of s 27(2) so that the three months' notice could expire at any time (para 3.2.34).

None of the above notices can be served by the tenant after the service of a s 26 request for a new tenancy: s 26(4). These procedures are mutually exclusive and the first to be served in time prevails: *Long Acre Securities Ltd* v *Electro Acoustic Industries* (1990);

- (c) by failure to adhere to statutory procedures. There are two ways in which procedural default can prevent the application of the security of tenure provisions. First, the tenant must respond within two months to a landlord's s 25 notice, by serving a counternotice expressing an unwillingness to give up possession. If he does not do this, the tenancy ends on the date set out in the landlord's notice: s 29(2). Second, the tenant must apply to the court for a new tenancy between two and four months after the service of a s 25 notice or s 26 request. If he fails to do this, no application can be entertained and the tenancy ends on the date set out in the notice or request: s 29(3) (see *Smith* v *Draper* (1990));
- (d) by serving a counternotice, in response to a s 25 notice, which indicates a willingness to give up possession: s 29(2);
- (e) by commencing and subsequently withdrawing an application for a new lease. In this instance, the current tenancy ends three months after the date of withdrawal: s 64(2).

3. Termination by the landlord

The landlord can bring the existing tenancy to an end by the following means:

- (a) by serving a statutory notice on the tenant in accordance with s 25 (see Chapter 5);
- (b) by the forfeiture of the tenancy (or a superior lease) for breach of covenant: s 24(2). In the case of the forfeiture of a tenancy to which Part II applies, the tenant has the normal rights of relief from forfeiture whether or not his

tenancy is a continuation tenancy. Any sub-tenant also has the right to relief at the discretion of the court. The tenant will lose all security of tenure and renewal rights unless the forfeiture can be averted. If forfeiture proceedings are stayed on condition that the tenant delivers up possession on a set date, the protection of the Act is lost. Where relief from forfeiture is applied for (even if an order for possession is made) the forfeiture is incomplete and the tenant can still benefit from the provisions of Part II: *Meadows* v *Clerical, Medical and General Life Assurance Co* (1980);

(c) in relation to a continuation tenancy which ceases to be one to which Part II applies (for example, the tenant no longer occupies for the purpose of a business) the landlord can terminate it by notice: s 24(3)(a). Unless the landlord takes steps to end the lease, it will continue under the terms of s 24(1).

Whether the original lease was periodic or for a fixed term affects the determination by the landlord in (c) above. As regards a periodic tenancy continued under the Act, determination can occur in accordance with the terms of the original agreement (for example, by an ordinary notice to quit). It is thought such termination involves the immediate and not the competent landlord. As regards a fixed term lease continued under s 24, the continuation tenancy can be ended by notice in writing served by the competent landlord. This notice must cover a period of between three and six months: s 24(3)(a). If the lease is to be determined in any other fashion as allowed by the original contract, it seems that this would involve the immediate landlord.

No difficulty emerges in the case where, immediately before the expiry of a fixed term, the tenancy is not one to which the Act applies. The tenancy will end by effluxion of time in the normal fashion. As the protection of the Act no longer extends to that tenancy, the service of a s 25 notice or a s 26 request is inappropriate. If, however, such steps had been initiated when the tenancy was within Part II, a continuation tenancy would arise and this would continue until the date set out in the notice or request: *Caplan (I & H) Ltd* v *Caplan (No 2)* (1963).

It should be appreciated also that where a periodic tenancy was originally outside the Act and, at such time, the immediate landlord served a notice to quit, that notice is not invalidated if the lease subsequently becomes one to which the statutory provisions apply: s 24(3)(b). This protects the landlord from a change of mind by the tenant following receipt of the notice.

4. Termination by agreement

The parties can jointly agree that the tenancy will be brought to an end in one of two ways:

(a) agreeing to a new lease

If there is an agreement, which is in writing (s 69(2)), between the competent landlord and the tenant as to the grant of a new lease, the current tenancy terminates on the date specified in the agreement: s 28. The agreement between the parties must, however, be binding: *RJ Stratton Ltd* v *Wallis Tomlin & Co Ltd* (1986). Once an agreement is reached, the tenant cannot later change his mind and argue for a new tenancy under the Act: s 28.

It is usual for the new lease to be negotiated so as to commence on the day after the previous one has expired by effluxion of time. If, however, a continuation tenancy has arisen, that tenancy comes to an end on the date specified by the agreement and in the intervening period ceases to be within the protection of the Act: s 28. Such protection is deemed unnecessary.

It is common for negotiations concerning a new lease to be stimulated by the service of a s 25 notice or a s 26 request. The purpose of s 28 is to avoid the need to go to court. If an agreement is reached after an application to the court for a new tenancy is lodged, that application (if not withdrawn by the tenant) is automatically invalidated by s 28: *Hancock & Willis* v *GMS Syndicate* (1983). This should not be confused, however, with the situation where the parties have agreed terms which the court is to be asked to incorporate into a new lease (if any) granted by it. In this case, s 28 is not relevant and the continuation tenancy remains within the Part II machinery.

(b) surrendering the lease

Surrender is the yielding up of the leasehold estate to the immediate landlord and the causing of the lease to be extinguished by the reversion. It may arise by agreement, operation of law, or because one party is given the right to surrender or to receive a surrender (for example, before assignment or following the damage to the premises by fire) by the lease. An effective

BUSINESS LEASES

surrender must usually be by deed (s 52 Law of Property Act 1925). Otherwise, for the purposes of the Act, it is likely to be an agreement to surrender: *Tarjomani* v *Panther Securities* (1983).

Surrender is one of the ways that a business tenancy protected by Part II can be terminated: s 24(2). As described in Chapter 3, where the tenancy comes within the Landlord and Tenant Act 1954, an immediate surrender is effective whereas, unless sanctioned by the court under s 38, an agreement to surrender in the future is void. Therefore any terms stipulating that surrender will occur upon specified contingencies, whether specified within or outside the lease, are invalid. There is also a further safeguard offered by s 24(2)(b) in that the tenant must have been in occupation of the premises, under the tenancy, for at least one month before surrender, or a sanctioned agreement to surrender, is made (see *Watney* v *Boardley* (1975)).

Chapter 5

The landlord's statutory notice

There are two ways in which the statutory renewal procedure may be activated: either the landlord may serve a s 25 notice to terminate the existing tenancy or the tenant may serve a s 26 request for a new lease. This chapter is concerned with the landlord's s 25 notice; the tenant's s 26 request is discussed in the next chapter.

It is usually the landlord who initiates the renewal procedure. As demonstrated in the previous chapter, the majority of business tenants will not wish to leave the premises demised and will be content to maintain occupation under a continuation tenancy at the existing rent. Accordingly, the service of a s 25 notice does not necessarily mean that the landlord seeks to regain possession. It is common for the landlord to initiate proceedings so as to ensure the negotiation of, or order for, a new lease at a market rent.

1. The server

The s 25 notice can be served only by the competent landlord. There can, of course, be joint landlords who together constitute the competent landlord. The general rule in this situation is that one of them alone may serve the statutory notice: *Leckhampton Dairies Ltd* v *Artus Whitfield Ltd* (1986), but such a notice must state the name(s) of the other joint landlord(s): *Pearson* v *Alyo* (1990). The notice may, moreover, be signed by an agent on the landlord's behalf.

As discussed in Chapter 2, the competent landlord is either the owner of the fee simple or, where underleases have been created, the landlord next above the tenant in the chain of tenancies who holds a reversion of at least fourteen months' duration: s 44(1). The competent landlord and the sub-tenant's immediate landlord need not, therefore, be one and the same person. There can only be one competent landlord at any given time, but his identity can change during the course of proceedings. As regards the service of the s 25 notice, the relevant time for ascertaining the identity of the competent landlord is at the date the notice is served. It is from this date that the fourteen-month time limit runs: *Diploma Laundry* v *Surrey Timber Co Ltd* (1955). The tenant can discover who is the competent landlord by serving a s 40 notice asking for this information (see Chapter 2).

If during the two months following the service of a s 25 notice the competent landlord changes, the notice can be withdrawn (Sch 6 para 6). To effect withdrawal, the new competent landlord must serve on the tenant notice in the prescribed form (Form 12).

2. Person to be served

The landlord's notice must be served on the tenant: s 25(1). The tenant for these purposes is the person entitled to claim a new lease. As regards a tenant in occupation of the whole premises, this raises no problems. Difficulties arise, however, where the premises have been sublet.

The following permutations may occur:

- (a) if the whole of the premises has been sublet and the sub-tenants are within the scope of Part II, the s 25 notice is to be served on them;
- (b) where the premises have been sublet in part only, if a new lease of the whole premises is to be granted, the landlord will serve the s 25 notice on his immediate tenant. The new tenancy will take effect subject to the sublease(s);
- (c) where the immediate tenant does not wish to have a new lease, the landlord has the alternative of serving the s 25 notice(s) directly on the sub-tenant(s). If necessary, the service of the statutory notice on the immediate tenant will result in the landlord becoming the competent landlord of the sub-tenants. The renewal process will then be fragmented in that each s 25 notice will relate to appropriate parts of the premises. Where notices are served on the tenant and sub-tenant on the same day, certain practical difficulties for the landlord are eased by the presumption that the notices are served in the correct order: *Keith, Bayley, Rogers & Co* v *Cubes Ltd* (1975).

3. Timing of service

The notice must be served by the competent landlord not less than six months nor more than twelve months before the date for termination specified in the notice: s 25(2). Where, however, the contractual tenancy requires a period of notice longer than six months, so as to end it at common law, the general rule gives way. The twelve months' period in s 25(2) is extended to a period equal to the duration of the contractual notice plus six months: s 25(3)(b). Accordingly, if the tenancy requires ten months' notice to quit, the s 25 notice may be served up to sixteen months before the date specified for termination. This does not apply if a continuation tenancy already exists.

The relevant date from which time runs is that of service of the notice. The rules as to service are considered in Chapter 2. The reference to "months" invokes what is known as the "corresponding date rule" (*Dodds* v *Walker* (1981)), which means that a period of months calculated from a specified date will end on the corresponding day in the appropriate subsequent month: *Hogg Bullimore & Co* v *Co-operative Insurance Society* (1984). In that case, a notice served on 2 April to terminate the tenancy on 2 October was held to be effective. If the appropriate month does not have a corresponding date (for example, 31 April), the period will end on the last day of that month: *Hodgson* v *Armstrong* (1967). It is clear, moreover, that the use of expressions "not less than" and "not more than" results in the period allowed, in which action is to be taken, including both the date of service and the corresponding date on which the notice expires: *E J Riley Investments Ltd* v *Eurostile Holdings Ltd* (1985).

If the tenant pre-empts the landlord, by the service of a s 26 request, the landlord cannot then serve a s 25 notice. The two procedures are mutually exclusive: s 26(4).

4. Form and content

Section 25(1) requires the statutory notice to be in writing and to adhere to the prescribed form (see Appendix B). A new form for the s 25 notice was issued to be effective from 29 September 1989 (see Landlord and Tenant Act 1954 Part II (Notices Amendment) Regulations (SI 1989 No 1548)). This amended version overcomes earlier doubts that the previous prescribed form did not satisfy the requirements of s 25. The problem had involved s 25(5), which requires the tenant to state whether or not he is willing to give up possession. While its predecessor did not satisfactorily cater for this reply, the amended model most certainly does. It is therefore advisable (but, since *Bridgers* v *Stanford* (1991), seemingly not crucial) for the new version of the statutory notice to be used.

It should be appreciated that different forms are to be used where there is no right to renew, or a limited one, on the grounds of national interest. In the following exceptional cases, the appropriate prescribed forms should be used:

- notice on the grounds of public interest: Form 2;
- notice that a change of use or occupation will be required on a future date on the grounds of public interest: Form 3;
- notice on the grounds of national security: Form 4;
- notice to achieve the objects of the Local Employment Act 1972: Form 5;
- notice that a change of use or occupier is required to produce employment as regards Welsh Development Agency property: Form 6; and as regards Development Board for Rural Wales premises: Form 7.

As discussed in Chapter 2, in most of the above special cases a ministerial or other certificate must be issued and a copy of it must be included in the notice.

Although it is normal for the appropriate documents to be purchased from law stationers, the Notice Regulations (see above and SI 1983 No 133) allow variation since a form "substantially to like effect" may be used (see *Sun Alliance & London Assurance Co Ltd* v *Hayman* (1975)). As will be discussed later, minor deviations from the prescribed form can therefore be overlooked.

The written notice must contain certain information:

(a) it must specify a date on which the tenancy is to terminate (ie, a date not more than twelve months and not less than six months after the date of the notice: s 25(2)). The date specified cannot be earlier than the date on which the tenancy could have been terminated at common law: s 25(3). This means that with a periodic tenancy this will be the date on which a notice to quit could have brought the tenancy to an end: s 25(3)(a). The same rule applies to a fixed term lease determinable on the exercise of a break

The landlord's statutory notice

clause. As regards other fixed term tenancies, the date will be the one on which it expires: s 25(4). If a fixed term or periodic lease is already being continued under s 24, only the time requirements of s 25(2) need be observed: *Lewis* v *MTC (Cars) Ltd* (1975). It matters not whether the termination date falls on a rent day or otherwise: *Westerbury Property & Investment Co Ltd* v *Carpenter* (1961). In addition, even if the wrong date is given, and provided that the tenant is not misled, the s 25 notice may still be valid: *Safeway Foodstores* v *Morris* (1980);

(b) it must require the tenant, within two months, to notify the landlord in writing whether or not possession will be willingly given up: s 25(5). If this clause is omitted, the notice *prima facie* is invalid; hence the recent change to the prescribed form considered above. Nevertheless, as was made clear in *Bridgers* v *Stanford* (1991), the court can take a purposive approach to this section. In this case, the old form was used and the notice did not require the tenant to serve a positive counternotice. The court held that the notice remained valid. First, as the provision benefited the landlord alone, it could be waived by him without the tenant's consent. Second, the notice as served gave the substance of the information required by the tenant. Third, Parliament could not have intended that the validity of a notice should be affected by a landlord's failure to demand a counternotice, expressing a willingness to give up possession, where the landlord himself did not require it. It is therefore difficult to see the purpose of the recent regulations. Certainly, *Bridgers* is a decision which decorously disregards the clear wording of s 25(5);

(c) it must state whether or not the landlord will oppose the grant of a new tenancy and, if so, on what statutory grounds (listed in s 30) he intends to rely: s 25(6). The grounds of opposition are examined in Chapter 8. The landlord should think carefully before stipulating any ground because the grounds specified cannot later be amended: *Nursey* v *P Currie (Dartford) Ltd* (1959). Furthermore, it may be necessary at a later stage to substantiate the ground stated and a cavalier citation of all or most of the s 30 grounds will reduce dramatically the credibility of the landlord's opposition. The landlord should also bear in mind that successful reliance on any of the grounds specified in s 30(1)(a)–(d) will preclude the tenant from claiming compensation for disturbance under s 37 (see Chapter 9).

With regard to (c) above, the landlord is not at this stage required to set out the grounds of opposition in full: *Bolton's (House Furnishers) Ltd* v *Oppenheim* (1959). It is sufficient that the grounds be identified by reference to the appropriate paragraph of s 30(1) (*Biles* v *Caesar* (1957)) or by other expression which indicates the particular ground(s) (*Philipson-Stow* v *Trevor Square Ltd* (1980)). It is necessary, however, that the tenant be given adequate warning of what contention he will have to refute at a subsequent hearing: *Morris Marks* v *British Waterways Board* (1963).

If the landlord does not state opposition in the s 25 notice, the tenant is seemingly entitled to a new tenancy provided that he takes the necessary procedural steps to obtain one. If opposition is stated, but no statutory ground is given, at first glance it appears that the landlord can raise no effective opposition to the tenant's application; nevertheless, the omission should render the notice invalid under s 25(6) and of no effect: *Barclays Bank Ltd* v *Ascott* (1961). In that case, the consent of the landlord to a new tenancy made conditional on the finding of a suitable guarantor was held to invalidate the notice (see later). The notice did not state on what ground a new tenancy would be opposed if no guarantor was found.

5. Defects and omissions

Although careful completion of the form should be standard practice, the requirements of s 25 are not always complied with. Despite the general rule that if there is a defect or omission the notice will be invalidated, the tenant is ill advised to ignore a notice in the belief that it is ineffective. There are two compelling reasons why the tenant should resist this temptation. First, minor defects will be condoned. Second, the tenant may be regarded as having waived the defect or may be estopped from relying upon it. The court, however, enjoys no jurisdiction to amend the notice: *Smith* v *Draper* (1990).

The courts have demonstrated a tendency to ignore minor deviations from the prescribed form and content of the s 25 notice. The decisive issue appears to be whether the tenant is given sufficient information to proceed and whether the landlord has clearly declared his intentions: *Morris* v *Patel* (1987). There the use of an outmoded form of notice did not adversely affect the tenant and was held to be valid. Any shortcomings might be cured by the landlord sending a covering letter containing the omitted information: *Stidolph* v *The American School in London Educational Trust Ltd* (1969). In *Falcon Pipes Ltd* v *Stanhope Gate Property Co Ltd* (1967), the failure to insert the date that the notice was signed did not invalidate the notice. Similarly, in *Tegerdine* v *Brooks* (1977) the omission of immaterial marginal notes on the form was condoned. A notice has been held to be effective even though it incorrectly stated the rateable value limits of the court's jurisdiction: *AJA Smith Transport Ltd* v *BRB* (1980). The validity of a s 25 notice was not undermined when the year of termination was omitted, but was ascertainable from the form itself: *Sunrose Ltd* v *Gould* (1962).

Serious defects and omissions cannot, however, be overlooked by the courts. It seems that an error is uncondonable where it would mislead the tenant or obscure the landlord's intentions: *Pearson* v *Alyo* (1990). Accordingly, in *Morrow* v *Nadeem* (1986) a notice which incorrectly stated the landlord's name and address was held invalid. Nicholls LJ did, however, concede that: "There might perhaps be an exceptional case in which, notwithstanding the inadvertent misstatement or omission of the name of the landlord, any reasonable tenant would have known that that was a mistake and known clearly what was intended". The notice must give the real substance of the information which is necessary to enable the tenant to serve an effective counternotice and to make his application for a new tenancy. Accordingly, a notice was held to be ineffective where it did not make clear to what property it was directed: *Herongrove Ltd* v *Wates City of London Properties plc* (1988). In similar vein, in *Barclays Bank* v *Ascott* (1961) the notice stated opposition to a new tenancy, without specifying a statutory ground of opposition, and was held to be invalid. The validity of the s 25 notice is to be judged, and judged objectively, at the date when it is given. As Nourse LJ in *Pearson* v *Alyo* made clear: "The question is not whether the inaccuracy actually prejudices the particular person to whom the notice is given, but whether it is capable of prejudicing a reasonable tenant in the position of that person".

The tenant can waive a defect and cure an otherwise invalid notice. It is clear that, where a tenant who is aware of the defect fails to raise the issue with the landlord, waiver can occur: *Morrow v Nadeem*. The consequence of waiver is that the tenant loses the right thereafter to object to its invalidity and the landlord also cannot go back on it: *Smith v Draper*. As Farquharson LJ explained in *Stevens & Cutting Ltd v Anderson* (1990):

> "This arises in a situation where a person is entitled to alternative rights inconsistent with one another. If he has knowledge of the facts which give rise in law to these alternative rights and acts in a manner which is consistent only with his having chosen to rely on one of them, the law holds him to his choice even though he was unaware that this would be the legal consequence of what he did."

Similarly, a tenant who accepts a landlord's s 25 notice (which is invalid by reason of a defect or omission) as being valid, and persuades the landlord either to take or not to take certain steps under Part II, can be estopped from setting up the invalidity of the notice: *Watkins v Emslie* (1982). Of course, in appropriate circumstances, the landlord may also be estopped from relying on the invalidity of his s 25 notice: *Smith v Draper*.

The appropriate action for a tenant, when faced with a potentially defective s 25 notice, is to serve on the landlord a counternotice (see later), and then apply for a new tenancy. This protects the tenant's position. It is crucial, however, that the tenant expressly reserves the right to challenge the notice: *Craddock v Fieldman* (1960). This can be done by taking the procedural steps "without prejudice" to his contention as to invalidity: *Rhyl UDC v Rhyl Amusements* (1959). Otherwise the tenant could be held to have waived the defect: *Tennant v LCC* (1957). If appropriate, a plea that the s 25 notice is invalid can be added to the tenant's application for a new lease: *AJA Smith Transport Ltd v BRB* (1980). The county court has the jurisdiction to make a declaration as to any matter arising under Part II whether or not any other relief is sought in the proceedings: s 43A. The High Court has this power by way of inherent jurisdiction.

An invalid s 25 notice will neither engage the renewal provisions nor terminate the continuation tenancy. It could, however, act as a notice to quit at common law and, by terminating the contractual tenancy, give rise to a continuation tenancy under s 24. It would still remain necessary for the landlord to serve subsequently a valid statutory notice.

The risk to the tenant, when faced with a seemingly invalid s 25

The landlord's statutory notice

notice, was made patently clear in *Smith* v *Draper* (1990). In that case the landlords served a statutory notice which they subsequently concluded was invalid (because it did not name all the joint landlords). The tenant responded by serving a counternotice and by initiating proceedings against the named landlords. The landlords' solicitors invited the tenant to join the other landlord to the proceedings. The tenant's solicitors refused to do so and continued to challenge the validity of the s 25 notice. The landlords then served a second (and valid) s 25 notice and, for good measure, added a further ground of opposition. A counternotice was served, but the tenant did not apply to court within the prescribed time limits following the second statutory notice. The landlords formally abandoned their first s 25 notice. It was held that the tenant had not waived the defect in the initial notice and that the landlord was not estopped from denying the invalidity of that statutory notice. The tenancy was terminated by the second notice and the tenant lost the right to renew through the unfortunate failure to take the necessary procedural steps following the service of the valid notice. As Ralph Gibson LJ concluded:

> "The result is harsh and in my view regrettable ... The statute gives no power in such circumstances to the court to give relief against the consequences of honest error on the part of the legal adviser. There is nothing that this court can do about it."

The moral of *Smith* v *Draper* is that the tenant should always respond to the landlord's actions. In short, it is advisable to serve a counternotice and to make an application to court following the service of each s 25 notice. The landlord remains free to withdraw an invalid notice unless estopped or the defect is waived by the tenant. The second notice can, moreover, contain additional grounds of opposition.

6. Split reversions

Although an ordinary notice to quit can be validly served in relation to part of the holding (see s 140 Law of Property Act 1925), no special statutory provisions apply to the s 25 notice. To be valid a s 25 notice must relate to the whole of the property let to the tenant: *Dodson Bull Carpet Co Ltd* v *City of London Corporation* (1975). This means that where the reversion is split (ie, different landlords own sepa ate parts of the property) no s 25 notice can be effective in relation to part only of the premises demised: *Southport Old Links Ltd* v *Naylor* (1985). As illustrated by *Herongrove Ltd* v *Wates City of London Properties plc* (1988), where two premises are demised to one tenant under one lease (for example, an office floor and a ground floor storage room), the s 25 notice must refer to both premises. The only exception to this rule is where the lease is of two distinct properties and it is made clear that the document can be construed as two separate leases. In that limited situation, a s 25 notice can refer to one property without relating to the other: *Moss* v *Mobil Oil* (1988).

It is of course true that the reversioners can join together and serve a single s 25 notice or separate notices operating at the same time. Together they can constitute the competent landlord, as jointly they are absolutely entitled to the whole reversion: *Nevill Long & Co (Boards) Ltd* v *Firmenich & Co* (1984). Nevertheless, this option is not always practicable and it ceases to be available where one landlord does not wish to oppose the grant of a new tenancy or cannot establish a s 30 ground of opposition. In such a case, when the leases are terminated in accordance with the contract, a continuation of the whole will arise under s 24. The tenancy cannot be terminated under the terms of s 25 unless and until the reversion of both parts becomes unified again in one landlord.

The Law Commission Working Paper (No 111) considered this issue and concluded that landlords with a split reversion could be placed in an impossible, inconvenient and unjust position (para 3.2.3). The problem has also been the subject of judicial recognition: "It may well be (and I think it is) that the Act is defective in not making provisions for this rather unusual situation" (*per* Oliver LJ in *Southport Old Links Ltd* v *Naylor* (1985)).

The Working Paper advocated that the law should be reformed, but was uncertain as to how that reform should be achieved. Although the desirability of allowing a s 25 notice to terminate part only of the property in such circumstances is undeniable, landlords should not be given any undue advantage over their tenants. It is necessary, therefore, to maintain a balance between the interests of the landlords and the tenant. In order to do so, the Working Paper differentiated between a landlord who originally let a property and then split the reversion (a "voluntary" landlord of part) and one who has only ever owned the reversion of part of the property (an "involuntary" landlord of part).

As regards a s 25 notice, relating to part of the premises, which is served by a voluntary landlord of that part, the Working Paper

The landlord's statutory notice

was of the opinion that the tenant should be allowed to require the notice to apply to the whole (para 3.2.12). The alternative of the notice being automatically applied to the whole of the premises demised was not mooted with enthusiasm.

In the case of a s 25 notice served by an involuntary landlord, the Working Paper envisaged two possibilities. The first possibility was that the notice would always apply only to the part of the property specified; the landlord (being involuntary) is not responsible for the split reversion and the tenant, therefore, would not have the right to apply the notice to the whole. The second possibility was that the tenant be given the right to apply to the court for an order that the s 25 notice be made referable to the whole. As both parties here are innocent (ie they were not responsible for the fragmentation of the reversion), the balance of justice could be drawn by the court in the light of all the circumstances (para 3.2.13).

The Working Paper continued its analysis by examining the circumstances in which a notice relating to part of the property could be served and by whom. Although a number of possibilities were explored, the Working Paper decided in favour of a general power to serve notices in relation to part of the property (para 3.2.17). The notice could be served by whoever is the landlord of the premises to which the notice refers (para 3.2.19). It was envisaged that the new rules could be made to apply to existing leases (para 3.2.22).

7. Tenant's counternotice

On the service of a landlord's s 25 notice, the tenant can respond in several alternative ways.

First, if the tenant does not wish to renew the lease, the tenant need do nothing. Such inaction will mean that the tenancy will end on the date specified in the termination notice.

Second, the tenant can prevent a continuation tenancy by serving a notice on the landlord, at least three months before the expiry of a fixed term lease, that he does not wish to renew: s 27(1). As discussed in Chapter 4, there is no prescribed form of notice for this purpose and any notice which makes clear the tenant's intentions will suffice: *Lewington* v *Trustees of the Society for the Protection of Ancient Buildings* (1983).

Third, as regards a tenancy for a fixed term continuing under s 24, the tenant may terminate the tenancy under s 27(2) by written notice to his landlord, which is of at least three months' duration and is to expire on a quarter day (see Chapter 4).

Fourth, where the tenant seeks a new tenancy, he must reply to the landlord's s 25 notice by serving a counternotice on the landlord which clearly states his unwillingness to give up possession: s 29(2).

The tenant's counternotice, stating whether or not he is willing to vacate the property at the end of the tenancy, must be given within two months of the service of the landlord's s 25 notice: s 29(2). Apart from it being in writing, there is no prescribed form for the counternotice. Provided that the intention of the tenant is manifest, it is possible to discern a counternotice from written negotiations for a new lease: *Lewington*. If the tenant states in the counternotice that he is willing to give up possession, that is an irrevocable election: *Re 14 Grafton Street London W1* (1971). The counternotice cannot be withdrawn. In addition, a counternotice posted within the time limit and never delivered is not sufficient notification and the tenant loses his right to apply for a new lease: *Chiswell* v *Griffon Land & Estates Ltd* (1975). In practice, the counternotice is served as a matter of routine and usually before the tenant has had the opportunity to give the matter deep consideration.

A counternotice should be served even when the landlord has indicated, in his s 25 notice, that he will not oppose the tenant's application for a new tenancy: *JT Development Ltd* v *Quinn* (1990). If there is any doubt as to the validity of the s 25 notice (see above) the counternotice should still be served, but marked "without prejudice". The tenant can then apply for a declaration of its invalidity before the hearing of the application for the new lease: *Airport Restaurants* v *Southend-on-Sea Corporation* (1960).

The tenant must apply to the court for a new lease not less than two nor more than four months after the giving of the landlord's s 25 notice: s 29(3). The "corresponding date rule" considered above applies also to these periods. The time limits are strict: *Kammins Ballrooms Co Ltd* v *Zenith Investments (Torquay) Ltd* (1971). Failure to apply to the court within these time limits is fatal to the tenant's claim even though he served a counternotice in time: *Polyviou* v *Seeley* (1979).

In its Working Paper, the Law Commission suggested that the present requirements for the service of a counternotice be changed.

The landlord's statutory notice

It considered whether counternotices should be abolished, but saw a danger that a landlord might then be kept in ignorance of the tenant's intentions. It favoured, however, a new procedure under which the tenant would serve a counternotice only when he wished to terminate the lease and not apply for a renewal (para 3.3.7). The tenant would not then need to serve a counternotice as a pre-requisite to applying for a new lease.

Chapter 6

The tenant's initiative

The Landlord and Tenant Act 1954 offers to the commercial tenant the fundamental right to obtain a new lease to follow on from the termination of the existing tenancy. This can be achieved in several ways.

First, there is nothing to prevent the parties from agreeing to a new lease without recourse to the statutory machinery. If an agreement is concluded, and is put into writing (s 69(2)), the current lease continues until the date set for the commencement of the new tenancy. In the intervening period, it is not a lease to which the provisions of Part II apply: s 28. On a binding agreement being reached, therefore, the tenant is precluded from making any application for a new tenancy.

Second, in the absence of agreement, the tenant can apply to the court for a new lease following the service of a landlord's s 25 notice and the tenant's subsequent counternotice (see Chapter 5).

Third, where there is no agreement and a s 25 notice has not been served, the tenant may be able to initiate the action for a new tenancy by the service of a s 26 request. The request terminates the current lease and paves the way for the grant of a new lease by the court. It is with this initiative that this chapter is concerned.

1. The "pre-emptive strike"

The standard advice to tenants is that the use of the s 26 procedure is, in most cases, inadvisable. As is made clear in Chapter 7, the tenant has much to gain by prolonging the existing lease, and the paying of the old rent, for as long as possible. In this light, and

The tenant's initiative

particularly when the landlord shows no sign of serving a s 25 notice, it is rarely advantageous for the tenant to terminate the existing tenancy. Such a step would be appropriate only where the tenant either seeks to gain a greater stability for his business by securing a new lease or wishes to make what is sometimes called "a pre-emptive strike".

The tactic of making a pre-emptive strike, when the landlord intends to serve a s 25 notice, focuses upon the tenant being able to maintain the status quo (and, subject to an interim rent, the old rent) for longer than might be desired by the landlord. In this context, the consequence of the s 26 request might be viewed as giving the tenant an unwarranted advantage over his landlord. The strategy is founded upon the tenant's request taking between six and twelve months to terminate the lease (s 26(2)) and the preclusion of the landlord from serving a s 25 notice: s 26(4). If the landlord has not yet served a s 25 notice, the tenant can effectively forestall him for twelve months. The Law Commission Working Paper (No 111) believed this to be an unfair manipulation of the rules and suggested that they be modified (para 3.2.30). The following possibilities were mooted:

(a) making it obligatory for the tenant's request to have effect as soon after its service as possible. This would be either at the expiry of six months or at the next following contractual term date, whichever is the later;

(b) ending the exclusivity of the s 25 and s 26 procedures. This would allow the landlord to serve a s 25 notice, on the heels of the tenant's request, specifying a termination date six months hence;

(c) allowing the landlord to serve a counternotice which would require the current tenancy to end on the earliest date on which the tenant's original s 26 request could have terminated it (ie six months). This was the alternative favoured by the Working Paper. It was viewed as being the most even-handed modification and a practical and acceptable way to eliminate the abuse associated with the pre-emptive strike.

It should not be overlooked that, once a s 26 request has been served, the competent landlord can apply for an interim rent under s 24A. As discussed in Chapter 7, this can mitigate substantially any loss associated with the tenant prolonging the continuation tenancy. It is conceivable that, if the Working Paper's recommendations on revamping the interim rent facility are acted upon, the changes to s 26 will be rendered unnecessary.

2. Availability of the right

Although any tenant who has been served with a s 25 notice is entitled (provided a counternotice is served by that tenant) to apply to the court for a new tenancy, not all tenants can make a request for a new tenancy under s 26. Only tenants under a tenancy originally granted for either a term of years certain (ie a fixed term) exceeding one year or a term of years certain and thereafter from year to year are entitled to make such a request: s 26(1). This excludes tenancies granted for a fixed term of up to one year and periodic tenancies. A request served by a tenant who does not qualify under s 26 is invalid and does not end the tenancy: *Watkins* v *Emslie* (1981).

It is a criticism of s 26 that the availability of the right is unduly restricted. The Law Commission Report (No 17) rejected this criticism:

> "We can see no merit in this proposal [to make the facility open to periodic tenants] since a periodic tenancy of its nature continues indefinitely until it is terminated. If the landlord serves notice under s 25 to terminate the tenancy, a weekly or monthly tenant has the same right as other tenants ... to apply for a new tenancy" (para 53).

The Working Paper (No 111), almost twenty years later, reconsidered the matter and arrived at the same conclusion (para 3.2.27), declaring that to extend the right to periodic tenants would result in a proliferation of applications and be of little benefit to such tenants.

Neither the Report nor the Working Paper considered whether a term of years certain for one year or less should continue to be excluded from the ambit of s 26. It does seem arbitrary that a current tenancy of exactly one year does not qualify under s 26(1), whereas a lease granted for one year and thereafter from week to week does qualify because the grant then exceeds one year by at least one week.

No request for a new tenancy can be made once the landlord has served a s 25 notice: s 26(4). As discussed in Chapter 5, the tenant

The tenant's initiative

must in that situation exercise his right to a new tenancy by serving a counternotice as to his unwillingness to give up possession and by applying for a new tenancy under the terms of that s 25 notice. No request by the tenant can be made after he has served a termination notice under s 27 or a notice to quit (see Chapter 4). Correspondingly, once a s 26 request has been given, the landlord cannot serve a s 25 notice; nor can the tenant serve a s 27 notice or notice to quit.

3. Form and content

The s 26 request must be served by the tenant on the competent landlord. The request must be in writing and in the format prescribed by the Part II (Notices) Regulations 1983 or in a form substantially to like effect: s 26(3). A specimen s 26 notice is set out in Appendix B. It should be appreciated that this is the only instance where a tenant is required to use a prescribed form in the Part II machinery.

The request must state the commencement date for the proposed new tenancy. This date cannot be earlier than that on which the tenancy could be ended at common law (ie, under the contract). This is not relevant when a continuation tenancy has arisen. The date set for commencement must be at least six, but no more than twelve, months after the service of the tenant's request: s 26(2). On the date so specified the new tenancy automatically terminates the current lease. The tenant cannot therefore serve a s 26 request until the last year of the fixed term lease.

A failure to comply with these time limits renders the request invalid. Nevertheless, landlords should be careful in dealing with any such request because defects can be expressly or impliedly waived. In *Bristol Cars* v *RKH Hotels* (1979), for example, neither party noticed the error as to the commencement date specified in the s 26 request. The landlords indicated that they would not oppose a new lease and applied for an interim rent. Subsequently, the defect in the tenant's request was spotted and the landlords served a s 25 termination notice. It was held that the landlords were estopped from denying the validity of the s 26 request (having led the tenants to expect that a new tenancy would not be opposed) and, in any event, had waived the defect by their application for an interim rent.

In addition to stating the commencement date for the new tenancy, the tenant's request must include the proposed terms of the tenancy requested: s 26(3). These proposals must concern:

(a) the property to be comprised in the new lease. This need not be identical to the premises demised under the current tenancy;

(b) the duration of the new tenancy. If the proposals are for a lease on the same terms as the original one, the court will (if the request is silent on the matter) assume that the tenant seeks a tenancy of the same duration: *Sidney Bolsom Investment Trust Ltd v E Karmios & Co (London) Ltd* (1956);

(c) the rent to be payable under the new tenancy;

(d) the other terms of the new lease. This usually consists of a statement that in all other aspects the renewal should be on the same terms as the original lease.

4. Effect of the request

The consequences of serving a s 26 request are as follows:

(a) it brings to an end the current lease (whether or not continuing by virtue of s 24) on the date specified in the request as being the commencement date for the new tenancy: s 26(5). This is, however, subject to any interim continuance under s 64 while the decision of the court as to the grant of a new tenancy is pending, and to any short extension under s 36(2) where the tenant elects not to accept the new tenancy on the terms decided by the court;

(b) it entitles the landlord to serve a counternotice stating opposition to the new tenancy: s 26(6);

(c) it enables the tenant to apply to the court, not less than two and not more than four months following the s 26 request, for a new lease: ss 24(1) and 29(3). If the tenant fails to make an application to the court, the current tenancy ends on the date specified in the request as the starting date for the proposed new tenancy: *Smith v Draper* (1990). The tenant, moreover, sacrifices his right to a new tenancy and ceases to be protected by the provisions of Part II: *Polyviou v Seeley* (1980). This is because the tenant is allowed to serve only one request for a new tenancy and that single request, provided it is valid, cannot be

The tenant's initiative

abandoned so as to make way for a fresh request: *Smith v Draper*. An invalid request is of no effect for these purposes.

5. Landlord's response

If the landlord seeks to oppose the grant of a new lease, he must serve a counternotice on the tenant within a period of two months of the request being served: s 26(6). There is no prescribed form for this counternotice, but it must state the landlord's opposition and the s 30(1) ground(s) upon which the opposition is based: s 26(6). As to the statement of opposition and the expression of the statutory grounds, the same considerations apply as previously discussed in the context of the s 25 notice (see Chapter 5). For example, a counternotice stating that the landlord will not oppose a new tenancy if a guarantor was found, but not providing a ground of opposition if that did not occur, is invalid: *Barclays Bank v Ascott* (1961). Moreover, the tenant must bear in mind the possibility that his conduct may give rise to waiver of the defect or estoppel.

The landlord must respond carefully because once the counternotice has been served it is both binding and limiting. The landlord and his successors remain bound by the grounds set out in the counternotice. Where a new competent landlord emerges within the two months following the service of the s 26 request, if a counternotice has already been served the new landlord cannot give his own counternotice. Where, however, the predecessor had not given a counternotice, the new competent landlord can serve a counternotice within the statutory period: *XL Fisheries v Leeds Corporation* (1955).

A landlord who does not serve a valid counternotice loses the right to oppose the tenant's application. If the landlord has no opposition to the tenant having a new lease, there is no need to respond to the s 26 request. It should be understood that where a counternotice is served (this applies also to a s 25 notice) which states a ground of opposition which is neither honest nor truthful, the landlord's counternotice (or s 25 notice) can be invalidated on the ground of fraudulent misrepresentation: *Betty's Cafes Ltd v Phillips Furnishing* (1958). This rationale extends also to a representation made recklessly: *Rous v Mitchell* (1991). Accordingly, the allegation of fraud could be a last gasp measure by which to save a tenant from the consequence of not adhering to the statutory time limits concerning the response to a s 25 notice and/or the application for a new tenancy.

6. The need to go to court

The fundamental right offered to the business tenant is to apply for a new tenancy to follow on from the termination of the existing lease. There is, however, no reason why the parties should not agree to the grant of a new lease without using the statutory machinery. If they do agree to the grant and terms of a new tenancy, the existing lease will continue, unprotected by the provisions of Part II, until the date agreed for the commencement of the renewal: s 28. Where a binding agreement is achieved, the tenant should ensure that the contract is registered as a C IV land charge (in the unregistered system) or by a notice or caution (in the registered system). As regards registered land, however, the contract is likely to constitute an overriding interest within s 70(1)(g) Land Registration Act 1925. The danger associated with non-registration is illustrated in *Stratton (RJ) Ltd* v *Wallis Tomlin* (1986) where the landlord sold his reversion before the termination date for the existing lease and the purchaser took free of the landlord's contract with the tenant. The tenant could not then apply for a new lease because s 28 provides that, when a written binding agreement is entered, the provisions of Part II cease to apply to the current tenancy.

It may be that there is agreement in principle only, and that the terms of the new tenancy are still in dispute. An application to the court will then be necessary to settle such outstanding terms and, in the intervening period, the existing lease will remain within the protection of the Act.

The tenant is given the right to apply to the court for a new tenancy by virtue of s 24(1). The right can, however, only be exercised following the service of the landlord's s 25 notice (plus the service, in response, of the tenant's counternotice) or the service of the tenant's s 26 request. The other means whereby a tenancy can be terminated under the Act do not carry with them the right to apply for a renewal.

7. Jurisdiction and some procedural matters

Since 1 July 1991, the date on which the Courts and Legal Services Act 1990 came into force, the county court has been given an unlimited jurisdiction to determine applications under the Landlord and Tenant Act 1954. The new law sweeps aside the now defunct s 63 of the 1954 Act and with it the jurisdictional limitations based upon rateable values. Although the venue of the High Court remains an option for the tenant, it is thought likely that such an election will infrequently occur in practice. The county court is now the primary agency dealing with lease renewals. It has long been the case that an application made to the wrong county court, provided it is received in time, does not invalidate the proceedings: *Sharma* v *Knight* (1986).

The parties to the application are termed the plaintiff and defendant in High Court proceedings; and the applicant and respondent in the county court. The plaintiff/applicant is the tenant of the holding in issue. Where there are joint tenants, the general rule is that all of them must join in the application: *Jacobs* v *Chaudhuri* (1968). However, the court has a discretion to order one joint tenant, as a trustee, to be party to the proceedings so as to protect the trust property: *Harris* v *Black* (1983). Even where the tenant is a trustee for the business occupier or where the tenant and the occupier are both members of a group of companies, it is the actual tenant who is a party to the proceedings. In addition, on obtaining probate, the executor of a deceased tenant can make the application to the court: *Re Crowhurst Park* (1974).

The appropriate defendant/respondent is the particular landlord who fulfils the definition of a competent landlord in s 44 (see Chapter 2). It is vital that the identity of the person intended to be sued is made unequivocal, but errors as to the landlord's name or mistakenly suing the wrong person will not necessarily render the proceedings nugatory. The distinction to be drawn is between a mistake as to the identity of the landlord and a mistake in the name of the landlord: *Evans Construction Co Ltd* v *Charrington & Co Ltd* (1983). As Donaldson LJ explained "... it is, in my judgement, important to bear in mind that there is a real distinction between suing A in the mistaken belief that A is the party who is responsible for the matters complained of and seeking to sue B, but mistakenly describing or naming him as A and thereby ending up suing A instead of B." In *Evans* the tenant intended to sue Bass Holdings, but mistakenly thought his landlord was Charrington & Co. The Court of Appeal concluded that it had the power to substitute an altogether different name and allowed the appropriate amendment. Nevertheless, the differentiation between name and identity is one of hair's breadth proportions: see *Sardinia Sulcis* v *Al Taiwwab* (1990).

If there is a change of competent landlord after the application to the court, the proceedings cease to be properly constituted unless the new landlord is made a party to the application: *Piper* v *Muggleton* (1956). Where a mortgagee of the landlord's interest is in possession, or a receiver has been appointed either under the mortgage or by the court, the mortgagee is substituted for the landlord (RSC O 97 r 1(2); CCR O 43 r 1(2)). If such developments occur after the application is made, the mortgagee must be joined to the proceedings: *Meah* v *Mouskos* (1964). In the situation where a reversionary tenancy will be granted, the landlord next superior to the competent landlord should also be joined: *Birch (A & W)* v *P B (Sloane) & Cadogan Settled Estates* (1956).

The application can cover a number of properties demised under different leases provided that the parties are the same and act in the same capacity, and the statutory procedures have been followed in relation to each property: *Curtis* v *Calgary Investments Ltd* (1984). Obviously, issues concerning individual premises will be argued separately. If appropriate, the court can order that each application be heard individually.

(a) County court

In the county court, proceedings are governed by CCR O 43 and commenced by originating application. There is no prescribed form for this application. Subject to the court directing otherwise, the return date will be that of the pre-trial review: O 43 r 2. The originating application must be served on the landlord within two months (O 43 r 6(3)), but the court does have the power to extend this time limit under O 7 r 20(2). This power is normally exercised only in exceptional circumstances (*Robert Baxendale Ltd* v *Davstone (Holdings) Ltd* (1982)) and will not be contemplated where the application for an extension is made more than two months after the time for service has passed (*Leal* v *Dunlop Bio-Processes International Ltd* (1984)). This latter limitation is not applicable, however, where the parties have agreed to waive the time limits while negotiations continue: O 13 r 4(1) (see *Ali* v *Knight* (1983)).

The application must set out the tenant's proposals for the new tenancy, but need not do so with precision: *Williams* v *Hillcroft Garage Ltd* (1971). The landlord has fourteen days within which to file an answer (O 44 r 2; O 9 r 18) and is required to state his objections to the tenant's application. There is no prescribed form for the answer (but see county court practice form N 4000) and the court has the discretion both to extend the time for filing the answer (O 13 r 4) and to allow the landlord to raise new objections at the hearing (*Morgan* v *Jones* (1960)). The landlord may insert into his answer an application for an interim rent.

The pre-trial review may be adjourned *sine die* pending negotiations or may be dispensed with if the parties agree directions by post. If the parties remain unable to reach an agreement, the matter will proceed to a hearing. Appeal from the county court is to the Court of Appeal: s 77 County Courts Act 1984.

(b) High Court

In the High Court, proceedings are instituted in the Chancery Division by originating summons and are governed by RSC O 97. The summons may be issued from the district registry within whose catchment the premises are situated. The tenant should, at the time of issue, file an affidavit verifying the statements made in the summons. Unless contrary affidavits are sworn (as is common with proceedings under the Landlord and Tenant Act 1954 because such matters as the landlord's intention, and the terms of the proposed lease, are often contested), the originating summons procedure operates to avoid cross-examination. At the latest, this affidavit must be filed fourteen days before the date fixed for the first hearing. It is in the summons that any dispute as to the validity of any statutory notices served should be raised specifically: *Bolton's (House Furnishers) Ltd* v *Oppenheim* (1959). If the parties are still in the process of negotiation, the summons will not usually state a date for the first hearing. Instead the tenant may insert the expression "on a day to be fixed".

The summons should be served within two months of its issue, but the court does enjoy the discretion to extend this time limit (O 97 r 6(3); O 6 r 8). The landlord must file an affidavit not less than four days before the date fixed for the first hearing of the summons (O 97 r 7(2)). The landlord's affidavit must state, as appropriate:

(i) whether the landlord opposes the grant of a new tenancy and, if so, on what s 30 ground(s);
(ii) the landlord's opposition to the tenant's proposed terms

for the new lease and the landlord's counter-proposals;
(iii) whether the landlord will have less than fourteen months unexpired on his own lease at the date specified for the termination of the current tenancy. In such a case, the name and address of the landlord's immediate landlord must be given (RSC O 97 r 7(2)).

Where the matter cannot be disposed of at the first hearing, the Master or District Judge (as appropriate) will give directions as to the further conduct of the proceedings. According to the Practice Direction [1990] 1 All ER 255 the general rule is that the Master will not deal with proceedings under the Landlord and Tenant Acts 1927 and 1954 except with consent or in so far as the proceedings relate to an interim rent or authorised contracting out under s 38(4). In special cases, the Master can be authorised by a High Court judge to deal with other matters. Discovery, however, will not usually be ordered: *John Miller (Shipping) Ltd v Port of London Authority* (1959). Discovery has to be justified on the facts of the case: *Wine Shippers (London) Ltd v Bath House Syndicate Ltd* (1960). An example of when it might be justified is where the production of accounts directly relates to the tenant's financial ability to perform the leasehold covenants: *Re St Martin's Theatre* (1959).

(c) Miscellaneous

In relation to both courts, several further observations need to be made:

(i) the issue of whether the tenant is to be granted a new tenancy may be tried as a preliminary matter before the court turns its attention to working out the terms: *Dutch Oven v Egham Estate & Investment Co Ltd* (1968);
(ii) the costs of the proceedings are at the discretion of the court: *Decca Navigator Co Ltd v GLC* (1974). Accordingly a landlord who withdraws opposition to the grant of a new tenancy after proceedings are commenced runs the risk of costs: *Demag Industrial Equipment Ltd v Canada Dry (UK) Ltd* (1969). Similarly, a tenant who is awarded a new lease, but then exercises his right to have that order revoked, will face the probability that costs will be ordered against him: *Re No 88 High Road, Kilburn* (1959);
(iii) the tenant's application to the court should be protected by

The tenant's initiative

registration as a pending land action in the Land Registry or under the Land Charges Act 1972, as appropriate (see *Selim Ltd* v *Bickenhall Engineering Ltd* (1981)).

8. Statutory time limits

The application for a new tenancy must be made not less than two and not more than four months after the service of the s 25 notice or s 26 request: s 29(3). Otherwise, the tenant loses the right to a new tenancy: *Polyviou* v *Seeley* (1979). The time that the application is made is when the relevant originating process is issued: *Kammins Ballrooms Co Ltd* v *Zenith Investments (Torquay) Ltd* (1971).

These time limits are strict, subject to waiver by agreement or implied waiver by the landlord's conduct: *Kammins Ballrooms* (see also *Stevens & Cutting Ltd* v *Anderson* (1990)). It seems that the parties can waive the time limits only up to the date for termination specified in the s 25 notice or s 26 request: *Meah* v *Sector Properties* (1974). After this time, the tenant no longer can be classified as a tenant for the purposes of Part II and no longer has rights to enforce. The *Meah* case, however, concerned implied waiver and has left some doubt as to whether it applies also to waiver by agreement. An estoppel might be raised to prevent the landlord relying on the irregularity of an out-of-time application. For this to operate, there must be a representation of fact; a reliance on the representation; and a detriment resulting from such reliance: *Stevens & Cutting Ltd* v *Anderson*. In this case, a premature application was held invalid because the landlord was neither debarred by waiver of the irregularity (he did not know of the defect and of any right to rely on it) nor estopped from relying on it (there was no representation by the landlord).

The courts have no jurisdiction to extend these statutory time limits: *Hodgson* v *Armstrong* (1967). One minor exception has, however, been permitted. If the last day for making the application is a Sunday or Bank Holiday, the application may be made on the next day that the court is open. In the county court this is permissible under CCR O 1 r 9(5) and, in the High Court, has been approved in *Kaur* (*Pritam*) v *S Russell & Sons Ltd* (1973).

In the calculation of the statutory periods, the corresponding date rule (considered in Chapter 5) applies. Accordingly, an application made exactly two months after the service of the s 25 notice or s 26 request will suffice (*EJ Riley Investments Ltd* v *Eurostile Holdings Ltd* (1985)) and the period will expire, on the same date as service, four months later (*Dodds* v *Walker* (1981)). Legal advisers should take care to satisfy these time limits, or they may face an action in professional negligence. There has been a spate of such cases in recent times. As to compensation for such negligence see *Hodge* v *Clifford Cowling & Co* (1990); *Teesside Indoor Bowls Ltd* v *Borough Council of Stockton on Tees* (1990); *Murray* v *Lloyd* (1990); and *Huxford* v *Stoy Hayward & Co* (1989).

Although the need to apply to the court within the time limits, as set out in s 29(3), is brought to the attention of the tenant by the prescribed forms of documentation involved in the renewal procedure, tenants often lose their rights by non-observance. This fact caused the Law Commission Working Paper (No 111) to criticise the rigidity of the present time conditions and to conclude that it is "undesirable that tenants should lose their statutory rights on what in some cases can be regarded as a technicality" (at para 3.3.9).

The Working Paper identified the aims of the renewal procedure as being fourfold (at para 3.3.10):

(i) to give the parties a reasonable time for negotiation so as to encourage renewal by agreement;

(ii) to ensure that neither party can create unreasonable delay and work it to their financial advantage;

(iii) to provide court proceedings as a last resort resolution of disputes;

(iv) to continue the current tenancy throughout the renewal process.

With these considerations in mind, the Working Paper speculated as to the scope for reform and the manner in which it could be achieved. The following possibilities were discussed:

(i) to give the court a statutory power to waive time limits. Although a simple expedient, this was not favoured because it did nothing to stimulate negotiation and to reduce the workload of the court (at para 3.3.12);

(ii) to allow the parties to vary the time limits by agreement, but to place such agreements on a statutory footing. Although this is a desirable move forward (it overcomes the uncertainty surrounding waiver: see above), the Working Paper concluded that it would not remove the trap of time limits for the unwary (at para 3.3.13);

The tenant's initiative

(iii) to remove time limits altogether from the statutory procedure. However, this would also remove the check upon unreasonable delay. This proposal was thought feasible provided that replacement safeguards are introduced (at para 3.3.14). The possible safeguards are that the landlord be able to ask the court to reimpose time limits (at para 3.3.15) or that the landlord be enabled to institute renewal proceedings (at para 3.3.16). The first option achieves little as the tenant would still be liable to fall foul of time limits. The second alternative was favoured by the Working Paper because it eliminates the statutory time-trap for the tenant and prevents the delay of the proceedings to the disadvantage of a helpless landlord.

9. Withdrawal of application

It may be that, after the tenant's application to court, the parties reach an agreement about the grant of a new lease and the terms of that lease. In such a case, there are two options open to the tenant. First, he may proceed with the application and have the agreement embodied in an order of the court. Second, he may withdraw the application on the terms agreed. The latter course is the most simple and inexpensive alternative.

If the agreement is that the tenant will abandon his claim for a new tenancy, this can be done either through a withdrawal of the application or by the tenant admitting the facts constituting a s 30(1) ground of opposition, whereupon the court will dismiss the application. The advantage to the landlord of withdrawal is that there can be no appeal and the existing tenancy will come to an end three months after the date of withdrawal. The disadvantage to the tenant of withdrawal is that it precludes any change of heart and any chance of compensation for misrepresentation under s 55. Although withdrawal does not disentitle the tenant to compensation for disturbance under s 37, the settlement may include a covenant by the landlord to pay compensation in appropriate circumstances. The settlement should also deal with the issue of costs.

In the county court, the tenant may withdraw his application as of right by giving notice to the district judge and serving a copy on the landlord: CCR O 18 r 1. In the High Court, the tenant can withdraw, without leave of the court, up to fourteen days after the service of the landlord's affidavit: RSC O 28 r 1A. Otherwise leave is necessary (see RSC O 21 rr 2 and 3). Leave is usually given unless the landlord will suffer injustice: *Young, Austen & Young* v *BMA* (1977). In exceptional circumstances, the court can attach conditions to its approval (for example, the tenant is not to claim compensation for disturbance): *Lloyd's Bank* v *City of London Corporation* (1983).

Chapter 7

The interim rent

As initially enacted, the 1954 Act provided that during a s 24 continuation tenancy the original contractual terms (other than those relating to termination) remained effective. Therefore the contractual rent payable to the immediate landlord was preserved until either the continuation tenancy was terminated or a new lease came into force. The tenant was offered the incentive to delay proceedings for as long as possible and thereby gain at the landlord's expense. The value of this tactic could be considerable. In *Re No 88, High Road, Kilburn* (1959), for example, the original annual rent of £250 was increased to £3,000 on the order for a new tenancy. The scope for this type of manipulation was great. There are many ways in which a tenant can stall for time (see Harman J in *Espresso Coffee Machine Co Ltd* v *Guardian Assurance Co Ltd* (1959)). Perhaps the most obvious method is to enter an appeal from a judge's refusal of a new lease. As a new tenancy does not operate until three months after the proceedings are complete (s 64), the advantage to the tenant is evident, even though there is no intention to proceed with the appeal.

The Law Commission (No 17) proposed that, in order to prevent this form of abuse, the landlord should be given the right to apply for an interim rent. As a result, a novel facility was incorporated into the 1954 Act (via the Law of Property Act 1969) by the insertion of the new s 24A. This gives the court the power to determine an interim rent in substitution for the contractual one, this new rent being a reasonable one for the tenant to pay while the old tenancy is statutorily continued. As will be shown, the interim rent is usually less than the market rent which is ordered on the grant of a new tenancy; some incentive for delay by the tenant, therefore, still persists. The tenant may maintain a financial advantage by keeping the continuation tenancy alive. As the Law Commission's Working Paper (No 111) asked: "Is there any justification for a tenant to enjoy the landlord's premises at less than the current market rent, and indeed is that not contrary to the policy of the Act?" (para 3.4.4). It should not be forgotten that such a benefit to the tenant brings with it a corresponding detriment to the landlord.

While recognising that the original justification for the interim rent facility remained, the Working Paper considered whether it should be replaced by a system which more fully protected the landlord's financial interests. The provisional conclusion reached was that the present system should be retained (with modification), but that new rent rules should apply where it would be unjust for the tenant to benefit, that is where:

(a) the landlord's s 25 notice or the tenant's s 26 request related to all the property let under the current lease;
(b) the tenant is in occupation of all the property; and
(c) the landlord stated that he will not oppose the grant of a new tenancy (para 3.4.8).

The Working Paper concluded that for this type of case no special interim rent would be necessary. An alternative suggestion was that, when the rent under the new tenancy is agreed or ordered by the court, it should be back-dated automatically to the date given in the s 25 notice or s 26 request for terminating the current lease (para 3.4.8). Under these new rules the tenant would be under a continuous obligation to pay a market rent.

As regards other situations, the interim rent (and associated benefit to the tenant) was thought to be justified. As the tenant does not have full security of tenure until the new lease is granted, if the renewal is being contested, the market rent for occupation in those circumstances could be well below the market rent payable by a tenant who enjoys full security (para 3.4.5). This is a justification for the tenant having a rent discount during the continuation period (see later).

1. Application for an interim rent

It is the competent landlord, and not the immediate landlord nor the tenant, who can apply for an interim rent. The Working Paper thought that this was anomalous and problematic. First, it saw no objections to the statutory right being extended to the tenant. Due to the trend of rising rents, such an extension would perhaps have

The interim rent

little practical value to a tenant, but it would " ... demonstrate the evenhandedness of the law" (para 3.4.10). There can be no justification in principle for a tenant, who at the end of the old lease is paying more than a market rent, being unable to apply for an interim rent. Although uncommon, it should not be overlooked that an interim rent can be less than the contractual rent: *O'May* v *City of London Real Property Co Ltd* (1983).

Second, the Working Paper envisaged no difficulties in allowing a landlord to make an application even though he was not the competent landlord (para 3.4.13). The current situation, that only a competent landlord (who is not necessarily the tenant's immediate landlord) can apply for an interim rent, can lead to injustice where the premises have been sublet in whole or part. It has long been recognised that, where the competent landlord and the immediate landlord are not the same person, there is no incentive for an application to be made; the interim rent benefits only the immediate landlord and yet he cannot make the application himself. The competent landlord has nothing to gain from the procedure. The problem is accentuated where the premises are partly sublet. The competent landlord might apply for an interim rent against his tenant, but that tenant cannot apply for an interim rent against the sub-tenant. If the rent is increased, the sub-tenant is under no obligation to pay an extra amount. This could result in the tenant being out of pocket to the extent that the increased rent is attributable to the part of the property sublet. The Law Commission saw a solution to this problem by allowing the interim rent for the whole premises to be apportioned between the parts of it (para 3.4.13), affected sub-tenants being given a right to join in any action.

The landlord's application must be express and can be made at any time after the service of either a landlord's termination notice under s 25 or a tenant's request for a new tenancy under s 26. In the county court, the application can be made under CCR O 13 rr 1 and 2; it can arise in the course of proceedings; in the landlord's answer to those proceedings; or within a separate originating application under O 3 r 4(1) (see *Thomas* v *Hammond-Lawrence* (1986)). In the High Court, the procedure is governed by RSC O 97 r 9A(1). This provides that if the tenant has not yet applied for a new lease, the application for an interim rent is made by originating summons whereas, otherwise, it is made by a summons in the tenant's proceedings. Although the summons does not have to be served within any fixed time limit, such action must be taken promptly as a summons can be invalidated by delay. If this occurs, a new summons may be issued: *Texaco Ltd* v *Benton & Bowles (Holdings) Ltd* (1983). In practice, a separate application for an interim rent is uncommon as it is not cost effective. Such a step is taken only to heighten pressure upon a tenant to quit the premises. It is more usual for the interim rent to be dealt with at the same time as the tenant's claim for a new tenancy. The tenant may then face substantial arrears as the sum is "back-dated" under the provisions of s 24A(2) (see later).

In both courts, the application may be heard any time after the service of a s 25 notice or s 26 request and might take place after the order for a new tenancy has been made: *Regis Property Co Ltd* v *Lewis & Peat Ltd* (1970). The application is not affected by the withdrawal of the tenant's application for a new tenancy because the landlord's application is in the nature of a counterclaim: *Artoc Bank & Trust Ltd* v *Prudential Assurance Co* (1984). Similarly, the assignment of the reversion does not prevent the new landlord (acquiring title after the application for an interim rent has been entered) from benefiting from the proceedings: *Bloomfield* v *Ashwright Ltd* (1984).

The court has a discretion and is not bound to fix an interim rent: *Bloomfield* v *Ashwright Ltd*. Refusals, however, appear to be rare (see *English Exporters (London) Ltd* v *Eldonwall Ltd* (1973)). If an interim rent is set, in effect it becomes the new contractual rent (s 24A(2)).

In its Working Paper, the Law Commission considered whether the landlord should continue to be required to make an express application, the alternative being that the landlord should be automatically entitled to an interim rent (para 3.4.14.). Although this alternative avoids unnecessary court applications, the Law Commission thought that the present system was preferable because it positively warns tenants that they may have to pay increased rents. Universal entitlement was, therefore, rejected. It is dubious, in any event, to what extent such a change would reduce the number of court applications; recourse to the court would still be necessary to settle disputes concerning quantum.

2. Commencement and quantum

If the court exercises its discretion to award an interim rent, the new rent becomes effective from the date when the landlord

The interim rent

applies for an interim rent or, if later, the date specified in the s 25 notice or s 26 request: s 24A(2) (see *Victor Blake (Menswear) Ltd* v *Westminster City Council* (1978)). Therefore the landlord should act expeditiously. Once the termination date for the current tenancy has passed, the new rent is payable only from the date of the application: *Stream Properties Ltd* v *Davis* (1972). In *Thomas* v *Hammond-Lawrence* (1986), the landlord was held to have commenced proceedings for an interim rent in his answer to the tenant's originating application for a new tenancy and not when the landlord (some two years later) served a notice applying for an interim rent. The change in rent operates prospectively and the interim rent continues to be payable until the continuation tenancy is brought to an end.

The interim rent is not usually the same as the market rent payable under a new lease. Admittedly, the starting point is to consider what the open market rent would be in accordance with s 34 (see Chapter 10), but the court must then "have regard to the rent payable under the terms of the [existing] tenancy" and calculate the rent payable for "a new tenancy from year to year of the whole property comprised in the tenancy": s 24A(3). It should also be remembered that s 24A(1) bases the calculation subjectively on what would be reasonable for the tenant to pay during the continuation period. These qualifications will operate to the tenant's advantage and produce an interim rent discounted below the market rent for that property. The Law Commission Report (No 17) thought that a market rent had no real meaning when related to a temporary situation of indeterminate duration, and advocated a "fair rent" as being an appropriate measure. Although the expression "fair rent" was omitted from s 24A, the legislature did give the court a discretion to fix the interim rent at a figure which achieves a balance between the interests of the parties. It is, therefore, the norm for the interim rent to be less than the market rent for that property. This is generally regarded as providing a cushion for the rent, bridging any steep increase between the old and the new rents: *English Exporters (London) Ltd* v *Eldonwall Ltd*.

The fact that the calculation is based on an annual tenancy can, in itself, produce a discount. This is justifiable because the tenant enjoys less security of tenure under a yearly tenancy than with a lease for a term of years certain. A yearly tenant, moreover, does not have the safeguard against increasing rent levels and inflation which is enjoyed by a fixed term tenant: *Janes (Gowns) Ltd* v

Harlow Development Corporation (1979). This does not mean that the court has an obligation to give a discount. A case for reduction must be made out: *Halberstam* v *Tandalco Corporation NV* (1985). The amount of discount built into the interim rent calculation can vary considerably. In *Regis Property Co* v *Lewis & Peat* (1970), the interim rent was initially assessed under the machinery of s 34 and then, due to the assumption of a yearly tenancy, discounted by 33 per cent. Being less generous to the tenant, the court in *English Exporters* v *Eldonwall* increased the original rent of £7,655 per annum to an interim sum of £14,000 where the market rent was approximately £15,000 per annum. The reduction (if any) is totally at the discretion of the court and no case sets a general principle to guide future decisions.

As mentioned earlier, the court must also have regard to the rent payable under the former business tenancy: s 24A(3). There has been some uncertainty as to how the court should do this. A very restrictive valuation approach was adopted by Stamp J in *Regis Property*. He concluded that the determination of the interim rent was a single operation, namely the calculation of the market value on the basis of a yearly tenancy. From this perspective, the existing rent was of relevance only in so far as it had evidential value in this calculation. It did not by itself justify the court making a seemingly arbitrary deduction. This approach has not, however, been followed in subsequent decisions. In *English Exporters*, it was held that the court could fix an interim rent lower than the market rent when it was reasonable to do so, taking into account the existing level of rent. Accordingly, a 20 per cent discount from the market rent valuation was made on this basis in *Ratners (Jewellers) Ltd* v *Lemnoll* (1980). Any uncertainty of judicial approach appears to have been resolved by the Court of Appeal in *Fawke* v *Viscount Chelsea* (1979). The view of Stamp J was rejected and the court accepted that the current rent is properly to be regarded as a cushion for the tenant, reducing the increase in rent that there otherwise might have been. Sometimes the value of this discount can be substantial (see *Charles Follett Ltd* v *Cabtell Investments Ltd* (1987) where the discount was 50 per cent).

In fixing the interim rent, any obligation of either party as to repairs may be taken into account when it involves expense during the continuation period: *Woodbridge* v *Westminster Press* (1987). Accordingly, the court can order a differential interim rent, varying with the state of repair of the property, with a

The interim rent

provision for the rent to increase once the repairs are executed: *Fawke* v *Viscount Chelsea*.

The court will have to look to comparable properties when assessing the interim rent. If there is nothing comparable, the rents of neighbouring premises may be used as a guide. It should be borne in mind that the comparable rents to be used in the calculation are those current at the time the interim rent period commences: *English Exporters* v *Eldonwall*. Therefore, where rents are rising steeply or a round of rent reviews is known to be due in the area, the landlord may be advised to hang fire and take advantage of more favourable conditions. Expert valuation advice is always necessary before negotiating or applying for an interim rent.

Where a continuation tenancy runs for a long time, an interim rent may become unrealistically low at its end. This does not, however, justify the court fixing initially an interim rent which is above the then market rent: *Halberstam* v *Tandalco Corporation NV*. It is also implicit in s 24A(3) that the interim rent must reflect the market rent throughout the whole period that it is payable. Accordingly, in *Conway* v *Arthur* (1988), where proceedings were delayed for three years and the interim rent was fixed eventually at over 300 per cent above the contractual rent, the sum was reduced on appeal because for part of that three year period the interim rent exceeded the market rent.

Although each case turns upon its own facts, it is common for modest discounts of between 5 and 10 per cent to be built into the calculation by the court. As regards interim rents achieved by negotiation, a standard practice of deducting 10 per cent from the agreed current market rental value appears to be emerging. Any appeal against valuation by the court will be entertained only if the court is manifestly wrong: *Halberstam* v *Tandalco Corporation NV*.

The existence of the discount may prompt the landlord to insert into the contractual tenancy a rent review clause to take effect upon the termination of that fixed term (usually the day before). This is based on the assumption that the tenant will remain in occupation under s 24. The rent obtainable on review is likely to be higher than any interim rent which would be set by the court. There is no need for the service of a s 25 notice or s 26 request to activate this rent increase.

Chapter 8

Grounds of opposition

The landlord can oppose the tenant's claim for a new lease on any of the grounds set out in s 30(1)(a)-(g), as stated in his s 25 notice or counternotice to the tenant's s 26 request. It should not be overlooked that the landlord can object also on the basis that the premises are not within the scope of the Act (for example, because the tenant has ceased any business activity); moreover, it is possible that the court will deny the grant of a new lease in circumstances where the tenant intends to use the premises for an illegal purpose: *Turner & Bell* v *Searles Ltd* (1977). The landlord should continue to bear in mind the alternative of forfeiture proceedings for breach of covenant which, if successful, will terminate the existing tenancy and prevent the tenant applying for a renewal.

There are seven statutory grounds of opposition and these are listed individually within paragraphs (a)-(g) of s 30(1). Each ground is distinct (*Housleys Ltd* v *Bloomer-Holt Ltd* (1966)) and, as demonstrated in Chapter 5, the landlord must take care to identify the correct ground(s) in his statutory notice or counternotice. It appears that the landlord can adduce evidence of an unspecified ground only to the extent that it may throw light on another ground and exert influence as to whether to decline renewal on that other ground: *Hutchinson* v *Lambeth* (1983).

Although paragraphs (a), (b), (c), and (e) offer the court a measure of discretion, when the landlord establishes any of the seven grounds the court must dismiss the tenant's application: s 31(1). In addition, regardless of grounds (e)-(g) involving a future element, it is now accepted that the relevant ground must be satisfied at the date of the hearing: *Betty's Cafes Ltd* v *Phillips Furnishing Stores Ltd* (1958). Where the landlord fails to establish a ground of opposition (or withdraws his

Grounds of opposition

opposition) the court must grant a new lease (see Chapter 10).

By way of a general observation, it can be said that the first three grounds require fault on the part of the tenant, whereas the other grounds do not depend upon default. It is necessary now to consider the seven grounds individually.

Ground A : Breach of repair

The first ground is that the state of repair of the holding, as a result of the tenant's failure to observe repairing obligations under the existing tenancy, is such that he ought not to be granted a new lease: s 30(1)(a). It is not sufficient merely to prove that there is a breach of a repairing covenant. The landlord must satisfy the court that the breach is so serious as to justify the tenant losing possession of the premises. This will involve the court considering the extent of the tenant's liability, the physical state of the premises and the consequences of the tenant's failure: *Lyons* v *Central Commercial Properties Ltd* (1958). This presents the court with a discretion and in its exercise the court will take account of, for example, the conduct of both parties, the reasons for the breach, issues of fairness and the willingness of the tenant to remedy the breach: *Lyons* (see also *Horowitz* v *Ferrand* (1956)). It should be noted that the disrepair of the premises demised is what is relevant under this head; it has no application to the disrepair of other premises (that might, however, be a valid consideration under para (c) below). Tenants are, therefore, well advised to carry out any repair work before the hearing for a new tenancy.

Ground B : Rent arrears

The second ground of opposition is that the tenant ought not to be given a new tenancy because of a persistent delay in paying rent: s 30(1)(b). The reference to "persistent" connotes either that there must have been delay on more than one occasion or that arrears have been outstanding for a considerable time. In short, the landlord must demonstrate a history of bad payment. Whether the delay is persistent or not is a matter of fact and degree. Although the arrears need not cover the whole duration of the lease (*Hopcutt* v *Carver* (1969)), they do need to be sustained over a period of time. It has been suggested, however, that the size or the duration of the arrears need not be substantial: *Horowitz* v *Ferrand*. Nevertheless, these factors will influence heavily the decision of the court.

The court will have regard to the frequency of delay, the reason for delay, the measures taken by the landlord to secure payment and any safeguards that the landlord has against future arrears: *Dellenty* v *Pellow* (1951). The latter may be offered by the tenant in the form of a rent deposit or a surety for the new lease: *Hopcutt*. The fact that a substantial rent increase will occur on renewal is another consideration that will be thrown into the melting pot: *Maison Kaye Fashions* v *Horton's Estate Ltd* (1967). If the tenant is withholding rent due to a breach of contract by the landlord, the court can take this into account. Nevertheless it appears that the tenant must inform the landlord in writing why the rent is being withheld: *Page* v *Sole* (1991).

The emphasis upon the discretion of the court, coupled with an absence of principle, brings with it uncertainty. As Russell LJ explained in *Page* v *Sole*: "Once he had made the finding that there had been persistent delay, there remained in the judge a discretion as to whether, in all the circumstances, this was a case where the landlord was entitled to possession". Accordingly, one decided case is no sure guide to another. In *Hurstfell Ltd* v *Leicester Square Property Co* (1988), a renewal was ordered where the tenant had been in arrears for eleven consecutive rent instalments and had given the landlord dishonoured cheques. The judge was satisfied that there would be no future repetition, notwithstanding certain question marks placed over the viability of the tenant's business. In *Rawasdeh* v *Lane* (1988), however, a new lease was denied to a tenant who had been late in rent payments regularly during the course of the lease, because it was regarded as being sufficiently serious to justify the refusal of the tenant's application. This was so even though the tenant was prepared to pay a quarter's rent in advance and agreed to rent being paid by a monthly standing order. With the Housing Act 1988 having introduced the notion of persistent arrears into the residential market, more litigation on this issue is expected. This may produce further guidance for the court as to how to exercise its discretion.

Ground C : Breaches of other obligations

The landlord may oppose the application on the basis that the tenant ought not to be granted a new lease in the light of

Grounds of opposition

other substantial breaches of his obligations under the lease or for any other reason connected with the use or management of the holding: s 30(1)(c).

This ground deals with two separate issues. First, any breach of the tenant's obligations under the lease (except those covered in paragraphs (a) and (b)) can be relied upon by the landlord. This could include a breach of repairing obligation concerning premises not forming part of the holding (compare s 30(1)(a)). For the landlord to be successful in his opposition, however, the breach must be more than trivial and its consequences must be serious. In exercising its discretion, the court will take into account the nature of the breach; whether it can be remedied; any proposals made by the tenant for remedy; and if the landlord has acquiesced in the breach or waived it: *Eichner* v *Midland Bank* (1970). In determining whether the breach is substantial, the court will look at the whole of the tenant's conduct during the tenancy and will not be restricted to the issues set out in the landlord's notice or counternotice: *Eichner*. It would appear that regard may be had also to the tenant's expected, future conduct: *Turner & Bell* v *Searles* (1977). The fact that s 30(1)(c) refers to "breaches", and does not confine itself to the singular, is seemingly of no consequence.

Second, the ground is widened considerably by the reference to "any other reason" relevant to the use and management of the premises. It is not certain how far this extension reaches. Clearly, it includes matters which are outside the tenant's legal obligations to his landlord. It covers for example, a breach of the criminal law or planning law by the tenant: *Turner & Bell* v *Searles*. It might possibly be invoked where, following a substantial change in the neighbourhood, it is no longer desirable that the tenant's business be continued on the premises or where the tenant has run his business in such a fashion that, although in compliance with the terms of his lease, it is undesirable that he continues to do so. The conduct of the tenant on land not comprised in the holding might also be relevant in so far as it reflects on the ability of the tenant to use or manage the holding properly: *Beard* v *Williams* (1986). The court is able to look at future conduct as well as past behaviour: *Turner & Bell* v *Searles*. The underlying consideration is whether the landlord will be prejudiced by the tenant's conduct: *Beard*.

The landlord should take care to specify all allegations made under s 30(1)(c) and support them with evidence (for example, the production of the tenant's accounts). A vague, general statement of the tenant's conduct will not suffice and should be avoided.

Ground D : Alternative accommodation

The landlord can successfully oppose the tenant's application on the ground that he has offered, and is willing to provide, suitable alternative accommodation for the tenant on reasonable terms: s 30(1)(d). The court enjoys no residual discretion here; if the landlord establishes certain facts, the court must refuse the tenant's application: *Betty's Cafes Ltd* v *Phillips Furnishing Stores Ltd*.

To succeed in his opposition, the landlord must prove four points:

(a) that he has offered alternative accommodation to the tenant. This offer must be *bona fide* and one which is capable of immediate acceptance. It must be such that, if accepted, a valid contract between the parties would thereby be created. The offer must, therefore, be a firm one and the landlord must be able to perform his side of the bargain;

(b) that he is willing to provide the accommodation to the tenant. Therefore the suitable alternative accommodation should remain available until the date of the hearing;

(c) that the alternative accommodation is available on terms which, having regard to the terms of the current lease and all other relevant circumstances, are deemed reasonable. The accommodation must remain available on those terms until the time of the hearing;

(d) that the accommodation is suitable for the tenant's requirements. The court is directed by s 30(1)(d) to consider a variety of issues: whether the goodwill attached to the existing premises will be preserved; the nature and class of the tenant's business; the size and situation of the existing holding; and the facilities afforded by the present purposes. It is thought that, because of the different considerations applicable to residential property, undue reliance should not be placed upon case law decided under the Rent Act 1977: *Singh* v *Malayan Theatres* (1953) (compare *Lawrence* v *Carter* (1956)). Provided that it is suitable, the alternative accommodation may consist of part only of the premises currently leased to the tenant: *Singh*. This case suggests also that the premises cannot be regarded as suitable when their occupation would cause the tenant to change the conduct of his business and carry it out in a different or diminished fashion. As Denning LJ explained in *Gold* v *Brighton Corporation* (1956):

> "Inasmuch as the tenant is to be protected in respect of his business, the terms of the new tenancy should be such as to enable him to carry on his business as it is. They should not prevent him from carrying on an important part of it."

Questions as to reasonableness and suitability are to be answered at the hearing. As mentioned earlier, if the above four requirements are satisfied the court cannot grant a new tenancy. The tenant, having had his application rejected, can then accept the offer of alternative accommodation. There is, however, no provision within the Act for the landlord's offer to be kept open for acceptance after the hearing. If the landlord withdraws his offer after the hearing, the tenant will have no redress unless the landlord can be shown to have misrepresented his intentions to the court (and thereby induced the court to reject the tenant's application). In such an instance, the tenant has a remedy for the landlord's misrepresentation under s 55 (see Chapter 9). Otherwise the tenant will have to quit the premises and will be unable to obtain compensation for disturbance (see Chapter 9).

Ground E : Uneconomic subletting

The landlord may object to the tenant's application on the basis that the current tenancy was created by subletting part only of the premises, themselves let under a superior tenancy by the landlord, and that he might reasonably expect to have a financial advantage if he relet or disposed of the property as a single unit: s 30(1)(e). Consequently, the landlord is seeking possession to effect a more lucrative reletting or sale.

This ground is rarely used in practice due to its difficulties and limited application. It is of relevance only where the following conditions are satisfied:

(a) it is a sub-tenant who makes the application for a new tenancy;

(b) the sub-tenancy is of part only of the premises (not the whole);

(c) the intermediate landlord's interest is due to end in the next fourteen months, as otherwise the head landlord would not be the sub-tenant's competent landlord for the purposes of the renewal procedure. This is crucial because the ground cannot be used by a landlord against his immediate tenant;

(d) the landlord would receive more rent (presumably calculated at a net value) if the premises are let/disposed of as a whole, rather than subject to separate lettings. This can be difficult to prove. It also ignores the possibility that the subletting may diminish the value of the landlord's reversion from an investment viewpoint, even if there is no diminution in the rental income. Unless the intermediate tenant's interest will end either before or around the same time as the sub-tenant's interest, the competent landlord will have the additional difficulty, due to the presence of the intermediate tenant, of establishing financial advantage as a reason for requiring possession;

(e) the court must be persuaded to exercise its discretion. The court will take into account all the circumstances of the case and, particularly, whether the superior landlord had consented to the subletting in the first place. Even if the landlord can prove the above matters, the court can still exercise its discretion and grant the tenant a new lease.

Ground F : Demolition and reconstruction

The tenant's application will be dismissed if the landlord can show that, on the termination of the lease, he intends to demolish or reconstruct the premises comprised in the holding, or a substantial part of them, or to carry out substantial works of construction on the holding or part thereof; and could not reasonably do so without first gaining possession: s 30(1)(f). Albeit fraught with difficulty, this ground is much used. It is convenient to analyse individually the constituent elements of the ground.

Intention: The landlord (ie the competent landlord: *Marks* v *British Waterways Board* (1963)) must have an unequivocal and fully formed intention to demolish or reconstruct. A vague or general assertion of intention will not suffice: *Reohorn* v *Barry Corporation* (1956). As Lord Asquith commented in *Cunliffe* v *Goodman* (1950), where the landlord had not secured planning permission for the proposed development:

Grounds of opposition

"Not merely is the term 'intention' unsatisfied if the person professing it has too many hurdles to overcome, or too little control of events; it is equally inappropriate if at the material date that person is in effect not deciding to proceed but feeling his way and reserving his decision until he shall be in possession of financial data sufficient to enable him to determine whether the payment will be commercially worth while ... In the case of neither scheme did she [the landlord] form a settled intention to proceed. Neither project moved out of the zone of contemplation – out of the sphere of the tentative, the provisional and the exploratory – into the valley of decision."

In order to move into the "valley of decision" the landlord must have a definite attitude to redevelopment, fully formed plans and overcome any serious obstacles in his way. Intention is, therefore, substantiated by the ability, financial and legal, of the landlord to put his plans into operation: *Reohorn* v *Barry Corporation*. The landlord should ensure that his financial arrangements are adequate (*DAF Motoring Centre (Gosport) Ltd* v *Hutfield & Wheeler Ltd* (1982)) and that planning and other consents are obtained (*Gregson* v *Cyril Lord Ltd* (1962)). If the work is to be entrusted to another (eg, a contractor or under a building lease), this will not prevent the landlord relying on paragraph (f) provided that he retains some form of control over the works: *Gilmour Caterers Ltd* v *St Bartholomew's Hospital* (1956). Nevertheless the word "intends" should not be equated with the expression "ready and able" so as to impose on the landlord the onus that he has not only made a final determination of the course proposed, but has also taken all necessary steps towards the achievement of that course: *AJ Levy & Son Ltd* v *Martin Brent Developments* (1987). This case made it clear that: "It is sufficient that there is a reasonable prospect that he will be able to bring about that which he says he intends. There must not be so many obstructions yet to be surmounted that he cannot truly be said to 'intend' it" (*per* Julian Jeffs QC). The court is expected to apply a degree of common sense to the matter.

The intention must be established as an issue of fact at the date of the hearing: *DAF Motoring Centre*. It can, however, be put into a provable form after the hearing has begun: *Betty's Cafes Ltd* v *Phillips Furnishing Stores Ltd* (1958). An objective test is applied: *Capocci* v *Goble* (1987). As the intention need not be supported at the date the s 25 notice or s 26 counternotice is served, the landlord need not set out his intentions precisely at that stage and it is sufficient merely to indicate that ground (f) is to be relied upon: *Biles* v *Caesar* (1957). The landlord can express alternative schemes of proposed development up to and throughout the hearing, provided that the landlord intends to carry out one of the schemes: *Austin Reed Ltd* v *Royal Insurance Co Ltd (No 1)* (1956).

As there is no need to substantiate or detail the intention at the time of service of the renewal documentation, it matters not that the identity of the competent landlord changes between that time and the hearing date. In such a situation, it is the new competent landlord's intention which is relevant and this is unaffected by the seriousness (or otherwise) of the intention of his predecessor. Accordingly, the landlord is able to advance his plans in the intervening period between service and the hearing: *Manchester Garages* v *Petrofina (UK) Ltd* (1974). Last minute changes to the proposals could, however, damage the strength of the landlord's claim.

In order to keep costs to a minimum, it is desirable that the determination of intention be dealt with as a preliminary matter before any other issue in the proceedings: *Dutch Oven Ltd* v *Egham Estate & Investment Co Ltd* (1968). Although it is at the date of the hearing that the competent landlord must establish the existence of the intention, that intention is necessarily one that will not be put into effect until the current lease is ended. As under s 64 (see Chapter 10) this date may be substantially later than the date of termination specified in the s 25 notice or s 26 request, the landlord must show an intention to start work on, or shortly after, that extended date. An intention to commence work within three months of termination has been held to be sufficient: *Livestock Underwriting Agency* v *Corbett & Newton* (1955). It has been held that the work must be intended to be commenced within a reasonable time of the date of termination: *London Hilton Jewellers* v *Hilton International Hotels Ltd* (1990). If the landlord cannot demonstrate his intention to start on (or near) the date of termination, but can show that he will do so within the next year, the court will allow the tenant to continue in possession only until that future commencement date: s 31(2) (see Chapter 9). This section applies also to grounds (d) and (e) (above). Certainly, the court will be unimpressed by the tenant arguing that, by his deferring the termination date (for example by lodging an appeal against the court's refusal to grant him a new tenancy),

Grounds of opposition

the landlord will be less able to effect the development: *AJA Smith Transport Ltd* v *British Railways Board* (1980). It should also be appreciated that, once possession is gained, the landlord is free to change his mind and the tenant (outside misrepresentation for the purposes of s 55) is left with no remedy: *Reohorn* v *Barry Corporation*. Hence the section requires a firm and settled intention on the landlord's part: *AJ Levy & Son Ltd* v *Martin Brent Developments*.

Where the premises are old and worn out, the court is more easily satisfied than when the premises are comparatively new or the desirability of the project is open to doubt: *AJ Levy & Son Ltd* v *Martin Brent Developments*.

The landlord can show a settled intention to redevelop in a variety of ways. The following examples may be distilled from the case law:

(i) obtaining planning permission (*Joss* v *Bennett* (1956)) or demonstrating a reasonable prospect of obtaining planning permission if the landlord is awarded possession (*Gregson* v *Cyril Lord*), the test here being what a reasonable man would expect (see also *Westminster City Council* v *British Waterways Board* (1985));

(ii) availability of adequate finance. In *DAF Motoring Centre (Gosport) Ltd* v *Hutfield & Wheeler Ltd*, a letter from a bank manager promising finance was held to suffice for this purpose. A faxed message from a bank was decisive in *Adams* v *JR Glibbery and Sons Ltd* (1991). In a similar fashion, the court can look at any documentation, even if not disclosed before the hearing, to evidence intention: *Mirza* v *Nicola* (1990);

(iii) demonstrating an intention for the work to be done by another. In *Gilmour Caterers Ltd* v *St Bartholomew's Hospital*, the landlord established his intention by showing that he had entered into an agreement for a building lease under which the lessees were to do the rebuilding. It is not necessary, however, that binding contracts have been entered: *P F Ahern & Sons Ltd* v *Hunt* (1988). In *Spook Erection Ltd* v *British Railways Board* (1988), the landlord had originally intended to develop through the sale of the site (this is outside paragraph (f)), but changed tactics, in order to gain possession, by then deciding to grant a long building lease to a developer who would execute the work. The landlord succeeded in opposing the tenant's application. If, as an alternative, the landlord had served a s 25 notice and sold to the developer, the developer would have been the competent landlord and would have had the necessary intention;

(iv) as regards a limited company, it is necessary to show a corporate intention. Normally, this will be contained in a board resolution: *Espresso Coffee Machine Co Ltd v Guardian Assurance Co Ltd* (1959). This should be coupled with an additional resolution authorising a specified director to give evidence of the company's intention, if required. Alternatively, a director could be given authority to take the necessary decisions and his intention would constitute the corporate intention: *Branhills Ltd v Town Tailors Ltd* (1956). It may, however, be possible to overcome the absence of a formal resolution where the intention of a number of directors is such that it is to be regarded as the intention of the company: *Bolton (HL) Engineering Co Ltd v Graham (TJ) & Sons Ltd* (1956). If the directors do not possess adequate powers either to pass a resolution or formulate the company's intention, a resolution of the company in general meeting will be necessary: *Birch (A & W) Ltd v P B (Sloane) Ltd* (1956);

(v) an undertaking given by the landlord to the court does not of itself prove that the landlord has the necessary intention. It may, however, add evidential weight to the landlord's case: *Chez Gerard Ltd v Greene Ltd* (1983). An undertaking was the decisive factor in *London Hilton Jewellers Ltd v Hilton International Hotels Ltd* (1990). As recognised in *Betty's Cafes Ltd v Phillips Furnishing Stores Ltd* an undertaking, coupled with other evidence such as a board resolution, can demonstrate a fixity of intention. If the undertaking is vague, it will not be of such value: *Lennox v Bell* (1957);

(vi) the uncorroborated sworn testimony of the landlord: *Mirza v Nicola* (1990). It is obviously a much safer course for the landlord not to rely on this alone: see *AJ Levy & Son v Martin Brent Developments* (1987).

The landlord must, therefore, show an ability to undertake the work and demonstrate the reasonable prospects of it being carried out: *Capocci v Goble*. In *Edwards v Thompson* (1990),

Grounds of opposition

for example, the landlord was deemed unable to carry out the work because at the time of the hearing he had not selected an independent developer and had not reached any agreement as to the cost of redevelopment. When the landlord initiates the renewal process (ie by the service of a s 25 notice), this can be fairly easily achieved. It is, however, more problematic where the tenant serves a s 26 request, because the landlord will have to act with some haste to ensure that his affairs are in order. Although the genuineness of the landlord's intention is of paramount importance, his motives are of no consequence. Accordingly, it matters not that the landlord wishes to reconstruct so that he can, for example, occupy the property himself: *Betty's Cafes Ltd* v *Phillips Furnishing Stores Ltd*. Nevertheless, if the landlord intends to sell immediately and leave the premises, this ground of opposition will be unavailable: *P F Ahern & Sons* v *Hunt*.

Nature of intended works: Paragraph (f) details what it is that the landlord must intend. It assumes that there are buildings on the holding or the landlord intends to erect some there: *Housleys Ltd* v *Bloomer-Holt Ltd* (1966). The paragraph requires the landlord to intend to demolish or reconstruct the premises (or a substantial part of those premises); or to carry out substantial construction work on the holding. These will now be segregated for analytical convenience, but it should at the outset be understood that it is a question of fact and degree whether the work can fit within one of these categories: *Bewlay (Tobacconists) Ltd* v *British Bata Shoe Co* (1959).

Where the landlord intends to demolish all the buildings on the holding, he is clearly within the scope of the paragraph. Similarly, if his intention is not to demolish all buildings, but to demolish a substantial part of the premises, he is within paragraph (f). The difficulty is in deciding what is "substantial". In *Atkinson* v *Bettison* (1955), the court interpreted "substantial" in general terms such as "big", "solid" and "considerable". This is hardly helpful guidance and it is left to be decided by the judge, as an issue of fact, on the circumstances of each case. The court will look to the totality of the work proposed.

It has been held that the term "reconstruct" is akin to a rebuilding exercise following a measure of demolition and is more than mere works of improvement or repair and mere changes of identity: *Percy E Cadle & Co Ltd* v *Jacmarch Properties Ltd* (1957). In *Cook* v *Mott* (1961), "reconstruction" was viewed as involving the demolition of an existing fixed structure in whole or part, whereas "construction" described works of an original or additional nature. The terms "demolition" and "reconstruction" are construed conjunctively. It is, therefore, the degree of building work and demolition that the court will assess, by evaluating how the premises will differ following the execution of the works: *Joel* v *Swaddle* (1957). Work which is not constructional, but is subsidiary to work which is, can be taken into account in this evaluation: *Barth* v *Pritchard* (1990). In *Housleys Ltd* v *Bloomer-Holt Ltd*, the demolition of a brick wall and a wooden garage was held to be sufficient. Similarly, in *Joel* v *Swaddle* the proposed change from a small shop with two storage areas into part of a large amusement arcade was held to be reconstruction. The physical removal of most of an office suite and its replacement with "something different", that is, a different floor level, new suspended ceilings, new partition walls and the removal of a wall had such a "far-reaching physical effect on the state of the demised property" that it constituted reconstruction: *City Offices (Regent St) Ltd* v *Europa Acceptance Group plc* (1990).

In *Percy E Cadle* v *Jacmarch*, however, the turning of three floors, in separate occupation, into a self-contained unit was not regarded as falling within this ground of opposition. In similar vein, the installation of a new shop front was held not to be reconstruction in *Atkinson* v *Bettison* (1955). The landscaping of a field, removal of material and infilling was not classified as work of reconstruction in *Botterill & Cheshire* v *Bedfordshire County Council* (1985).

The next portion of paragraph (f) deals with new construction, whether on the whole holding or on part (for example, an extension to an existing building). The construction work needs to be substantial (see above) and this is again a question of fact and degree: *Cook* v *Mott*. It was recognised in *Housleys Ltd* v *Bloomer-Holt* that the laying of a sufficient area of concrete and the resurfacing with hard standing might be regarded as construction for the purposes of this paragraph. However, the work must directly affect the structure of the building in some way and not merely be refurbishment or improvement: *Barth* v *Pritchard*. In *Barth*, electrical re-wiring, provision of new toilet facilities and installation of a new central heating system were neither works of construction nor substantial. The court rejected an argument that, as none of the items could separately be regarded as construction, the works as a whole could be so classified.

In a comprehensive redevelopment scheme, the landlord will have

Grounds of opposition

no difficulty in showing that the nature of the proposed works falls within s 30(1)(f). Difficulties can be experienced, however, where the intention is to refurbish an existing building, because of the court's need to look at the project as a whole. It should also be remembered that the works contemplated must be on the "holding" and, accordingly, the landlord cannot rely on works to be carried out on premises not part of the tenant's demise (for example, common parts).

Landlord's need for possession: The landlord has to show that he could not reasonably carry out the demolition, reconstruction or construction without obtaining possession of the tenant's holding: s 30(1)(f). "Possession" in this context means both physical and legal possession, and this requires the landlord to establish that the work could not be undertaken without bringing the tenancy to an end: *Heath* v *Drown* (1973). It was concluded in *Heath* that, where the landlord has a right to enter and to carry out the works reserved in the lease, he cannot successfully oppose the tenant's application because legal possession is not dependent upon the termination of the lease. This general rule will give way, however, where the work when completed would deprive the tenant of facilities necessary to carry on his trade and amount to derogation from the landlord's grant: *Leathwoods Ltd* v *Total Oil (GB) Ltd* (1986).

The tenant can still obtain a renewal if it can be demonstrated that it is not necessary for the landlord to have possession of the whole holding to carry out the proposed works. This brings into relevance s 31A which, by way of an escape route for the tenant, can defeat the landlord's opposition when the landlord requires possession of part only of the holding or possession for a short time only. It is provided by s 31A that the landlord is unable to show the need for possession if either (i) or (ii) below applies.

(i) The tenant agrees to the inclusion in the new lease of terms which allow the landlord access and facilities for carrying out the work, and the landlord could reasonably execute the work without obtaining possession and without disrupting to a substantial extent, or for a substantial time, the tenant's business use of the holding: s 31A(1)(a).

This is appropriate only where the tenant's existing lease does not contain a term allowing the landlord to carry out the work. In addition, the assessment of interference is one of fact and degree: *Blackburn* v *Hussain* (1988). The terms "extent" and "time" are to be read conjunctively: *Cerex Jewels* v *Peachey Properties* (1986). The key issue is whether the work can go ahead with only temporary and minor inconvenience to the use of the property by the tenant or whether it will involve a total disruption of that use: *Cerex Jewels*. The onus is on the tenant to show that the proposed term will allow the landlord to undertake the work; the determination is one of fact for the judge, based upon a detailed description of the works intended: *Spalding* v *Shotley Point Marina (1986) Ltd* (1989). It is, moreover, the effect on the tenant's use which is relevant and not the effect on the tenant's business: *Redfern* v *Reeves* (1978). In *Cerex Jewels* a closure of business for two weeks was regarded as a "minor" interference, whereas in *Blackburn* a closure of twelve weeks was a sufficient disruption to prevent s 31A(1)(a) assisting the tenant. These examples illustrate the point that the longer the interruption, the less likely it is that the court will protect the tenant. The tenant is, perhaps surprisingly, unable to waive the interference with his use of the holding. In *Redfern*, it was made clear that s 31A(1)(a) did not confer on the tenant an option to disregard any disruption. As the landlord is under no duty to minimise any interference, this may prove to be a major obstacle for the tenant who wishes to invoke the provision. Nevertheless, the aim of s 31A(1) is to reduce the ability of the landlord to recover possession, except where a complete demolition or reconstruction is proposed.

Guidance as to how s 31A(1)(a) should be applied was provided by the Court of Appeal in *Cerex Jewels Ltd* v *Peachey Properties*. The following propositions can be distilled from the judgment of Slade LJ. First, only works which cannot be carried out under a right reserved in the current lease are relevant. Second, the court must look to the physical effect of the work on the tenant's use of the holding, and not to any interference with the goodwill or profitability of the business carried on there. Third, the assessment of interference concerns only the period where the work is being carried out and does not relate to any future effect on use.

> (ii) The tenant is willing to accept a tenancy of an economically separable part of the holding and either the landlord can still carry out the intended work if given access and facilities in respect of that part, or possession of the remainder of the holding would be reasonably sufficient to enable him to carry out such work: s 31A(1)(b).

The meaning of "an economically separable part" is given in

Grounds of opposition

s 31A(2). This provides that a part is economically separable where, after the completion of the intended work, the aggregate of the rents which would be reasonably obtainable on separate lettings of that part and the remainder of the premises is not less than the rent which is reasonably obtainable on a letting of those premises as a whole. This is a partial shield for the tenant and cannot lead to more than a new tenancy of part.

This alternative course for the tenant requires the landlord to be able to carry out the work on the part not to be re-let, or that any incursions on the economically separable part to be let will not substantially affect the tenant's use of that part. The burden of proof lies with the tenant: *Spalding* v *Shotley*. His willingness must be established at the date of the hearing. The tenant cannot insist that the landlord alter his plans so as to minimise the impact of the redevelopment: *Decca Navigator Co Ltd* v *GLC* (1974). Therefore, if the *bona fide* intention of the landlord is to work on the whole holding, the tenant cannot resist the landlord on the basis that he is willing to accept a tenancy of the part. It was made clear in *Decca Navigator* that the court cannot consider whether the landlord's proposals are reasonable and, most certainly, cannot modify the development plans (see also *AJ Levy & Son Ltd* v *Martin Brent Developments* (1987)).

The relationship between the various statutory provisions was considered in *Romulus Trading Company Ltd* v *Trustees of Henry Smith's Charity* (1990). It was made clear by the Court of Appeal that the court is bound to consider s 30(1)(f) in the light of s 31A. This means that the tenant can put forward conditional arguments. Accordingly, it is perfectly proper for the tenant to argue alternatives on the following lines: first, to dispute the genuineness of the landlord's intention; second, if the intention is genuine, that the work does not satisfy s 30(1)(f); third, if the work is within paragraph (f), that the work can be carried out by the means of access and facilities contemplated by s 31A(a); fourth, if the facilities are insufficient, that the work can be done if the tenant accepted part only of the premises (and was willing to do so) under s 31A(b). There is, therefore, no need for any election on the tenant's part.

Ground G : Own occupation

The landlord can oppose the tenant's application for a new tenancy on the ground that he intends to occupy the whole premises fully or partly as his residence or for a business carried on by him or by a company which he controls: s 30(1)(g). As will be shown, this is qualified by the so-called "five year rule" imposed by s 30(2). To succeed under paragraph (g) the landlord must satisfy certain conditions.

Intention: The requirement of the landlord's intention is subject to the same standard of proof as considered above in connection with s 30(1)(f): *Chez Gerard Ltd* v *Greene Ltd* (1983). Accordingly, in *Europark (Midlands) Ltd* v *Town Centre Securities* (1985) the landlord's intention to occupy was demonstrated by the minutes of a board meeting, an affidavit of a director, and the receipt of quotations for equipment to be used by the landlord on regaining possession. In *Page* v *Sole* a minute of a partnership meeting and the evidence of one business partner was sufficient to enable the court to make a factual finding of intention. If the landlord has alternative accommodation available for his occupation, this may prevent him establishing his settled intention: *Espresso Coffee Machine Co Ltd* v *Guardian Assurance* (1959). As Lord Evershed commented, the landlord cannot always " ... have his bun and his penny". Similarly, if the competent landlord wishes to occupy for the purposes of a business, which is prohibited under a head lease, that landlord will not be able to satisfy paragraph (g): *Wates Estate Agency Services Ltd* v *Bartleys Ltd* (1989). The financial resources of the landlord are again a crucial issue, particularly so when the premises need expensive refurbishment before they can be occupied: *Adams* v *JR Glibbery*.

Occupation: The landlord need not seek to occupy the premises personally, and it is well established that there are a number of other ways in which a landlord can occupy. He can occupy through an agent (*Skeet* v *Powell-Sheddon* (1988)); a manager (*France* v *Shaftward Investments* (1981)); a partnership (*Re Crowhurst Park* (1974)); a beneficiary under a trust (s 41(2); *Morar* v *Chauhan* (1985)); and a company which is a member of a group of companies which includes the landlord company (s 42(3)). As regards occupation by a beneficiary under a trust, the occupation must be by virtue of his interest under the trust and not otherwise: *Meyer* v *Riddick* (1990).

It is expressly mentioned in s 30(1)(g) that occupation can be through a company controlled by the landlord: *Adams* v *JR Glibbery*. A landlord has a controlling interest in a company when either he holds over half of the equity share capital of that company (disregarding nominee and fiduciary holdings) or he is a shareholder and can alone appoint or dismiss the holders of a majority of the directorships: s 30(3). Where a family company owns the property and its majority shareholders wish to carry on a business there, this is outside the scope of s 30(1)(g) because it is necessary for the landlord to be an individual.

There is no mention in s 30(1)(g) as to how the landlord must intend to occupy the premises. It will not be enough if the landlord intends to occupy for a short time before selling the property: *Willis* v *Association of Universities of the British Commonwealth* (1965). In some circumstances, an intended occupation of a number of months might suffice, but only where there is then no outright sale of the premises to a cash purchaser: *Jones* v *Jenkins* (1986). In *Willis*, the court expressed the view that such a short period of occupation before, for example, passing over the business to a successor, could be sufficient. It should also be appreciated that the landlord must intend to occupy the whole of the tenant's holding and not merely part of it, no matter how substantial that part may be (compare s 31A regarding part-development).

The occupation must be of the holding. This has been narrowly interpreted to mean that ground (g) is unavailable where a landlord intends to demolish the building, because then he can no longer occupy the holding as it was: *Nursey* v *P Currie (Dartford) Ltd* (1959). This view is highly dubious and, not surprisingly, has been the subject of much criticism: see *Cam Gears Ltd* v *Cunningham* (1981). It is thought unlikely that Parliament intended the landlord to recover the holding only on the understanding that it remained in an unaltered state. The *Nursey* decision remains, however, but it is confined to the demolition and replacement of existing buildings and does not apply where the site is vacant: *Leathwoods Ltd* v *Total Oil (GB) Ltd* (1986). In the situation where a landlord intends to demolish or to carry out substantial work before taking up occupation, it is advisable to rely on both grounds (f) and (g). Provided that the necessary intentions are established, it is practicable for both to be relied upon together: *Fisher* v *Taylor's Furnishing Stores Ltd* (1956).

A further point for discussion arises in the context of the amalgamation of premises. It has been held that a landlord who wishes to demolish partition walls, between his present premises and those of the tenant, and to occupy the enlarged premises for his business can be within paragraph (g): *J W Thornton Ltd* v *Blacks Leisure Group* (1986). This decision also confined the *Nursey* approach to demolition. It should, however, be appreciated that in Thornton the demolition and reconstruction work was not substantial.

Occupation need not be immediate and the court may accept the landlord's undertaking to occupy at a later date: *Chez Gerard Ltd v Greene*. In *Method Developments Ltd v Jones* (1971) it was made clear that occupation must be intended to be within a reasonable time from the date of termination.

Business or residential purposes: The occupation needs to be for the landlord's business or his residence. The term "business" is widely interpreted. It has been held to include a community centre managed in conjunction with a nearby church: *Parkes v Westminster Roman Catholic Diocese Trustee* (1978). It extends to storage purposes ancillary to the business and advantageous to the development of the business in the future: *Page v Sole*. It is also sufficient where the landlord is in the business of letting accommodation and intends to let the property to others, while providing services and management: *Jones v Jenkins*. Although the landlord must occupy the whole of the holding, it is not necessary that he uses the whole for the purposes of a business or residence: *Method Developments Ltd v Jones* (1971).

Five years as landlord: The right of a landlord to oppose the tenant's application under s 30(1)(g) is subject to an important qualification, commonly called "the five year rule". This is contained in s 30(2) and provides that a landlord is precluded from relying upon paragraph (g) if his interest was purchased or created within the five years preceding the termination of the tenancy, and the holding has throughout been the subject of a business tenancy. This prevents a new landlord buying over the head of a sitting tenant and then claiming possession on this ground. Landlords should, however, be aware that the five year rule does not apply to ground (f) and that reliance on this other ground may be an attractive possibility. Clearly, the rule has no application where the landlord himself granted the tenancy: *Northcote Laundry Ltd v Frederick Donnelly Ltd* (1968). It does, however, mean that a landlord who has acquired his interest in the last five years will be unable to use ground (g) unless there was no Part II tenancy in existence at any given time in that period. Some observations need to be made concerning the application of s 30(2):

  (i) the landlord's interest may be either the reversion or a leasehold estate. The five year rule applies if the landlord has been granted a reversionary lease: *A D Wimbush &*

Grounds of opposition

Sons Ltd v Franmills Properties Ltd (1961). It appears not to matter that the capacity in which the landlord held the interest has changed in the five years: *Morar* v *Chauhan* (1985);

(ii) "purchased" is given its ordinary meaning (ie buying for money) and does not include a surrender by operation of law or acquisition in consideration of a covenant: *Frederick Lawrence Ltd* v *Freeman Hardy & Willis Ltd* (1959);

(iii) "created" can give rise to difficulties where the landlord's interest is subject to a trust and a beneficiary wishes to be treated as the landlord and to rely on s 30(1)(g). In this situation, the landlord's interest is treated as being created when the trust was declared and not the date when the landlord acquired his interest. This does not apply, however, where the landlord himself (*qua* trustee) seeks possession: *Morar* v *Chauhan*;

(iv) the date of acquisition of the landlord's interest is the date when it initially arose and not, if the interest is leasehold, the date of any later lease granted after the original had expired: *Artemiou* v *Procopiou* (1965);

(v) where the landlord's interest is leasehold the date of acquisition is at the execution of the lease: *Northcote Laundry Ltd* v *Frederick Donnelly*. If the lease was executed before it became effective, the date of commencement is arguably the relevant date: *Denny Thorn & Co Ltd* v *George Harker & Co Ltd* (1957);

(vi) if a contract preceded the acquisition of the landlord's freehold or leasehold estate, the date of acquisition is the date of the contract;

(vii) the date of termination of the current lease is the date specified in the landlord's s 25 notice or the tenant's s 26 request: *Frederick Lawrence* v *Freeman Hardy & Willis*. Any possible extension under s 64 is ignored. When issuing a s 25 notice or a s 26 request, the date selected for termination should take into account the five year rule. This might influence the landlord to insert a date more distant in time and the tenant to choose an earlier date;

(viii) the five year rule does not operate where the landlord is a company and the interest has been acquired by another company landlord within the same group of companies: s 43(2).

Even though the operation of s 30(2) may prevent the landlord opposing the tenant's application for a new tenancy, it may be to the advantage of the landlord still to rely on s 30(1)(g). If the landlord can satisfy the other elements of ground (g), the court might be persuaded to order a new tenancy of shorter duration than it would otherwise have granted: *Upsons Ltd* v *E Robins Ltd* (1956). If the landlord attempts to delay matters until the five year period is satisfied, the tenant might be able to defeat this tactic by the service of a s 26 request.

Chapter 9

Rejection of the tenant's application

If the landlord successfully opposes the tenant's application for a new tenancy on one or more of the grounds listed in s 30(1), the court cannot grant a new tenancy: s 31(1). Otherwise, the court must make an order for a new tenancy: *Morar* v *Chauhan* (1985).

By way of an exception to these general rules, a compromise is achieved where the landlord's opposition is based on grounds (d): alternative accommodation; (e): uneconomic subletting; or (f): demolition and reconstruction. If the landlord cannot establish such ground at the date of the hearing, but the court is of the view that the landlord would be able to do so within one year of the date for termination set out in the s 25 notice or s 26 request, s 31(2) comes into operation. This provides that the court must dismiss the tenant's application and make a declaration to that effect stating on which of those grounds, and as at what date, the court would have been satisfied. The tenant then has fourteen days in which to require the court to substitute that date, as specified in the declaration, for the original termination date. If the tenant fails to respond to the declaration, the tenancy will end on the date specified in the renewal documentation, or later if s 64 applies (see below). On the tenant taking the positive step envisaged by s 31(2), the existing tenancy continues beyond the original termination date until the later date as specified in the declaration. It is necessary to appreciate that the fourteen day period cannot be extended.

An example of the operation of this provision is provided by *Accountancy Personnel Ltd* v *Worshipful Company of Salters* (1972), where it was established that the landlord's redevelopment plans were dependent on planning permission which would be granted in the near future. The provision leaves unaltered the date when intention must be established, but focuses rather on when it is to be implemented.

1. Final disposal (s 64)

The date of termination set out in the s 25 notice or s 26 request is not necessarily the date on which (whether the tenant's application is successful or not) the current tenancy will end. Under s 64, where the tenant makes an application to the court for a new tenancy and the termination date specified in the renewal documentation expires within three months of the final disposal of the matter, the current tenancy automatically continues until the end of that three month period. No application need be made under s 64; it is the whole tenancy that is continued.

Final disposal occurs when all proceedings (including an appeal) have been determined and any time for further appeals has expired. Alternatively, it arises when an application has been withdrawn or any appeal discontinued. In *Austin Reed* v *Royal Insurance Co (No 2)* (1956), for example, the date of final disposal, where the Court of Appeal refused leave to appeal to the House of Lords, was held to be the date on which time to petition the Appeals Committee of the House of Lords expired.

Although intrinsically reasonable, these provisions have fostered much criticism. First, where a tenant enters a genuine appeal, the period of three months is hardly sufficient to locate new premises. If the tenant attempts to find alternative accommodation, he must be aware that he is under a continuing condition to remain in occupation of the demised premises throughout all of the proceedings: *Caplan (I & H)* v *Caplan (No 2)* (1963). If he does not remain in occupation, he ceases to have the protection of the Act and thereby loses any hope of a new lease. The Law Commission in 1969 (No 17) thought it unreasonable to expect a business tenant to wait three months before he seeks other premises and unrealistic to suppose that he will always find other accommodation in that time (at para 45). The Law Commission recommended that the tenant should be required only to occupy up to the time of the court order, any later and intermediate period being of no relevance. This recommendation was not to find its way into the Law of Property Act 1969 and has not been championed since.

Rejection of the tenant's application

Second, the more cynical (and less genuine) tenant can exploit s 64 so as to extend, for as long as possible, the current tenancy. The tenant can delay the time of final disposal by entering a notice of appeal, even where there is no reasonable prospect of an appeal being successful. Such an appeal is often abandoned at the last possible moment. This tactic secures for the tenant time to look for alternative accommodation and meanwhile brings with it (as considered in Chapter 7) considerable rental advantages. There remain other tactical advantages associated with dubious appeals. In *Photo Centre Ltd* v *Grantham Court Properties (Mayfair) Ltd* (1964), the aim was merely to gain the tenant an extra period of occupation, whereas in *AJA Smith Transport* v *British Railways Board* (1980) the tenant delayed in the hope that it would cost his landlord extra money (by way of rising building costs) and deter his landlord's redevelopment plans. In the latter case, the court thought that the tenant was close to an abuse of the judicial process.

The attitude of the court towards unmeritorious appeals is encapsulated in *Burgess* v *Stafford Hotels Ltd* (1990). In this case, the tenant "played the system" by entering an appeal which had no chance of success. Glidewell LJ concluded:

> "One cannot say that a person who is granted such rights [to appeal] and takes advantage of them is behaving disgracefully or is deserving of moral condemnation. The landlord's remedy ... is either to apply for an order to strike out ... or to apply for an order for security of costs, or to make both applications."

The Court of Appeal made the point, however, that appeals will be struck out only in clear and obvious cases and not when an extensive inquiry into the facts is going to be necessary. It was also said that to raise an issue on appeal, which had not been raised below, would be an abuse of process when its argument would entail a rehearing.

2. Compensation for disturbance

Where the tenant is unable to obtain an order for a new lease, the question of compensation may arise. Compensation may be payable for tenant's improvements (see Chapter 11) and/or for what is termed "disturbance". The latter expression is believed to have been coined by Lord Reid in *Cramas Properties Ltd* v

Connaught Fur Trimmings (1965). More technically, it is compensation for loss of the contingent right of renewal.

Compensation for disturbance reflects the fact that a tenant's failure to obtain a new lease can prove costly. Apart from a loss of business and goodwill, the tenant will incur expense in finding, and moving to, alternative premises. This is particularly harsh on the tenant when the loss of a new lease is not due to any default (for example, rent arrears and breach of covenant) on his part. It is this mischief against which the compensation provisions in s 37 are aimed.

Before an amendment introduced by the Law of Property Act 1969, compensation was payable only where the tenant had made an application for a new tenancy and the court was precluded from making the order on grounds (e): uneconomic subletting; (f): demolition and reconstruction; and/or (g): own occupation. This was a cause for much complaint. As the Law Commission Report (No 17) concluded:

> " ... tenants may be put to unnecessary trouble and expense in making applications for new tenancies, which they know will be refused, in order simply to enforce their rights to compensation under the Act. Moreover, these rights are often lost through failure to make an application by tenants who are unaware that this is necessary" (at para 46).

Accordingly, the Law Commission recommended that compensation should not be limited to where an application had been made and refused and that it should be available whether or not the tenant bothered to make such an application (at para 47). This recommendation is now enacted in s 37(1), but was not made retrospective in effect: *Re 14 Grafton Street, W1* (1971).

Compensation for disturbance is available under s 37(1) when either:

(a) the court is precluded from making an order for a new tenancy solely on any of the grounds (e), (f) and (g). Where the court makes a declaration under s 31(2) (see above) that one of the grounds (e) and (f) will be satisfied at a later date, compensation remains payable because the tenant is denied a new lease; or

(b) the landlord has served a s 25 notice, or counternotice in response to the tenant's s 26 request, stating one or more

Rejection of the tenant's application

of the grounds of opposition contained in s 30(1)(e) – (g) and no other ground.

Compensation is available under (b) above where the tenant does not apply for a new tenancy or withdraws any application made. After some uncertainty, it is now clear that a tenant can discontinue his action for a new tenancy without any undertaking that he will not seek compensation: *Fribourg & Treyer* v *Northdale Investments* (1982). A possible tactical advantage for the tenant can emerge where the landlord opposes the tenant's application on one of the three specified grounds and the tenant has found alternative premises. The finding of alternative premises is one ground on which his application would be dismissed (ie, he no longer wants a new lease) and, if he proceeded with the application, no compensation would then be payable. If the application is withdrawn, he will still be able to claim compensation. Accordingly, the tenant here is in a better position by discontinuing the action than he would if he continued to pursue it. The landlord also cannot avoid paying compensation by withdrawing his opposition to the tenant's application. If this occurs, the tenant has two options: either to obtain a new tenancy or to discontinue the application and obtain compensation: *Lloyd's Bank* v *City of London Corporation* (1983).

A court refusing a new tenancy on any of the three specified grounds is, on the application of the tenant, obliged to certify that fact: s 37(4). A request for such a certificate is usually made at the end of the hearing, but it can be entertained subsequently. The procedure is governed by RSC O 97 r 10(1) (High Court) and CCR O 43 r 9 (county court).

3. Special provisions

Where the right to renew is excluded on the grounds of public interest or national security, or a certificate on those grounds prevents renewal beyond a specific date (see Chapter 2), compensation for disturbance is payable (s 59). This right extends also to where the certificate is issued for the purposes of the Local Employment Act 1972 and the provision for employment in Wales (ss 60, 60A and 60B). Concerning property in Wales, however, no compensation is payable in the following instances (s 59(1A) and (1B)):

    (a) where the tenant took the lease after the Welsh Development Agency or the Development Board for Rural Wales acquired its interest, by virtue of which the certificate was issued;

(b) where the premises were transferred to the Agency after formerly being the property of the Welsh Industrial Estates Corporation;

(c) where the premises, before their transfer to the Agency, were held by a Minister for the purposes of the Local Employment Act 1972;

(d) where industrial premises were transferred by the Agency to the Board, having been acquired by the Agency as in (c) above or when no tenancy was in existence.

As regards partly residential premises included within a business tenancy, the abolition of domestic rates has entailed modification of the compensation scheme. The general rule is that the domestic property is excluded when the rateable value of the premises is calculated (ie, the domestic property does not figure in the calculation of compensation under s 37). None the less, the tenant can claim reasonable removal expenses for that part, as agreed with the landlord or ordered by the court (s 37(5A) and (5B)). The general rule does not apply in relation to certain transitional arrangements. Under s 37(5)(a) and (b), the tenant can opt for statutory compensation, on the basis of the rateable value of the whole premises as at 31 March 1990, provided that:

(a) the tenancy was entered before 1 April 1990 (or pursuant to a contract entered before that date);

(b) the landlord served his s 25 notice or counternotice before 1 April 1990; and

(c) on the date of service of such documentation, a rateable value was shown in the valuation list for the property or could be arrived at by appointment or aggregation of the value shown between the constituent parts of the property.

4. Amount of compensation

The tenant is entitled to a flat rate compensation geared to the rateable value of the premises, that he occupies for his business, on the date the landlord serves his s 25 notice or counternotice: s 37(2). The amount payable is the product of an appropriate multiplier (currently one) and either the rateable value of the

Rejection of the tenant's application

holding or twice the rateable value: s 37(2). These rates can be changed by ministerial order: s 37(8). The appropriate multiplier to be used is that applicable when the tenant vacates the premises: *Cardshops Ltd* v *John Lewis Properties Ltd* (1983). Similarly, compensation is payable from the date the tenant quits the premises: s 37(1). The compensation scheme is, therefore, attractive by reason of its simplicity and certainty, but it is unarguably based on an arbitrary calculation.

Compensation is payable in respect of the "holding" (as defined in s 23(3)), which is not necessarily the whole of the premises comprised in the current tenancy. There will usually be no dispute as to the property which constitutes the holding. If such dispute arises, the court is empowered to determine the issue: s 37(5) and (6).

The rateable value is that as shown on the valuation list in force at the date of service of the landlord's s 25 notice or counternotice: s 37(5)(a). If no separate value is given, a proper apportionment or aggregation needs to be made: s 37(5)(b). Where the rateable value of the holding cannot be ascertained under s 37(5)(a) or s 37(5)(b), it is taken to be the value which, apart from any exemption from assessment to rates, would on a proper assessment be the value which would have been entered in the valuation list as the annual value of the holding: s 37(5)(c).

In *Plessey Co plc* v *Eagle Pension Funds* (1990), a dispute arose as to whether the rateable value was to be ascertained in accordance with s 37(5)(b) (as argued by the landlord) or under s 37(5)(c) (as argued by the tenant). The difference between these calculations was considerable. The landlord was claiming that the rateable value, on apportionment, was £17; the tenant was claiming that the rateable value was £21,097. The discrepancy stemmed from the premises being damaged by fire and the valuation list consequently being altered to reflect a massively reduced rateable value. Although the premises were put into a restored state, due to disagreement between the parties the rateable value was not upgraded until after the tenant had quit. It was decided by the Lands Tribunal that the relevant rateable value was that at the time when the landlord's s 25 notice was served (ie £17). It was with regret that the tribunal came to this conclusion, but the language of s 37(5)(b) is clear and the landlord's argument was irrefutable.

Any dispute concerning the determination of the rateable value must be referred to the Commissioners of the Inland Revenue for evaluation by an authorised valuation officer: s 37(5) and (7). Subject to an appeal to the Lands Tribunal, the decision of the valuation officer is final. The court has no jurisdiction to determine rateable values: s 37(5). Pursuant to s 37(6), rules have been made by the Inland Revenue governing the procedure for such references (Landlord and Tenant (Determination of Rateable Value Procedure) Rules 1954). Reference may be made either by one party or jointly and the prescribed form must be adhered to. Unless all parties join in the reference, copies of the form must be forwarded immediately to all other parties to the dispute. The valuation officer is also obliged to inform all parties that referral has occurred and invite them to make written representations to him (usually within twenty-eight days). The valuation officer can request the parties to supply such information as he may reasonably require to assist him in his determination. He decides the issue in his capacity as an expert, on such evidence as he considers relevant. There is no duty to consider any evidence from the parties, other than their written representations. The valuation officer has the power to hold a meeting with all the parties before making the determination. All must be invited, but the meeting can proceed even if some decline the invitation. On reaching the determination of the rateable value, the officer will send notification of his decision to all the parties and to the Inland Revenue Commissioners. Such notification will state the right of appeal to the Lands Tribunal.

5. The higher rate valuation

As mentioned above, in certain cases the rateable value is doubled for the purposes of compensation. The conditions for this higher rate to become payable are set out in s 37(3) and are:

(a) that during the whole of the fourteen years immediately preceding the termination of the current tenancy, the premises (being or comprised in the holding) have been occupied for the purpose of a business carried on by the occupier or for those and other purposes. This deals with the case of mixed user and makes it unnecessary that in such cases the residential occupation should have been for fourteen years. The requirement of fourteen years' business occupation is strict. In *Department of Environment* v *Royal Insurance* (1987), the fact that occupation had been for two days less than fourteen years defeated the claim for higher rate compensation. As the period is calculated retrospectively from the date of termination specified in the landlord's s 25 notice or tenant's s 26 request, the effect of any interim continuation under s 64 is discounted from this calculation;

(b) that if during those fourteen years there was a change of occupier of the premises (ie, the holding or, if relevant, the part occupied for the purpose of a business), the new occupier succeeded to the business of the predecessor. What is relevant here is, therefore, the continuity of business user and not the identity of the occupier. For these purposes, one government department is deemed to succeed to the business of another: s 56(3).

A particularly illustrative case is *Edicron* v *William Whitely* (1984) where the tenants had occupied the first floor of a building for over fourteen years. During that period, they had surrendered their original lease and obtained a new lease comprising the first, second and third floors. Although the second and third floors had not been occupied for the requisite period, the tenants, by virtue of the occupation of the first floor, were able to claim double compensation on the basis of the rateable value of their entire holding. The Law Commission Working Paper (No 111) thought it unsatisfactory that occupation of some part of the property for fourteen years suffices to qualify the tenant for higher rate compensation in respect of the whole property (at para 3.6.10). It was correctly pointed out that: "The amount of compensation could change materially, to the profit of one party and the loss of the other, because of the period of occupation of an insignificant part of the property" (*ibid*). As the law stands, no other construction of s 37(7) is possible. Although doubting whether such situations often arise, the Working Paper saw as the obvious cure a requirement that compensation be payable on the respective parts of the property according to the periods of occupation of each part (at para 3.6.11). If this had been the law when *Edicron* was decided, double compensation would have been payable with regard to the first floor only. The second and third floors would have attracted compensation at only the lower rate. The Working Paper, however, was uncertain as to whether reform was appropriate.

If the fourteen years' qualification is not satisfied, the tenant (no matter how short his period of occupation) is entitled to compensation at only the lower rate.

6. Contracting out

Chapter 3 considered how the parties can contract out of the Act altogether. In relation to the right to compensation, different principles apply. The general rule is that the right to compensation (including tenancies terminated in the public interest or due to national security: s 59(2)) can be excluded or modified by an agreement in writing: s 38(3). This general rule gives way, however, where the premises, which comprise the holding or a part of it, have been occupied for the purposes of the occupier's business (or for those and other purposes) for five years before the date on which the occupier is to quit: s 38(2). In such cases, any agreement which purports to exclude or reduce compensation before its accrual, is void. When the occupier has changed in that five year period, the agreement is invalidated only if the new occupier was a successor to the business of the previous occupier. Merely being a successor in title to the previous tenant is not sufficient to continue the chain of occupation. The exclusion agreement is invalid in the above circumstances regardless of whether (a) it is contained in the lease or outside it, and (b) it is entered into before or after the termination of the tenancy.

It is not uncommon for compensation to be "excluded" in a lease for a term longer than five years. This exclusion is not void *ab initio* and will be rendered inoperative only when five years' occupation is achieved. Until that time, the agreement will be effective if the lease is prematurely terminated (for example, as a result of a break-clause) or there is a late change in tenant and the nature of the business carried out on the premises. From the landlord's perspective, such exclusions should always be included in leases for a term not exceeding five years.

In all cases, the timing of the s 25 notice should be keyed in to termination before the five year period is reached. Conversely, the tenant's s 26 request should attempt to ensure that the five year mark is passed before the lease can be terminated under the Act. Both parties will be aware of the extensions possible under ss 31(2), 36(2) and 64, and the landlord, in particular, must build such possibilities into his calculations.

An agreement as to the amount of compensation made after the right to compensation has "accrued" is always valid: s 38(2). Accordingly, s 38(2) does not affect any agreement concerning the amount of compensation, provided that the agreement is entered into after the right has accrued. There is, as yet, no definitive interpretation of what is meant by the term "accrued". It seems, however, that the right accrues when the landlord serves his s 25 notice or counternotice, specifying in the document grounds (e), (f) and/or (g). It is unclear whether any of the other grounds can also be cited. Technically, it appears that if the landlord relies on grounds (a) – (d) in his stated opposition, the right to compensation has not accrued. This may be correct; if so, it does prevent the parties from making sensible agreements as to the amount of compensation.

The provisions of s 38 do not prevent the parties from entering an agreement which increases the amount of compensation beyond that payable under the statutory calculation. In addition, where the lease contains a provision as to compensation payable on termination, the tenant can choose whether to claim under s 37 or the lease. He cannot, however, choose both: Sch 9 para 5.

7. Misrepresentation

The Act contains a separate provision for compensation for misrepresentation. The tenant can obtain compensation under s 55 if his application is rejected because of any misrepresentation to, or concealment of a material fact from, the court. This remedy is in addition to any other common law remedies, such as deceit and negligence: *French v Lowen* (1925). The scope of s 55 is not keyed into any particular ground of opposition relied upon by the landlord (compare s 37), but is likely to be relevant where the landlord bases his opposition upon either ground (f): demolition and reconstruction; or ground (g): own occupation. This is because, in both instances, the landlord will have to demonstrate the necessary intention, and it is to that intention that any misrepresentation and concealment will normally strike.

Misrepresentation (which can be innocent, negligent or fraudulent) or concealment (which recognises that the landlord must act in utmost good faith) must induce the court to reject the tenant's application. This gives rise to certain observations. First, the tenant must have applied to the court for a new tenancy. The Law Commission Working Paper (No 111) thought that this requirement was illogical, because it necessitates the tenant going through the motions of a seemingly hopeless application so as to be eligible for compensation under s 55 (compare s 37). The Working Paper did, however, stress that there was no known case in which this potential lacuna had caused injustice (at para 3.6.16). It should not be overlooked that the tenant may still be entitled to damages at common law. It is only on the basis of symmetry between the compensation provisions (ie, in s 37 and s 55) that any reform will, it seems, be made.

Second, the tenant must establish that the misrepresentation or concealment actually induced the court to reject the tenant's application. Accordingly, if the tenant consents to the court refusing to make an order for a new tenancy, it seems that the tenant cannot rely on s 55 because it cannot be shown that landlord's actions induced the court's decision: *Thorne* v *Smith* (1947). As indicated above, s 55 does not take into account any misrepresentation or concealment which induced the tenant not to apply for a new tenancy or to consent to an order of the court rejecting a renewal.

Third, s 55 is inapplicable where the landlord sets up a ground of opposition *bona fide* and then, after the hearing, changes his mind.

Fourth, the compensation payable by the competent landlord under s 55 is not punitive: *Engleheart* v *Catford* (1926). The measure of damages is that which is sufficient to compensate the tenant for any loss sustained as a result of the refusal. If the tenant is entitled to compensation for disturbance under s 37, that compensation will be taken account of in the assessment of damages under s 55. Loss of expected profits and removal expenses may, however, be included in the calculation: *Clark* v *Kirby-Smith* (1964).

Chapter 10

The new lease

Where the landlord does not oppose the tenant's application for a new tenancy, or his opposition proves unsuccessful, the court must make an order for a new lease: s 29(1). The terms of the new lease may, in whole or part be agreed between the parties without recourse to the court: s 28. Any agreement must be in writing (s 69(2)) and it is possible, for example, for a formal offer to be made in the pleadings of the application which, on acceptance, becomes binding: *Lovely & Orchard Services Ltd* v *Daejan Investments* (1977). Once a binding agreement is reached, neither party can unilaterally withdraw from it. If no enforceable agreement is reached, it is left to the court to divine the terms of the new tenancy and its discretion must be exercised in accordance with ss 32–35.

Once the tenancy is granted by the court, the tenant is given an opportunity to reconsider. He may, within fourteen days of the order, apply to the court for revocation: s 36(2). In such a case, the court must accede to the tenant's application. The purpose of s 36(2) is to ensure that the tenant is not bound to accept a new lease on the terms dictated by the court. As mentioned above, the tenant has no right to withdraw from a tenancy which is the subject of agreement with the landlord. Unless the tenant does so apply in fourteen days, or the landlord agrees not to proceed, the landlord is bound to grant the lease and the tenant is bound to accept it: s 36(1). If required by the landlord, the tenant is obliged also to execute a counterpart or duplicate of the lease. In *Broadmead* v *Corben-Brown* (1966), it was recognised that, where more than one tenancy has been granted by the court, the tenant can apply for the revocation of any of those tenancies.

Revocation does not, of itself, affect any order for costs made, but the court can, if it thinks fit, cancel or vary any such order or, where no order has previously been made, make an award of costs taking into account the tenant's actions: s 36(3). In *Rom Tyre & Accessories Ltd* v *Crawford Street Properties Ltd* (1966), for example, a tenant who exercised his right to revoke the new tenancy was ordered to pay the landlord's costs.

On revocation, the current tenancy continues for any such period as the parties may agree or, in default of agreement, for as long as the court deems necessary so as to allow the landlord a reasonable opportunity to re-let or otherwise dispose of the premises: s 36(2).

As referred to above, in the absence of agreement between the landlord and the tenant, the court will determine the terms of the new tenancy. Several provisions in the Act govern issues such as the property to be comprised in the new tenancy, its duration, the rent and any other terms. Some of these provisions have attracted criticism. The Law Commission Working Paper (No 111) declined to consider many potential changes because it feared that such alterations would shift the fundamental balance of the Act (at para 3.6.1). Despite this aversion, the Working Paper did feel able to concentrate attention on the duration of the new lease (see below).

1. Property

The general rule is that the property comprised in the holding at the date of the order will be the subject of the new tenancy: s 32(1). The term "holding" is defined in s 23(3) as including those parts that are occupied by the tenant (or the tenant's employee) for the purposes of a business, but excluding those parts of the demised premises not so occupied. The parties may, however, come to an agreement as to what property will be comprised in the lease. In default, it is for the court to determine with reference to the circumstances prevailing at the date of the order: s 32(1). Accordingly, a tenant who intends to sublet part or whole of the premises should first be advised of the effect that this can have on renewal. It should also be understood that the court cannot enlarge the holding so that the premises are greater than under the original lease: *G Orlik (Meat Products)* v *Hastings & Thanet Building Society* (1974). In this case, it mattered not that the landlord had subsequently allowed the tenant to enjoy that particular amenity.

The general rule contained in s 32(1) does not apply in two situations. First, where the tenant is willing to accept a new

The new lease

tenancy of an economically separable part of the holding (see s 31A(1)(b) and Chapter 8) so that the landlord can carry out works on the remainder, the new tenancy is confined to the part he accepts. Second, where there are other premises included in the lease as well as the holding, the landlord can insist that the new tenancy is of the whole premises: s 32(2). This is to protect the landlord against the fragmentation by reason of sub-interests in the property. The status quo between the landlord and the tenant is thereby preserved.

Subject to contrary agreement between the parties, other rights of a proprietary nature, enjoyed by the tenant under his current tenancy, are to be included in the new tenancy: s 32(3). This extends to such rights as access, drainage and light. In *Re No 1 Albermarle Street* (1959), a right (held under a mere licence) to maintain advertising signs on premises retained by the landlord was included in the order for a new tenancy. The court has no jurisdiction, however, to grant rights which were not appurtenant to the original lease: *Kirkwood* v *Johnson* (1979). *De facto* enjoyment will not suffice: *Orlik* v *Hastings & Thanet*.

As regards rights reserved for the landlord, s 32 is silent. It is to be assumed that s 32 (and s 35 below) does not allow the court to add to or alter such provisions contained in the old tenancy: *Fernandez* v *Walding* (1968). This approach could cause problems for a landlord who may wish to refurbish a building in which the tenant has a lease of a part. If the landlord cannot establish a ground of opposition, when the new lease is granted the landlord cannot be given any new rights over the part demised. The refurbishment scheme could thus be thwarted. There is some force in the argument that the court should be given power to extend the landlord's rights beyond that envisaged under s 35 below.

2. Duration

Unless the parties agree in writing to the term of the new tenancy, the court can order a term, up to a maximum of fourteen years, as it considers reasonable in all the circumstances: s 33. An agreed duration can be incorporated into the court order, even though it exceeds the maximum length that could otherwise be ordered: *Janes (Gowns) Ltd* v *Harlow Development Corporation* (1979). There appears no reason why the court cannot order a periodic tenancy, if deemed appropriate. The court is given a wide discretion, but must have particular regard to certain factors, when exercising that discretion, so as to protect the interests of both parties. These factors include:

(a) the duration of the original lease: *London & Provincial Millinery Stores* v *Barclays Bank* (1962). The court will rarely grant a lease for a term longer than the current lease: *Betty's Cafes Ltd* v *Phillips Furnishing Stores Ltd* (1959). In practice, this often means that the new lease is of the same duration as its predecessor;

(b) the length of time that the tenant has been holding over under a s 24 continuation tenancy: *London & Provincial Millinery Stores*. This could be used to justify a new lease longer than the original;

(c) hardship to, and needs of, either party: *Upsons Ltd* v *E Robins Ltd* (1956). In this case, the landlord owned only one shop, whereas the tenant was a company with some two hundred and fifty retail outlets. When looked at from the perspective of comparative hardship, this inequality justified the grant of a short-term lease. Hardship can become relevant in other ways. If the tenant seeks a short-term lease which would damage the value of the landlord's reversion, the court may order a lease of longer duration (perhaps including a tenant's break clause) than the tenant wishes: *Charles Follett Ltd* v *Cabtell Investments Co Ltd* (1986). A similar result could give the landlord a fair opportunity to re-let the premises: *Re Sunlight House* (1959). As Morris LJ said in *Upsons*: "A consideration of 'all the circumstances' of a case, if it is careful and complete ... may inevitably involve considering how the 'circumstances' tell on the fortunes of those concerned";

(d) the landlord's future plans for the property. If the landlord intends to demolish and reconstruct or to occupy the premises himself, but cannot establish this intention at the date of the hearing, this may persuade the court to grant a short letting: *London & Provincial Millinery Stores*. Alternatively, a break clause could be inserted (see s 35) into the tenancy for the benefit of the landlord: *Amika Motors Ltd* v *Colebrook Holdings Ltd* (1981). The courts have shown willingness, moreover, to insert a mutual break clause in these circumstances: *Reohorn* v *Barry Corporation* (1956). A break clause is appropriate where the development is not immediately in prospect, but is reasonably likely: *Adams* v *Green* (1978). Similarly, it might properly be inserted into the new tenancy to allow comprehensive redevelopment, provided that it is a real possibility, according to plans not yet finalised: *NCP Ltd* v *Paternoster Consortium Ltd* (1990). As Fox LJ made clear in *JH Edwards & Sons Ltd* v *Central London Commercial Estates Ltd* (1984):

> "If it is likely that the superior landlord for the time being may wish to develop the property, then (since it is not the policy of the 1954 Act to inhibit development) he should not be saddled with a lease which may prevent such development. In that connection a present intention to redevelop immediately is not necessary ... Accordingly, it seems to me that it must be wrong in principle in the present case to order the grant of new leases for such substantial periods as 12 and 10 years respectively without development 'break' clauses."

In order to offer the tenant some security, the break clause can be made to be operative only on the expiry of an initial fixed period: *JH Edwards & Sons Ltd* v *Central London Commercial Estates Ltd*. If the current lease has a break clause, it is likely (but not certain) that the new lease will contain such a provision: *Leslie & Godwin Investments Ltd* v *Prudential Assurance Co Ltd* (1987);

(e) the relationship between the parties (good or bad): *Orenstein* v *Donn* (1983);

(f) the nature of the business and the age and state of the property.

Unless the judge errs at law (for example, by taking account of an irrelevant circumstance), the Court of Appeal will not interfere with the length of term ordered by the judge: *Upsons* v *E Robins*. For the court's power to grant reversionary leases, and the provisions concerning the public interest and national security, see Chapter 2.

The new tenancy starts when the current one terminates under the provisions of the Act, taking into account any interim continuance under s 64. When the duration of the new lease is set by the court, it is standard practice for the order to state that the new term will commence from the date of final disposal and end on a specified date: *Chipperfield* v *Shell (UK)* (1980). In this situation, the court will not know exactly when the lease will commence, but will be sure of when it will end. The parties can, however, agree a different commencement date; the agreed date will then be incorporated into the court order: *Bradshaw* v *Pawley* (1980). Such an agreed date might, for example, be the day immediately following the expiry of the original contractual term.

The present maximum of fourteen years, imposed by s 33 with regard to the court's power to order a new tenancy, is open to criticism. The Law Commission Working Paper (No 111) identified three areas for concern (at para 3.6.2):

(a) the original lease may have been for a considerably longer term than the fourteen years. Since the landlord's interest can be protected by the inclusion of a rent review clause, this unrealistic ceiling was thought to have no justification;

(b) the maximum term of fourteen years is inconvenient because the common rent review pattern is now for a review at five year intervals. It was argued that the court should, therefore, be able to order a term of years divisible by five (for example, a fifteen or twenty year lease). An increased maximum term would be a practical and useful step forward;

(c) although fourteen year terms were once common, they are now considered unfashionable. Rents negotiated for new lettings are usually based on five, fifteen, twenty-five and thirty-five year terms. These rents are used as yardsticks for the purpose of assessing rents upon renewal (see s 34(1) below). The comparison would, therefore, be more accurate if the court could order a lease for the same duration as would be found in the open market.

The Working Paper was unsure whether the best course was to abolish the maximum ceiling altogether or merely to increase the present power of the court (para 3.6.5). If the former option is followed, it would be appropriate to provide the court with statutory guidance as to how the discretion should be exercised. If the latter course is adopted, the selection of a new ceiling would have to be made. The Law Commission expressed no preference as to whether the increase should be to fifteen, twenty-five or thirty-five years.

3. Rent

The rent is to be that which is agreed between the parties or, in default of such agreement, determined by the court: s 34. The Act sets out a formula by which the rent is to be fixed by the court. The rent is to be that at which, having regard to the terms of the new tenancy, the holding might reasonably be expected to be let in the open market by a willing lessor: s 34(1). The requirement that the court is to have regard to the terms of the new tenancy leads to the rent being determined after all other terms are settled: *O'May v City of London Real Property* (1982). Accordingly, if on appeal any terms other than that as to rent are varied, this variation must be reflected in a reconsideration of the rent ordered: *Cardshops Ltd v Davies* (1971). The date at which the level of the new rent is to be calculated is at the date of the hearing, but the court should take into account any foreseeable changes that might occur between this date and the time the new lease will take effect: *Lovely & Orchard Services v Daejan Investments Ltd* (1977). The reference in s 34(1) to a "willing lessor" is to a hypothetical landlord and not to the actual landlord: *FR Evans (Leeds) Ltd v English Electric Co* (1977). It should be noted that the section does not, unlike many rent review clauses, expressly assume a letting to a "willing tenant". It seems that, because the application is at the tenant's instigation, this is tacitly assumed. In addition, the reference to "the open market rent" in s 34 might imply the existence of both a willing landlord and a willing tenant, as otherwise it cannot be said that any "market" exists. The objective yardstick employed also prevents the court from fixing a rent, below the market level, on the basis that the tenant cannot afford the market rent: *Giannoukakis Ltd v Saltfleet Ltd* (1988).

The state of repair of the premises may also be relevant. Where the premises are in disrepair due to the tenant's default, a question arises as to whether the premises should be valued as they stand or on the assumption that the tenant has performed his repairing obligations. The courts have not always spoken in one voice on this issue, but support for the assumption that the covenants have been observed is to be found in *Re 5 Panton Street, Haymarket* (1959). The court in *Family Management v Gray* (1979) drew a similar conclusion. In *Fawke v Viscount Chelsea* (1980), moreover, the court decided that it could take cognisance of the disrepair (here due to the landlord's breach of covenant) and concluded that the proper market rent was less than it would have been had the repairs been effected. The court decided also that it had the discretion under s 34, in exceptional circumstances, to order a differential rent for the property until the repairs were carried out. The principle running through these cases appears to be that the tenant cannot set up his own breaches of covenant in reduction of the rent and the landlord cannot profit from his non-observance of repairing obligations.

The calculation of the open market rental value, in practice, turns on expert valuation evidence. An important feature of this evidence is the rent reserved on recent lettings of comparable properties in the area, taking into account the terms of the new tenancy. If there is nothing comparable, general rent increases in the area might be applied: *NCP* v *Colebrook Estates* (1983). Such evidence must be introduced without resort to hearsay: *English Exporters (London) Ltd* v *Eldonwall Ltd* (1973).

There is, however, an absence of authoritative guidance as to how the rent is to be calculated for the purposes of s 34. In *Re 52 Osnaburgh Street* (1957), the landlord proved that he had a firm offer of a particular rent for the premises from a prospective tenant. This was held to be good evidence of the open market rent and was preferred to the valuations of experts based on a square-foot basis. Such a departure from expert valuation will, however, be rare.

Evidence of the profitability of the tenant's business is, as a general rule, inadmissible: *WJ Barton Ltd* v *Long Acre Securities Ltd* (1982). This case involved an ordinary shop, of which there were ample comparable properties which could be adduced in evidence. Issues of profitability were therefore irrelevant. In exceptional situations, however, such evidence can be allowed. In *Harewood Hotels Ltd* v *Harris* (1958), for example, the profitability of a hotel business was a relevant factor. It was indicated that profit could be relevant also in relation to petrol stations, theatres and race courses. Nevertheless, it is not usual for the tenant to disclose his trading accounts.

Where the premises could be used for a more profitable purpose, provided that the user is not prohibited under the terms proposed for the new tenancy, the more valuable use must be considered. In *Aldwych Club Ltd* v *Copthall Property Co Ltd* (1962), the fact that club premises could have been used more valuably as offices affected the calculation of the new rent. The court will not, however, relax a user covenant merely to justify a higher valuation: *Gorleston Golf Club* v *Links Estate* (1959).

Although the court may also have regard to the rateable value of the holding, such value is not a reliable guide to rental value. Rateable value is thought to be of influence only where the new lease is to be a yearly tenancy; otherwise, it is of no consequence: *Davies* v *Brighton Corporation* (1956).

There is no mention in s 34 of the effect of sub-tenancies. There is no express assumption that the whole premises are being let with vacant possession. Since *Oscroft* v *Benabo* (1967), it is arguable that the court should take account of the right of an existing sub-tenant to renew his lease under the Act. This would work to reduce the open market rent.

The rent currently payable under the existing lease is not a factor to be taken account of, in the setting of the new rent, unless it constitutes direct evidence of the market rent. This, of course, it will rarely do.

The Act provides that four matters must be disregarded in assessing the rent for the new tenancy: s 34(1). These disregards are:

(a) any effect on rent attributable to occupation by the tenant (or a predecessor in title) of the holding. The tenant does not, therefore, benefit from any sitting tenant discount: *O'May* v *City of London Real Property Co* (1982). The disrepair of the premises, due to the tenant's non-observance of covenants, can also be disregarded: *Family Management* v *Gray*;

(b) any goodwill attaching to the premises by reason of the business carried on by the tenant (or by his predecessor both in title and in business). This involves the court in calculating whether there is any difference in the value of the holding with or without goodwill. If such a difference exists, it must be disregarded by the court in assessing the new rent. The burden of proof lies with the tenant; for the disregard to occur, it must be shown that the goodwill has enhanced the letting value of the holding. Lord Macnaghten defined goodwill, in *Commissioners of Inland Revenue* v *Muller & Co* (1901), as " ... the benefit and advantage of the good name, reputation, and connection of a business. It is the attractive force which brings in custom. It is the one thing which distinguishes an old established business from a new business at its first start." Whether a person is a predecessor in business is entirely a question of fact. Relevant issues include whether, for example, the new tenant continued to trade under the same name; the goodwill was assigned to him; and the new tenant purchased his predecessor's stock-in-trade;

(c) any increase in value attributable to relevant improvements carried out by the tenant, other than in pursuance of an obligation to his landlord. It has, somewhat dubiously, been suggested that a moral obligation might be relevant here: *Appleton* v *Abrahamson* (1956). Traditionally, a legal obligation on the tenant is required: *Godbold* v *Martin the Newsagents Ltd* (1983). This disregard is also dependent on the work being carried out by a tenant; therefore it does not operate where the improvement was made either pre-term or during a licence agreement: *Euston Centre Properties Ltd* v *H & J Wilson* (1982). Improvements are considered in detail in Chapter 11. This disregard requires the improvement to have been carried out during the current tenancy; or if this is not the case, that certain conditions specified in s 34(2) be complied with. These conditions are:

(i) that the improvement was completed not more than twenty-one years before the application for the new tenancy was made. This ceiling reflects the fact that, as time passes, it is impossible to say what effect the improvement has had on the letting value. Beyond twenty-one years, it is presumed to have no beneficial effect. Serious problems can arise if details of what improvements were carried out, when and by whom are misplaced. It is important that such documentation is preserved. The twenty-one year period was preferred by the Law Commission (No 17); ten and fourteen years were viewed as being too short;

(ii) that the holding or any part of it affected by the improvement has, at all times since the completion of the improvement, been comprised in tenancies within the scope of the 1954 Act;

(iii) that, at the termination of each of those tenancies, the tenant did not quit. If a tenant did quit, he might be compensated under the Landlord and Tenant Act 1927 (see Chapter 11).

A valuation difficulty arises with this particular disregard. It is unclear whether the valuer is to assume that the works

The new lease

have never been carried out; or is to value the premises as improved, but adjust the rental value by making complex valuations as to cost of the work, amortisation and so forth. There is some force in the argument that the Act should be amended so as to simply require a "fair deduction" or "fair allowance" to be made;

(d) in the case of a holding comprising licensed premises, any addition to its value attributable to that licence where it appears to the court that the benefit of the licence belongs to the tenant. This provision is relevant to those licensed premises which are within the Part II provisions. As mentioned in Chapter 3, the Landlord and Tenant (Licensed Premises) Act 1990, subject to certain transitional provisions, will place all on-licensed premises within the protection of Part II from 11 July 1992. From that date, this disregard will assume more importance.

Since 1969, the court has been expressly enabled by s 34(3) to order that the new tenancy must include a rent review clause. The insertion of a review clause is now standard practice. The court usually orders review clauses which permit the rent to be raised upwards or downwards: *Janes (Gowns) Ltd* v *Harlow Development Corporation* (1979); the fact that upwards-only reviews are the norm in the open market is immaterial. It is unclear what influence a review clause in the current tenancy will have on the court. Unlike s 35 (see below), s 34(3) does not require the court to have regard to the current tenancy. Nevertheless, any provisions in the current lease will undoubtedly be of evidential value. The court will usually take the opportunity to update the review clause in the light of recent developments in the drafting of such clauses.

4. Other terms

In the absence of agreement between the parties, the onus is placed on the court to determine the remaining terms of the new tenancy: s 35. It is standard for these other terms (for example, as to service charges) to mirror those contained in the current tenancy: *O'May* v *City of London Real Property Co Ltd* (1983). The court can order a variation of the existing terms, but the burden of persuading the court to impose a change of terms, against an unwilling party, rests heavily on the shoulders of the party proposing the change. He must convince the court that the variation is fair and reasonable in the circumstances: *O'May*. As Lord Wilberforce explained:

> "This section [s 35] contains a mandatory guideline or direction to 'have regard to' the terms of the current tenancy and to all relevant circumstances. The words 'have regard to' are elastic: they compel something between an obligation to reproduce existing terms and an unfettered right to substitute others. They impose an onus upon a party seeking to introduce new, or substituted, or modified terms, to justify the change, with reasons appearing sufficient to the court ... If such reasons are shown, then the court ... may consider giving effect to them: there is certainly no intention shown to freeze or ... to 'petrify' the terms of the lease."

Therefore, it is unlikely that the court will impose new terms which serve merely to improve the position of one party; this is particularly so where the change would prove detrimental to the other party: *Cardshops Ltd* v *Davies* (1971). In that case the landlord did not succeed in the proposed change of a qualified covenant against assignment into an absolute covenant. Similarly, the court will be wary of giving the tenant a more valuable lease than he previously held: *Kirkwood* v *Johnson* (1979). The tenant there unsuccessfully sought the insertion of an option to purchase into the new lease. In *Gold* v *Brighton Corporation* (1956), the Court of Appeal did not allow a more restricted user clause to be put in the new lease because the proposed change would have prevented the actual business of the tenant being carried on at the premises.

It is clear that the party seeking a change of terms must support his case with cogent reasons. In *Adams* v *Green*, for example, the need to permit subsequent redevelopment of the property was a sufficient justification for the insertion of a break clause. A change may be justified so as to bring the lease into line with current practice: *Hyams* v *Titan Properties Ltd* (1972). Similarly, a new term might be introduced to overcome the previously demonstrated unreasonableness of one of the parties (*Re 5 Panton St* (1959)) or to ensure that there is no default in rent payments by the imposition of a guarantor (*Cairnplace Ltd* v *CBL (Property Investment) Co Ltd* (1984)). Faced with an insoluble conflict, the court will decide the issue according to fairness and justice: *Becker* v *Hill St Properties* (1990).

The court cannot use its discretion under s 35 to insert a term in

The new lease

the new lease to the effect that the tenant will pay the landlord's costs of the grant. This is so even if there is such a term in the current lease: *Cairnplace Ltd*. Such a term can be included only as a result of agreement in writing between the parties.

Where a landlord is the Department of Industry or the English Industrial Estates Corporation, and the premises are within a development or intermediate area, the Department may certify that the new tenancy must include terms regulating assignment, subletting and user: s 60(2). A similar right extends to the Secretary of State for Wales where the landlord is the Welsh Development Agency or the Development Board for Rural Wales: s 60A(2). The court must then include such terms in the order for a new tenancy.

Chapter 11

Compensation for tenant's improvements

At common law, any improvements made by a tenant (unless classified as "tenant's fixtures" and thereby, removable) form part of the freehold and, at the end of the lease, must be left for the reversioner: *New Zealand Govt Property Corporation* v *HM & S Ltd* (1982). Subject to the law of waste and to any contrary stipulation in the lease, the tenant remains free to carry out improvements, but is not entitled to compensation. This common law approach is of particular benefit to landlords when the improvement adds to the value of the reversion.

Admittedly, there has never been anything to prevent the parties to a lease negotiating terms to deal with the subject of improvements. Indeed, most commercial leases contain a covenant (either qualified by the need for the landlord's consent or absolute in its prohibition) not to make alterations or improvements to the property demised. Seldom, if ever, is there any agreement for payment of compensation to the tenant for improvements made.

Such remained the position until the enactment of Part I Landlord and Tenant Act 1927. The purpose of Part I was clear:

> "Parliament intended that a landlord whose property had been improved by a tenant so that its letting value at the end of the tenancy had been increased, should pay compensation for the benefit he had received" (*per* Ormrod LJ in *Pelosi* v *Newcastle Arms Brewery (Nottingham) Ltd* (1981)).

The mischief at which the provisions of Part I were aimed was to prevent landlords from gaining an unmerited windfall at their tenants' expense: *Stuchbery & Son* v *General Accident Fire and Life Assurance Corporation Ltd* (1949). Accordingly, where uncertainty or ambiguity arises, the statutory provisions fall to be interpreted in a manner favourable to the tenant: *Owen*

Compensation for tenant's improvements

Owen Estate Limited v *Livett* (1955). It is unfortunate that the statutory machinery is cumbersome and complex. In 1987 the mechanics of the compensation scheme was scrutinised in the Law Commission Working Paper (No 102) and was heavily criticised. The future of compensation for improvements by business tenants is in some doubt. The Law Commission, in its 1989 report, *Landlord and Tenant Law: Compensation for Tenants' Improvements* (No 178), recommended the abolition of the scheme. The reasons underlying this recommendation will be outlined later, but it should be appreciated that statutory reform is unlikely in the foreseeable future. The low political profile of the subject area will ensure that the present system will continue for some years to come.

The Landlord and Tenant Act 1927 derogates from the parties' common law freedom to contract by giving the tenant a series of potentially valuable rights:

(a) by virtue of Part II of the Act there is implied, into all qualified covenants prohibiting improvements, the proviso that the landlord's consent cannot be unreasonably withheld: s 19(2). Although this does nothing to override absolute covenants, in other cases it can assume importance where the tenant needs to act with urgency or where the proposed improvement will not add to the subsqent letting value of the premises. In the context of s 19, works can be classified as an improvement even though they produce a diminution of the letting value: *Lambert* v *F W Woolworth & Co Ltd* (1938). This conclusion was reached because what constitutes an improvement is adjudged from the tenant's perspective: *Haines* v *Florenson* (1990). It is of no surprise, therefore, that s 19(2) allows the landlord to attach reasonable conditions to the consent, concerning compensation and reinstatement. The meaning ascribed to an improvement within s 19(2) does not always apply to other sections in the Act or to other statutory provisions: *National Electric Theatres* v *Hudgell* (1939). It is an oft-repeated judicial warning that a different subject matter (for example, a different Act or a different section within the same Act) can produce a wholly dissimilar interpretation: *Re "Wonderland", Cleethorpes* (1965);

(b) Part I of the Act enables qualifying tenants to obtain the authority of the court to carry out improvements which are prohibited by the lease: s 3. This mechanism can be applied against both qualified and absolute covenants (compare s 19(2)) and allows the tenant to sidestep the objections of a non-consenting landlord. Provided that (a) the preliminary notification procedure is followed and the improvement will add to the letting value of the premises; (b) the improvement is reasonable and suitable to the character of the property; and (c) it will not diminish the value of any other property of the landlord, the improvement is deemed to be a "proper improvement": s 3(1). Due to the time limits set out in Part I, the authorisation procedure is certainly not expeditious. Delay can be worked by a landlord to the disadvantage of a tenant. As Staughton LJ remarked in *Hogarth Health Club Ltd v Westbourne Investments Ltd* (1990):

> "There may in these days be some injustice in this area of the law. A landlord may object to the tenant's proposed improvement for little or no reason, and thus hold it up until the county courts can provide a hearing with no penalty other than costs".

The tenant does, however, have the additional benefit that, once the improvement is certified as proper, the foundation for a later claim for compensation is laid. It may also be prudent to ensure that, in fixing the rent for a new tenancy, the added value of an improvement is disregarded under s 34 Landlord and Tenant Act 1954 (see Chapter 10).

The Law Commission Report recommended that the authorisation function of the 1927 Act be retained with some minor modification (para 5.3);

(c) provided that the eligibility and procedural requirements of Part I are satisfied, there is the right to claim compensation, at the end of the tenancy, for improvements made by the tenant or predecessors in title: s 1(1). It is with this aspect of the legislation (as amended by ss 47–50 of Part III Landlord and Tenant Act 1954) that this chapter is concerned.

Stage 1: Tenancies within the Act

Part I Landlord and Tenant Act 1927 applies to holdings as defined in s 17. The improvement must have been made to the holding by the tenant or the tenant's predecessor in title (who are both defined in s 25(1)), and it is the current tenant of a s 17 holding who can invoke the authorisation and compensation provisions: s 1(1).

In order to ascertain the scope of Part I, it is necessary to look to the Act for guidance and to the common law for elaboration. The commencement point is s 17(1) which defines "holdings" as:

> "... any premises held under a lease, other than a mining lease, made whether before or after the commencement of this Act, and used wholly or partly for carrying on thereat any trade or business, and not being agricultural holdings within the meaning of the Agricultural Holdings Act 1986."

Further assistance is given by s 17(3) which states that a profession regularly carried on at the premises is deemed to be a trade or business and, thereby, within the scope of Part I. Beyond this, the Act is unhelpful, and it is left to the courts to breathe meaning into these key terms.

1. Premises

The meaning of the word "premises" is, in practice, rarely disputed. At common law, premises include the land and (if any) the erections upon it: *Bracey* v *Read* (1963). This is discussed further in Chapter 3. In the context of the 1927 Act, and in the desperation of litigation, it has been contended that the wording of s 16 lends itself to the interpretation that the terms "holding" and "premises" are given distinct meanings: the former signifying the land, the latter referring to the buildings on the land. Regardless of the curious juxtaposition of the words within s 16, this contention proved too much for Morton J, in *National Electric Theatres* v *Hudgell*, who concluded that both words were ascribed a composite meaning by virtue of s 17(1).

In *Whitley* v *Stumbles* (1930), Viscount Hailsham defined "premises", for the purposes of s 17, as being:

> "... not merely the actual buildings in which a trade is carried on, but also the land surrounding them, the easements granted as appurtenant to them, and any other incorporeal hereditaments which may form part of the premises in the strict legal sense of the term".

The term "premises" is therefore one of technical meaning and encompasses everything which is contained in the parcels clause of the lease (ie the subject matter of the grant). This does not, however, allow an incorporeal hereditament standing alone (such as a right of way or right to fish) to be classified as "premises". It is apparent from the wording of s 17(1), and in particular the use of the expression "thereat", that a physical context and connotation is intended by the legislature (*Land Reclamation Co Ltd v Basildon DC* (1979)). Accordingly, rights in the nature of an easement are of relevance only in so far as they form part of a comprehensive demise.

2. Lease

The requirement for a "lease" in s 17 (and the reference to a "tenant" in s 1(1)) operates to exclude licences from the ambit of Part I: *Euston Centre Properties Ltd v H & J Wilson Ltd* (1982). The difficult distinction between a lease and a licence is drawn in Chapter 3.

A wide definition of lease is contained in s 25(1) and extends to tenancies; under-leases; assignments; and agreements for a lease, under-lease or assignment. There is no minimum term of lease stated and the definition covers both fixed term and periodic tenancies. Part I applies to a lease whether it was granted before or after the commencement date of the Act (25 March 1927): s 17(1). By analogy with Part II Landlord and Tenant Act 1954, it seems that an unlawful subletting (ie, one in breach of the head lease) is still within the extensive s 25 definition (*D'Silva v Lister House Developments Ltd* (1970)), whereas a tenancy at will is excluded (*Hagee (London) Ltd v A B Erikson & Larson* (1975)).

3. Exclusions

Although the Act is vague as to what holdings are within s 17, it clearly states that certain holdings are outside its scope. The specified exclusions are:

    (a) mining leases, defined in s 25(1) as "a lease for any mining purposes or purposes connected therewith". The expression "mining purposes" is further explained in s 25(1) as including:

"the sinking and searching for, winning, working, getting, making merchantable, smelting or otherwise converting or working for the purposes of any manufacture, carrying away, and disposing of mines and minerals, in or under land, and the erection of buildings, and the execution of engineering and other works for those purposes".

Tenants under mining leases may receive some security by virtue of the Mines (Working Facilities and Support) Act 1966, but there is no right whatsoever to compensation for improvements. This is justifiable in the light of the fact that mining necessarily involves the wasting of assets and resources;

(b) agricultural holdings within the Agricultural Holdings Act 1986: s 17(1). An agricultural holding is a tenancy used for agriculture and so used for the purposes of a trade or business: s 1 of the 1986 Act. In relation to mixed user (for example, partly agricultural and partly non-agricultural business), the classification can, as shown in Chapter 3, prove difficult to make. Despite the legal niceties, however, it must not be overlooked that tenants of agricultural holdings can receive security of tenure and compensation for improvements under the 1986 Act;

(c) holdings let to a tenant as the holder of any office, appointment or employment from the landlord provided that, if the lease was granted after 24 March 1927 (as will inevitably be the case), the agreement is in writing and expresses the purpose for which the tenancy is created: s 17(2). The requirement is that the letting be made dependent upon the tenant continuing to hold the position. Accordingly, most service tenancies fall outside the provisions of Part I;

(d) premises used for the business of residential subletting: s 17(3). This is regardless of whether the provision of meals or services to the occupants is undertaken by the tenant. Such tenants, it should be remembered, may attract security of tenure under Part II Landlord and Tenant Act 1954;

(e) premises used to carry on a profession on an irregular basis: s 17(3). This is discussed further below;

(f) tenancies terminated under the Sch 2 Leasehold Reform

Act 1967 and those excluded under the Coal Mining (Subsidence) Act 1957.

4. Used wholly or partly for a trade or business

Although it is the tenant of a holding who can take advantage of Part I of the Act (s 1(1)), there is no requirement (unlike Part II Landlord and Tenant Act 1954, s 23(1)) that the tenant occupy the premises. The terms "use" and "occupy" are not interchangeable in this area of the law (*Land Reclamation Co* v *Basildon DC*). It is, therefore, important to consider whether this is a distinction with any practical difference. Clearly, the wording of s 17(1) places the emphasis upon the *de facto* use of the holding rather than upon the user by the tenant. The emphasis upon use, as opposed to occupation, avoids a variety of difficulties (for example, as regards companies and partnerships) and seemingly does not require that the business, trade or profession be that of the tenant. There appears to be no need for a trade or business to be regularly carried out at the premises, whereas a profession must be practised on a regular basis in order to qualify: s 17(3). The conclusion, therefore, is that seasonal, occasional and part-time business use will suffice, but irregular professional use most certainly will not. It can be argued, moreover, that ancillary or incidental use (eg, lettings to garage business vehicles, to accommodate staff and to store goods) will not constitute the carrying on thereat of a trade or business. It is fortunate that such issues are rarely encountered in practice, but the absence of litigation does leave a variety of matters unresolved.

The reference within s 17(1) to partial or whole business use contemplates that a mixed use (eg, trade and residential) may be made of the holding. This is also recognised by s 17(4) which provides that, in such cases of mixed use, Part I applies if, and so far as, the improvements relate to the trade, business or profession. Unlike the 1954 Act, Part I does not prevent a holding being within the compensation scheme because it is (as a result of the mixed use) protected by other legislation such as the Rent Act 1977. As Lord Greene in *Stuchbery & Son* v *General Accident* explained:

> "What that appears to mean is this. Once you have shown that a trade or business has been carried on on the premises, you are not to have your claim for

compensation ... defeated by having it pointed out to you that, in addition to the trade or business, you are doing something else there. A very common class of case is where you have a shop and dwelling rooms over it. It is not to be said that a tenant is not entitled to compensation when the lease of his shop comes to an end merely because the demised premises include the dwelling rooms".

The Act does not attempt to define the words "trade", "business" or "profession". The wide definition of trade and business within s 23(2) Landlord and Tenant Act 1954 does not apply here. Accordingly, it is for the court to determine, as a question of fact, whether a particular activity falls within one category or another and "... although there may be difficult cases, in general any person with a reasonable knowledge of affairs would not have much difficulty in saying what the legislation intended in regard to some particular activity" (*per* Greene MR in *Stuchbery*). Nevertheless, there has been much litigation as to what constitutes each of the three categories and how to distinguish between them. This is examined in Chapter 3.

In the context of Part I the distinction between a trade and a business is unimportant. What is of import, however, is the segregation of these types of activity from a "profession". For a profession to qualify for the compensation (and authorisation) provisions, it must be regularly carried on at the holding: s 17(3). As mentioned earlier, there is no such requirement for a trade or business.

5. Comparison with the 1954 Act

While in general it can be said that both Part I of the 1927 Act and Part II of the Landlord and Tenant Act 1954 cater for business tenancies, it needs to be appreciated that the Acts do have dissimilar catchment provisions and contain different sets of exclusions. Consequently, a tenant may qualify under one Act while not being within the scope of the other. This lack of uniformity is largely unjustifiable and can be the cause of much confusion and complexity.

The 1954 Act (as discussed in Chapter 3) extends the definition of a business to include a trade, profession, employment and any activity carried on by a body of persons, whether corporate or unincorporate (s 23(2)). This is clearly more extensive than the s 17 definition, under the 1927 legislation, which does not extend its protection to activities carried on by a members' club, or lettings for recreational purposes, for example.

Like the 1927 Act, the Landlord and Tenant Act 1954 excludes from its scope agricultural holdings and mining leases. Similarly, the later Act also disentitles tenancies granted by reason of the holding of any office or employment, provided that they are in writing and express the purpose for which they were granted. Nevertheless, as mentioned, the specific exclusions from both Acts are not identical. The differences between them are that:

(a) tenants of licensed premises can claim compensation for improvements, but not necessarily security of tenure (see Chapter 3 and note the effect of the Landlord and Tenant (Licensed Premises) Act 1990);

(b) tenants in the business of residential subletting cannot claim compensation for improvements, but can have security of tenure;

(c) short tenancies and tenancies which are lawfully contracted out of the 1954 Act have no security of tenure, but are within the compensation provisions concerning improvements;

(d) a tenant carrying out a business in contravention of a blanket prohibition against business use in the lease will usually be deprived of security of tenure, but will still be entitled to claim compensation under the 1927 Act.

The Law Commission Working Paper advocated that the definitions of "business" contained in the two Acts should be harmonised (para 6.8), but was more diffident concerning the unification of the classes of specific exclusions (para 6.5). It recommended that on-licensed premises and short-term tenancies continue to be within the ambit of the compensation scheme, but concluded that coverage should not extend to cases where the business user is in breach of the lease (paras 6.5 and 6.8).

Stage 2: What is an improvement?

Not every change to the holding can be classified as an "improvement"; it is therefore unfortunate that there is neither a definition of the term within the Act, nor a schedule of works (as in the Agricultural Holdings Act 1986) expressed to be within the scope of the statutory scheme. To discover what is to be categorised as an improvement, it is necessary to look to the Act and the common law.

At common law, an improvement is an addition or alteration which makes the demised property in some way better than before: *Wates* v *Rowland* (1952). As Denning LJ concluded: "If the work which is done is the provision of something new for the benefit of the occupier, that is, properly speaking, an improvement" (*Morcom* v *Campbell-Johnson* (1956)). The improvement must be assessed from the perspective of the tenant (*Balls Brothers Ltd* v *Sinclair* (1931)) and regard must be had to the demised premises and to the context in which the issue arises (*Haines* v *Florenson*). Although a matter of construction in each case, the central issue is whether the tenant has achieved a more beneficial use of the holding (*ibid*). In some contexts (but not for the purposes of the compensation scheme), works could constitute an improvement even though the value of the demised property is diminished as a result: *Lambert* v *FW Woolworth*.

As far as possible, the courts will give effect to the ordinary meaning of the word "improvement" (*Leathwoods Ltd* v *Total Oil* (1986)); this will normally involve some alteration or addition to the existing building (*Re Scottish & Newcastle Breweries Ltd* (1985)). In the 1927 scheme, however, an improvement is expressed to include "the erection of any building" (s 1(1)). Accordingly, in *National Electric Theatres* v *Hudgell* the demolition of a cinema and its substitution by a row of shops and flats was held to be an improvement. It mattered not that a different business was then to be carried on or that no part of the original structure remained. The decision may, however, be confined to its particular statutory context, and it has been said that such a redevelopment is rarely to be so classified elsewhere in the law: *Sainty* v *Minister of Housing and Local Government* (1964). Nevertheless, in *Price* v *Esso Petroleum Co Ltd* (1980) the demolition of a service station and its replacement by another was held to be an improvement both in the ordinary meaning of the word and in the framework of the lease in question.

The term "improvement" is generally given a liberal interpretation. Examples of improvements for the purposes of Part I of the 1927 Act are the installation of a WC (*Bresgall & Sons* v *London Borough of Hackney* (1976)); the replacement of granite cladding with stainless steel cladding (*Land Securities* v *Receiver for the Metropolitan Police District* (1983)); the removal of internal walls and installation of a lift (*Billson and others* v *Residential Apartments Ltd* (1991)); and the building of a wall, connecting electricity and fitting locks (*C & P Haulage* v *Middleton* (1983)).

One common thread which runs through the types of improvement within the compensation provisions is that they all relate to the physical property. Incorporeal "improvements" (for example, securing better access over neighbouring land and obtaining covenants restricting business competition) are, evidently, outside the scope of the compensation scheme: *Haines* v *Florenson*. This conclusion is consistent with the wording of s 1(1) and the approach of the Court of Appeal in *Land Reclamation Co* v *Basildon DC*. The Law Commission Working Paper suggested, however, that such "improvements", provided they enhance the value of the holding, should be catered for (paras 6.10 and 6.12).

Once the work has been classified as an "improvement", the tenant must still establish that certain qualifying conditions are met before there is a chance of compensation.

1. Qualifying conditions

For an improvement to merit compensation, a number of hurdles, which are set out in Part I Landlord and Tenant Act 1927, must be overcome. These are as follows:

(a) the improvement must be carried out "on" the holding (s 1(1)); therefore the work must concern either the land or the buildings on it and result in some physical change (*Land Reclamation Co Ltd* v *Basildon DC*). Improvements to land other than that demised are totally discounted. This omission gained the approval of the Law Commission in its Working Paper (para 6.16);

(b) the improvement must not consist of a trade or other tenant's fixture (ie, one which the tenant can lawfully remove at the end of the lease). It is irrelevant whether such fixtures are actually removed or left for the landlord. Fixtures introduced by the tenant which are not removable (ie, the landlord's fixtures) can, however, constitute improvements: *New Zealand Government Property Co* v *HM & S Ltd*;

(c) the improvement must be calculated to add to the net

Compensation for tenant's improvements

letting value of the holding: s 1(1). This contemplates that an improvement can have detrimental as well as beneficial aspects: *National Electric Theatres Ltd*. If it does not add to the subsequent rental value then, regardless of its utility to the tenant, the improvement does not qualify. The Law Commission Working Paper advocated, moreover, that compensation should be made payable by the tenant if the landlord's reversion was, on balance, diminished (para 6.24);

(d) the improvement must be reasonable and suitable to the character of the holding and must not diminish the value of any other property of the landlord: s 3(1). This raises issues of fact for the court to determine, and in this regard the landlord and superior landlords enjoy the right to present evidence: s 3(2);

(e) the improvement was not made before 24 March 1927 (s 2(1)(a));

(f) unless completed after 1 October 1954, the improvement was not made in pursuance of a statutory obligation: s 48(1) Landlord and Tenant Act 1954;

(g) the improvement was made by the tenant or the tenant's predecessor in title: s 1(1). The meaning of "tenant" has been discussed above, but it should be appreciated that an improvement by a sub-tenant is not included unless the tenant has paid, or is liable to pay, compensation to that sub-tenant. The statutory definition of a "predecessor in title" is given in s 25(1) as "any person through whom the tenant or landlord has derived title, whether by assignment, by will, by intestacy, or by operation of law". This has been interpreted as meaning a person who had the title to the premises to which the tenant succeeded (*Corsini* v *Montague Burton Ltd* (1953)) or a predecessor in title to the interest of the tenant in the premises (*Pasmore* v *Whitbread & Co Ltd* (1953)). Although it is important that the expression is not too narrowly defined, it is not sufficiently wide to encompass each and every person who at any time had some interest in the premises: *Trustees of Henry Smith's Charity* v *Hemmings* (1983). Accordingly, improvements made by tenants under previous tenancies are not within the scheme. The Law Commission Working Paper did, however, advocate a system of roll-over from one tenancy to the next (para 6.26).

In *Pelosi* v *Newcastle Arms Brewery (Nottingham) Ltd*, Ormrod LJ passed comment about the curious nature of the statutory definition and the peculiar conjunction between "any" and "person" and "has" and "derived". Nevertheless, on complicated facts, the court experienced little difficulty in ensuring a common-sense application of the definition. It was held in *Pelosi* that, where the improvements had been made by a sub-tenant who subsequently assigned the sub-tenancy to an assignee who, in turn, later acquired the head lease, the sub-tenant was the predecessor in title of the assignee. Regardless of the fact that the assignee ended up with a different title from that of the predecessor, the assignee's title was historically derived from the sub-tenant;

(h) the improvement was not undertaken by the tenant or predecessor in consequence of an obligation in a contract (including a building lease) supported by valuable consideration: s 2(1)(b). An obligation merely to carry out the works in a certain way, if the tenant decides to undertake the improvement, is insufficient to preclude compensation: *Godbold* v *Martin The Newsagents Ltd* (1983). It is also irrelevant whether the contract was entered into before or after the commencement of the 1927 Act. It is, however, important to appreciate that s 2(1)(b) is drafted in such general terms that the obligation need not be within a contract between landlord and tenant. In *Owen Owen Estate Ltd* v *Livett* (1955), the tenant was precluded from claiming compensation because of an obligation to carry out improvements which was contained in a contract with a sub-tenant.

As discussed later, there is no reason why the contractual obligation cannot be contained in the same instrument which grants the landlord's consent to carry out the works. The problem lies in supporting this with valuable consideration; normally, it requires the landlord to offer some form of payment or rent reduction to the tenant.

Stage 3: Procedures for obtaining compensation

The carrying out of work which can be classified as an improvement, and which satisfies the above qualifying conditions, will not automatically entitle the tenant to compensation. The tenant must

Compensation for tenant's improvements

follow strict procedural steps as set out in Part I Landlord and Tenant Act 1927 (as amended). This is so even if the improvement is carried out under a statutory obligation. Both the Law Commission Working Paper (1987) and the subsequent Law Commission Report (1989) criticised the somewhat convoluted procedures as being inherently wasteful and unwieldy.

Eight separate, procedural steps may have to be taken before compensation is paid. Some are taken before the work, some immediately afterwards and others at the end of the lease. It is possible to summarise these procedural matters as follows:

(a) a preliminary notice of intention must be served by the tenant on the landlord;

(b) the tenant must, following the service of the notice, allow the landlord three months within which to object. If no objection is raised, the tenant is authorised to carry out the improvement;

(c) on objection by the landlord, the tenant must apply to the court for a certification that the improvement is a "proper" improvement;

(d) if a certificate is refused on the ground that the landlord has offered to execute the improvement personally, and has failed to do so, the tenant must again apply to the court for certification;

(e) after the works are completed, the tenant may apply to the landlord for a certificate of due execution;

(f) if no such certification is given by the landlord within one month, the tenant may apply to the court for the completion certificate;

(g) within strict time limits (which vary according to how the lease was terminated), the tenant may lodge an application for compensation with the landlord;

(h) unless agreement is reached between the parties, the tenant must then apply to the court within three months for a compensation award.

1. Preliminary notice of intention

In order to lay the foundation for a future claim for compensation, the tenant or the tenant's predecessor in title must have served on the landlord (which includes the Crown: s 24(1)) a preliminary notice of the intention to make the improvement: s 3(1) and (5). The notice must contain a specification and plan showing the proposed improvement and the part of the demised premises affected by it: s 3(1). The Act offers no prescribed form for the notice to adopt and states only that it must be in writing: s 23(1). The initial plan can be in outline form, but it must provide sufficient detail as to allow the landlord to identify and assess the proposal. Where further details are requested, the effective date of the notice is not the original date of service, but the date when the information is provided: *Deerfield Travel Services Ltd* v *Leathersellers' Company* (1983). Failure to request additional details, provided that the landlord was aware of the purpose of the notice, will imply that the stated details are sufficient (*ibid*).

The notice must be served even when there is no prohibition within the lease preventing alterations to the premises. It is a possibility, as recognised in *Deerfield*, that a tenant's application for the landlord's consent to carry out the improvements could satisfy the s 3 requirements, even though no reference is made to the compensation provisions. In such a case, the court will be astute to ensure that the landlord had sufficient opportunity and information to object to the tenant's proposal.

2. Landlord's objection

Upon service of the tenant's preliminary notice, the landlord has two options:

> (a) to raise no objection or to serve a notice of consent. Either allows the tenant to go ahead and undertake the improvements regardless of any prohibition in the lease: s 3(4). The tenant need do nothing more (except carry out the works) to lay the ground for a claim for compensation. The Law Commission Working Paper recommended that, although the authorisation procedure was useful to a tenant, the tenant should not be allowed to claim compensation for an improvement which contravenes a provision of the lease (para 6.17);
>
> (b) to object within three months of the service of the preliminary notice: s 3(1). The objection can be on the basis that (i) the landlord will carry out the improvements personally for a reasonable increase in rent (or such increase as determined by the court); (ii) the proposed works do not

constitute an improvement within the meaning of the Act; or (iii) the occupier is outside the compensation scheme (for example, is a licensee). An objection raised outside the time limit is ineffective. Although compensation is now payable for such works, no objection can be raised where the improvement is to be made in pursuance of a statutory obligation.

Where an objection is raised, which cannot be resolved by agreement between the parties, the onus is upon the tenant to obtain the authorisation of the court. In the absence of agreement, all matters fall to be determined by the court: s 1(3).

3. Application to the court

If, following an objection by the landlord, the tenant wishes to pursue the matter, he must obtain from the court a certification that the improvement is a "proper improvement": s 3(1). In the High Court, the action must be commenced by originating summons in the Chancery Division. In other cases, commencement is by originating application in the county court.

The court will seek to ascertain whether the preliminary notice was served upon the landlord and all superior landlords and that such persons have been offered the opportunity to be heard. The court can grant a certificate either on a conditional (for example, with modification of the plans and specifications, time limits or other terms) or on an unconditional basis: s 3(1) and (5). As was made clear in *English Exporters (London) Ltd* v *Eldonwall Ltd* (1973), in order to establish the improvement as "proper", and before the court can issue a certificate, the tenant must show on a balance of probabilities that the proposed improvement:

(a) is of such a nature as to be calculated to add to the letting value of the holding at the termination of the tenancy: s 1. Expert evidence, on behalf of both parties, might be appropriate here; and

(b) is reasonable and suitable to the character of the holding: s 1. The court is directed by s 3(2) to have regard to evidence of the landlord or superior landlord that the improvement is calculated to injure the amenity or convenience of the neighbourhood; and

(c) will not diminish the value of any other property belonging to the landlord or any superior landlord: s 1. Again, expert testimony may assist the parties; and

(d) is not one which the landlord has undertaken to execute in consideration of a reasonable increase in rent: s 3(1). The defence gives way if the landlord fails to carry out the undertaking: s 3(1). The landlord or agent is given the right to enter the holding to inspect or carry out such an improvement: s 10. Unless there is some contractual obligation, the tenant cannot enforce the landlord's undertaking. It is left open to the tenant to reapply to the court on the landlord's failure.

The certification of the court has a two-fold effect: first, the court authorises the tenant, subject to the plans or specifications, to make improvements which might otherwise have been unlawful under the lease; and second, it establishes (in part) the right of the tenant to compensation at the end of the lease. The certificate can be issued only before the work is done and not after it has been completed: *Hogarth Health Club Ltd* v *Westbourne Investments Ltd* (1990).

The Act provides, in addition, that where the landlord is obliged to pay fire insurance premiums or is liable to pay water rates and/or non-domestic rates and, as a result of the authorised improvement, the amount of such payment is increased, the tenant is liable to pay such additional amount to the landlord: s 16.

4. Certificate of execution

On completion of the works by the tenant, the landlord may be asked to provide a certificate to confirm that the work has been duly completed: s 3(6). There is no obligation upon the tenant to obtain such a certificate, but the documentation could be of evidential benefit because it proves that the improvement was carried out and establishes the date of completion. This is of particular worth when the compensation claim is to be made many years in the future. The tenant is liable to pay the landlord's reasonable expenses (s 3(6)) and these might include the fees of a surveyor or architect.

If the landlord declines to issue this certificate, or fails to do so within one month of the tenant's request, the tenant may apply to the court which, if satisfied that the improvement has been duly completed, must issue the certificate to that effect: s 3(6).

5. Claiming compensation

Although compliance with the above procedures is a pre-requisite to any claim for compensation, it does not guarantee payment. As Ormrod LJ, in *Pelosi*, explained: "In my judgement s 1 of the 1927 Act clearly distinguishes between the right to compensation and the right to payment." The tenant must overcome additional hurdles before compensation will actually be paid.

A further notice must be served on the landlord towards the end of the lease, and the tenant must establish, as fact, that the improvement has satisfied the requirements of s 1 (above), and in particular has added to the letting value of the property. Accordingly, the "right to claim" may be earned at an early stage by taking the appropriate procedural steps, but the "right to payment" remains throughout defeasible if the landlord can show that there is no enhancement of rental value (for example, by proving that the premises are to be substantially altered or demolished, or that the improvement has worn out): s 1(2).

Compensation is payable only when the tenant has quit the holding at the expiration of the lease: *Smith* v *Metropolitan Properties Co Ltd* (1932). A tenant who leaves in mid-term (for example, by surrender, assignment or forfeiture) or stays on as a trespasser is, therefore, not entitled to compensation. It will often be of importance to the tenant to know whether the right to payment exists before the expiry of the lease. Accordingly, the court is empowered to consider this issue (including, if appropriate, the amount of compensation) in advance of the tenant quitting the premises (*Pelosi*). If difficulties exist as to quantum, the court can adjourn that issue until a convenient date.

Under s 1(1), the tenant's claim for compensation must be made in the prescribed manner and served within the strict time limits set out in s 47 Landlord and Tenant Act 1954. No particular form of notice of claim is required, but if an important matter is omitted (for example, the amount of compensation claimed) the notice is likely to be invalidated: *British & Colonial Furniture Co Ltd* v *William McIlroy Ltd* (1952).

The claim must be in writing and signed by the claimant (or agent). It should provide the following information:

(a) the names and addresses of the claimant and the immediate landlord;

(b) the holding to which it refers and the trade or business carried on thereat;

(c) the nature of the claim;

(d) the cost and other particulars of the improvement (including its completion date);

(e) the amount of compensation claimed.

6. Time limits

The notice of claim must be served within the various time limits prescribed in s 47 of the 1954 Act. The time limits vary according to how the lease was terminated and cannot be extended by the court: *Donegal Tweed Co Ltd* v *Stephenson* (1928). These are as follows:

(a) where the tenancy expires by effluxion of time. The notice must be served within a period not earlier than six nor later than three months before the expiry date (s 47(2));

(b) where the lease is ended by the service of a notice to quit or s 25 notice. The claim must be made within the period of three months beginning on the date when the notice was served (s 47(1));

(c) where the tenancy is terminated by forfeiture or re-entry. The notice of claim must be served within the three months commencing with the effective date of the possession order (or the date on which it ceases to be the subject of appeal, if later); or, if there is no order, on actual re-entry (s 47(3));

(d) where the tenancy is terminated by the tenant's s 26 request for a new tenancy under the 1954 Act. The claim must be made within three months starting from the date on which the landlord gives his counternotice, or if none, the latest date on which such counternotice could have been given: s 47(1).

The Working Paper recommended the simplification of these diverse time conditions and concluded that a claim should be made only during the three months following the end of the tenancy (para 6.55), and that no earlier or later applications should be entertained.

Compensation for tenant's improvements

7. Quantum

In the absence of agreement, all issues of quantum are to be determined by the court: s 1(3). The tenant will have stated in his application the amount claimed. A statutory formula is, however, employed to calculate compensation so as to ensure that the compensation payable mirrors the actual value of the improvement to the landlord: s 1. As the value is calculated as at the end of the lease, inflation may make compensation an onerous obligation for the landlord. According to the Working Paper, there should be no change to the existing method of evaluation (para 6.35). This formula provides that the compensation payable cannot exceed:

(a) the net addition to the value of the holding as a whole which may be determined to be the direct result of the improvement. This is the benefit of the improvement less any detriment; or

(b) the reasonable cost of carrying out an identical improvement at the end of the tenancy: s 1(1). Unless the tenant is under a covenant to repair or to meet the cost of repair, this takes into account a deduction equivalent to the cost (if any) of putting the improvement into a reasonable state of repair.

Within this calculation, the court is directed to discount any benefits which the tenant (or predecessors in title) may have received from the landlord (or predecessors in title) in consideration of the improvement: s 2(3). Normally, such benefit will form part of a contractual obligation on the tenant to carry out the improvement and preclude the operation of the compensation scheme: s 2(1)(b). Nevertheless, in cases where the provisions apply, the benefit must be expressly or implicitly referable to the improvement and cannot arise from any source other than the landlord or predecessor. An example of where this discount might arise is where the landlord has gratuitously contributed to the tenant's expenditure or, in some cases, where the landlord has forgone or reduced rent as a result. The word "consideration" in s 2(3) should not be interpreted in any technical sense; it seemingly requires only that there be some nexus between the benefit and the improvement.

The claim may also be refused or reduced where the landlord intends to demolish or alter the premises, or establish a different business user, at the end of the lease. Much turns on the time scale for the proposed change. This is appropriate because the measure of compensation is geared to the value of the improvement to the landlord. The tenant has the safeguard, however, that if the landlord fails to translate the intention into reality within such time as fixed by the court (s 1(3)), a fresh application may (and, usually, will) be entertained.

Other factors may produce a depressive effect. The landlord can deduct any sum outstanding from the tenant under the lease. Rent arrears, or an agreed claim for lack of repair or dilapidations, for example, can be set-off against the compensation payable: s 11(1). The tenant can, in turn, deduct any amounts owed to the landlord from any compensation payable by the landlord: s 11(2).

The satisfaction of a claim for compensation for a tenant's improvement is amongst the purposes for which a tenant for life, statutory owner, trustee for sale or personal representative may raise money under the Settled Land Act 1925. Capital money can also be applied in the payment for improvements executed by the landlord, and costs and charges incurred pursuant to the Act: s 13.

The landlord, where appropriate, may obtain an order from the Secretary of State charging the premises (in whole or in part) with repayment of any sums paid by way of compensation and/or costs (s 12 and Sch 1). The order is registrable as a Class A land charge in the unregistered system and is capable of being protected as a minor interest as regards registered land.

8. Reclaiming compensation from a superior landlord

Where a chain of tenancies exists in relation to the holding, the tenant will make the claim for compensation against the immediate landlord (the mesne landlord) as defined in s 25(1). The mesne landlord can recover from a landlord immediately superior in title provided that copies of all documentation relating to the tenant's compensation claim and payment are served upon the superior landlord within the time limits (see above): s 8(1). The indemnity becomes payable at the expiry of the mesne landlord's tenancy, and the claim should be made at least two months before the expiration of that lease: s 8(1). It remains necessary, however, to show that the superior landlord obtains a reversionary benefit from the improvement: s 1.

Special provisions apply where there has been a change of ownership of the reversion; these are contained in s 23(2) which states that, unless and until a tenant has received notice of the change and notice of the name and address of the new landlord, the original landlord will be deemed to be qualified so as to accept service or delivery of documents.

9. Landlord's tactics

Irrespective of the safeguards and restrictions contained in the Act, a landlord can be placed in a vulnerable position as against a tenant committed to the carrying out of improvements. In *National Electric Theatres* v *Hudgell*, Morton J provided an illustration of how "grave hardship" for the landlord can arise:

> "For instance, an investor might invest a small sum in a comparatively modest property, which was subject to a lease, and the lessee might pull down this small property and erect, for example, an expensive block of shops with flats over it and thereby impose upon the landlord against his will an obligation to pay a very substantial sum by way of compensation at the end of the lease."

Nevertheless, as Morton J realised, the Act has to be applied as it stands and the courts can do nothing to assist the landlord.

There are, however, two methods which a landlord can adopt by way of self-protection and as a means of sidestepping the compensation provisions. The first is to take a covenant from the tenant requiring reinstatement, at the end of the lease, on the landlord's demand. If reinstatement occurs, then there is no addition to the letting value of the property and no compensation becomes payable. The second concentrates on s 2(1)(b) of the Act which excludes from compensation an improvement carried out under a contractual obligation. This provides that, where the lease obliges the tenant to carry out the improvement (a term commonly found in building leases), compensation for that improvement is unavailable. A similar end can be achieved where the landlord issues a licence for alterations to be made by the tenant (ie, under a qualified covenant or on the relaxation of an absolute covenant). Provided that the landlord's consent obliges (as opposed to permits) the tenant to carry out the improvement; is unconditional and immediate; and, crucially, is supported by valuable consideration, the compensation provisions will not apply. Consideration can be inserted into the licence itself or may be found in the relaxation of an absolute (but not, it is thought, a qualified) covenant.

It should not be overlooked that landlords are compelled to take such indirect routes because, since 10 December 1953, it has not been possible expressly to contract out of the compensation provisions (s 49 Landlord and Tenant Act 1954). Nevertheless avoidance, it is feared, is widespread and is simple to achieve. The Working Paper thought that control of such measures should be tightened (para 6.48) and recommended specifically that reinstatement provisions should be limited in their effect (para 6.49).

10. Recommendations for abolition

It has been assumed, for well over half a century, by Parliament, and in a wide-ranging series of official reports, judicial decisions and academic writings, that compensation for improvements and security of tenure protect two distinct values. For over thirty-five years they have co-existed on the statute book, presumably upon the basis that each has its separate role to play. This understanding has now, for the first time, met with serious challenge. It is the claim of the Law Commission (No 178) that: "The statute book would be simplified by deleting a complex procedure, of little practical use" (para 3.21).

The Law Commission bases its abolitionist stance upon the ground that the compensation provisions are seldom invoked and are thereby devoid of practical worth.

Several causes are identified in the Report as being responsible for the compensation provisions falling into some disuse:

(a) the impact of the Landlord and Tenant Act 1954. The argument here is that the general availability of security of tenure has undermined any need for a right to compensation for improvements. Although this view has a ring of truth, it overlooks the position of tenants who either cannot or do not seek a new tenancy;

(b) the complexity of the claims procedure. There can be no doubt that the elaborate nature of the procedure involved in making a claim for compensation contributes to the unpopularity of the scheme. This, however, seems a ground for reform and not abolition;

(c) their unsuitability to retail properties. This inappropriateness is alleged to be due to the slow and cumbersome nature of the claims procedure, but this is merely a repetition of paragraph (b) above and adds little to the abolitionist case. Curiously, the Report admits that the British Retailers' Association is in favour of retaining the scheme. Presumably, the retailers themselves see some merit in the right to compensation;

(d) the ease with which the compensation scheme can be side-stepped by landlords. The Law Commission considered avoidance to be widespread and drew the conclusion that this evidenced the willingness of landlords and tenants to do without the scheme. This line of reasoning is hard to support. The tendency of landlords to use avoidance measures indicates that there is still potential value for tenants in the statutory right. As there is little scope in landlord and tenant law for the courts to consider the inequality of bargaining power, it must be left for Parliament to tighten any loop-holes in the existing system;

(e) the short life-span of improvements. Although a tenant will often calculate the value of an improvement in the context of the remaining years of the lease and, accordingly, write off the expenditure over the period, such sensible accounting cannot always be relied upon. Improvements can be forced on a tenant by way of a statutory obligation; there is no certainty that there will be a renewal under the Landlord and Tenant Act 1954; and a tenant may wish to make a long-term improvement (redevelopment, for example). All of these factors can distort the balance sheet approach and leave a residual role for the compensation scheme;

(f) ignorance of the scheme. This ground, rather than being an argument in support of the abolition of the statutory right, suggests that the scheme should be more available and accessible. In addition, the prevalence of landlord's avoidance tactics clearly shows that the landlords are certainly not unaware of the existence of the compensation provisions.

Although the weight of a Law Commission recommendation is undeniable, its judgements are not beyond question. It is to be hoped that this recommendation is never adopted and that the potentially valuable right to compensation is retained (with reform) on the statute book.

Appendices

Contents

	page
Appendix A – Statutory sources	171
1. Part I Landlord and Tenant Act 1927	171
2. Parts II, III and IV Landlord and Tenant Act 1954	178
Appendix B – Forms	213
Table of contents	213

Appendix A: Statutory sources

1. Part I Landlord and Tenant Act 1927

Tenant's right to compensation for improvements
s.1. **1.** Subject to the provisions of this Part of this Act, a tenant of a holding to which this Part of this Act applies shall, if a claim for the purpose is made in the prescribed manner and within the time limited by section 47 of the Landlord and Tenant Act 1954 be entitled, at the termination of the tenancy, on quitting his holding, to be paid by his landlord compensation in respect of any improvement (including the erection of any building) on his holding made by him or his predecessors in title, not being a trade or other fixture which the tenant is by law entitled to remove, which at the termination of the tenancy adds to the letting value of the holding.

Providing that the sum to be paid as compensation for any improvement shall not exceed –

(a) the net addition to the value of the holding as a whole which may be determined to be the direct result of the improvement; or

(b) the reasonable cost of carrying out the improvement of the termination of the tenancy, subject to a deduction of an amount equal to the cost (if any) of putting the works constituting the improvement into a reasonable state of repair, except so far as such cost is covered by the liability of the tenant under any covenant or agreement as to the repair of the premises.

2. In determining the amount of such net addition as aforesaid, regard shall be had to the purposes for which it is intended that the premises shall be used after the termination of the tenancy, and if it is shown that it is intended to demolish or to make structural alteration in the premises or any part thereof or to use the premises for a different purpose, regard shall be had to the effect of such demolition, alteration or change of user on the additional value attributable to the improvement, and to the length of time likely to elapse between the termination of the tenancy and the demolition, alteration or change of user.

3. In the absence of agreement between the parties, all questions as to the right to compensation under this section, or as to the amount thereof, shall be determined by the tribunal hereinafter mentioned, and if the tribunal determines that, on account of the intention to demolish or alter or to change the user of the premises, no compensation or a reduced amount of compensation shall be paid, the tribunal may authorise a further application for compensation to be made by the tenant if effect is not given to the intention within such time as may be fixed by the tribunal.

Limitation on tenant's right to compensation
[NB See amendments in Part III of Landlord & Tenant Act 1934 s.48]
s.2. 1. A tenant shall not be entitled to compensation under this Part of this Act —

(a) in respect of any improvement made before the commencement of this Act; or

(b) in respect of any improvement made in pursuance of a statutory obligation, or of any improvement which the tenant or his predecessors in title were under an obligation to make in pursuance of a contract entered into, whether before or after the passing of this Act, for valuable consideration, including a building lease; or

(c) in respect of an improvement made less than three years before the termination of the tenancy; or

(d) if within two months after the making of the claim under section 1, subsection (1), of this Act the landlord serves on the tenant notice that he is willing and able to grant to the tenant, or obtain the grant to him of, a renewal of the tenancy at such rent and for such term as, failing agreement, the tribunal may consider reasonable; and, where such a notice is so served and the tenant does not within one month from the service of the notice send to the landlord an acceptance in writing of the offer, the tenant shall be deemed to have declined the offer.

2. Where an offer of the renewal of a tenancy by the landlord under this section is accepted by the tenant, the rent fixed by the tribunal shall be the rent which in the opinion of the tribunal a willing lessee other than the tenant would agree to give and a willing lessor would agree to accept for the premises, having regard to the terms of the lease, but irrespective of the value attributable to the improvement in respect of which compensation would have been payable.

3. The tribunal in determining the compensation for an improvement shall in reduction of the tenant's claim take into consideration any benefits which the tenant or his predecessors in title may have received from the landlord or his predecessor in title in consideration expressly or impliedly of the improvement.

Landlord's right to object
s.3. 1. Where a tenant of a holding to which this Part of this Act applies proposes to make an improvement on his holding, he shall serve on his landlord notice of his intention to make such improvement, together with a specification and plan showing the proposed improvement and the part of the existing premises affected thereby, and if the landlord, within three months after the service of the notice, serves on the tenant notice of objection, the tenant may, in the prescribed manner, apply to the tribunal, and the tribunal may, after ascertaining that notice of such intention has been served upon any superior landlords interested and after giving such persons an opportunity of being heard, if satisfied that the improvement —

Appendix A

    (a) is of such a nature as to be calculated to add to the letting value of the holding at the termination of the tenancy; and

    (b) is reasonable and suitable to the character thereof; and

    (c) will not diminish the value of any other property belonging to the same landlord, or to any superior landlord from whom the immediate landlord of the tenant directly or indirectly holds;

and after making such modifications (if any) in the specification or plan as the tribunal thinks fit, or imposing such other conditions as the tribunal may think reasonable, certify in the prescribed manner that the improvement is a proper improvement.

Provided that, if the landlord proves that he has offered to execute the improvement himself in consideration of a reasonable increase of rent, or of such increase of rent as the tribunal may determine, the tribunal shall not give a certificate under this section unless it is subsequently shown to the satisfaction of the tribunal that the landlord has failed to carry out his undertaking.

2. In considering whether the improvement is reasonable and suitable to the character of the holding, the tribunal shall have regard to any evidence brought before it by the landlord or any superior landlord (but not any other person) that the improvement is calculated to injure the amenity or convenience of the neighbourhood.

3. The tenant shall, at the request of any superior landlord or at the request of the tribunal, supply such copies of the plans and specifications of the proposed improvement as may be required.

4. Where no such notice of objection as aforesaid to a proposed improvement has been served within the time allowed by this section, or where the tribunal has certified an improvement to be a proper improvement, it shall be lawful for the tenant as against the immediate and any superior landlord to execute the improvement according to the plan and specification served on the landlord, or according to such plan and specification as modified by the tribunal or by agreement between the tenant and the landlord or landlords affected, anything in any lease of the premises to the contrary notwithstanding.

Provided that nothing in this subsection shall authorise a tenant to execute an improvement in contravention of any restriction created or imposed –

    (a) for naval, military or air force purposes;

    (b) for civil aviation purposes under the powers of the Air Navigation Act 1920;

    (c) for securing any rights of the public over the foreshore or bed of the sea.

5. A tenant shall not be entitled to claim compensation under this Part of this Act in respect of any improvement unless he has, or his predecessors in title have, served notice of the proposal to make the improvement under this section, and (in case the landlord has served notice of objection thereto) the improvement has been certified by the tribunal to be a proper improvement and the tenant has complied with the conditions, if any, imposed by the tribunal, nor unless the improvement is completed within such time after the service on the landlord of the notice of the proposed improvement as may be agreed between the tenant and the landlord or may be fixed by the tribunal, and where proceedings have been taken before the tribunal, the tribunal may defer making any order as to costs until the expiration of the time so fixed for the completion of the improvement.

6. Where a tenant has executed an improvement of which he has served notice in accordance with this section and with respect to which either no notice of objection has been served by the landlord or a certificate that it is a proper improvement has been obtained from the tribunal, the tenant may require the landlord to furnish to him a certificate that the improvement has been duly executed; and if the landlord refuses or fails within one month after the service of the requisition to do so, the tenant may apply to the tribunal who, if satisfied that the improvement has been duly executed, shall give a certificate to that effect.

Where the landlord furnishes such a certificate, the tenant shall be liable to pay any reasonable expenses incurred for the purpose by the landlord, and if any question arises as to the reasonableness of such expenses, it shall be determined by the tribunal.

Rights of mesne landlords
s.8. **1.** Where, in the case of any holding, there are several persons standing in the relation to each other of lessor and lessee, the following provisions shall apply: –

> Any mesne landlord who has paid or is liable to pay compensation under this Part of this Act shall, at the end of his term, be entitled to compensation from his immediate landlord in like manner and on the same conditions as if he had himself made the improvement ... in question, except that it shall be sufficient if the claim for compensation is made at least two months before the expiration of his term.

A mesne landlord shall not be entitled to make a claim under this section unless he has, within the time and in the manner prescribed, served on his immediate superior landlord copies of all documents relating to proposed improvements and claims which have been sent to him in pursuance of this Part of this Act.

Where such copies are so served, the said superior landlord shall have, in addition to the mesne landlord, the powers conferred by or in pursuance of this Part of this Act in like manner as if he were the immediate landlord of the occupying tenant, and shall, in the manner and to the extent prescribed, be at liberty to appear before the tribunal and shall be bound by the proceedings.

2. In this section, references to a landlord shall include references to his predecessors in title.

Restriction on contracting out
s.9 This Part of this Act shall apply notwithstanding any contract to the contrary, being a contract made at any time after the eighth day of February, nineteen hundred and twenty-seven.

Appendix A

Right of entry
s.10 The landlord of a holding to which this Part of this Act applies, or any person authorised by him may at all reasonable times enter on the holding or any part of it, for the purposes of executing any improvement he has undertaken to execute and of making any inspection of the premises which may reasonably be required for the purposes of this Part of this Act.

The right to make deductions
s.11. 1. Out of any money payable to a tenant by way of compensation under this Part of this Act, the landlord shall be entitled to deduct any sum due to him from the tenant under or in respect of the tenancy.

2. Out of any money due to the landlord from the tenant under or in respect of the tenancy, the tenant shall be entitled to deduct any sum payable to him by the landlord by way of compensation under this Part of this Act.

Application of 13 and 14 GEO 5, c.9 s.20
s.12 Section 20 of the Agricultural Holdings Act 1923 (which relates to charges in respect of money paid for compensation), as set out and modified in the first Schedule to this Act, shall apply to the case of money paid for compensation under this Part of the Act, including any proper costs, charges, or expenses incurred by a landlord in opposing any proposal by a tenant to execute an improvement, or in contesting a claim for compensation, and to money expended by a landlord in executing an improvement the notice of a proposal to execute which has been served on him by a tenant under this Part of this Act.

Power to apply and raise capital money
s.13. 1. Capital money arising under the Settled Land Act 1925 (either as originally enacted or as applied in relation to trusts for sale by section 28 of the Law of Property Act 1925), or under the University and College Estates Act 1925, may be applied –

- (a) in payment as for an improvement authorised by the Act of any money expended and costs incurred by a landlord under or in pursuance of this Part of this Act in or about the execution of any improvement;
- (b) in payment of any sum due to a tenant under this Part of this Act in respect of compensation for an improvement ... and any costs, charges, and expenses incidental thereto;
- (c) in payment of the costs, charges, and expenses of opposing any proposal by a tenant to execute an improvement.

2. The satisfaction of a claim for such compensation as aforesaid shall be included amongst the purposes for which a tenant for life, statutory owner, trustee for sale, or personal representative may raise money under section 71 of the Settled Land Act 1925.

3. Where the landlord liable to pay compensation for an improvement ... is a tenant for life or in a fiduciary position, he may require the sum payable as compensation and any costs, charges, and expenses incidental thereto, to be paid out of any capital money held on the same trusts as the settled land.

In this subsection "capital money" includes any personal estate held on the same trusts as the land, and "settled land" includes land held on trust for sale or vested in a personal representative.

Power to sell or grant leases notwithstanding restrictions
s.14 Where the powers of a landlord to sell or grant leases are subject to any statutory or other restrictions, he shall, notwithstanding any such restrictions or any rule of law to the contrary, be entitled to offer to sell or grant any such reversion or lease as would under this Part of this Act relieve him from liability to pay compensation thereunder, and to convey and grant the same, and to execute any lease which he may be ordered to grant under this Part of this Act.

Provisions as to reversionary leases
s.15. **1.** Where the amount which a landlord is liable to pay as compensation for an improvement under this Part of this Act has been determined by agreement or by an award of the tribunal, and the landlord had before the passing of this Act granted or agreed to grant a reversionary lease commencing on or after the termination of the then existing tenancy, the rent payable under the reversionary lease shall, if the tribunal so directs, be increased by such amount as, failing agreement, may be determined by the tribunal having regard to the addition to the letting value of the holding attributable to the improvement.

Provided that no such increase shall be permissible unless the landlord has served or caused to be served on the reversionary lessee copies of all documents relating to the improvement when proposed which were sent to the landlord in pursuance of this Part of this Act.

2. The reversionary lessee shall have the same right of objection to the proposed improvement and of appearing and being heard at any proceedings before the tribunal relative to the proposed improvement as if he were a superior landlord, and if the amount of compensation for the improvement is determined by the tribunal, any question as to the increase of rent under the reversionary lease shall, where practicable, be settled in the course of the same proceedings.

3. ...

Landlord's right to reimbursement of increased taxes, rates or insurance premiums
s.16 Where the landlord is liable to pay any rates (including water rates) in respect of any premises comprised in a holding, or has undertaken to pay the premiums on any fire insurance policy on any such premises, and in consequence of any improvement executed by the tenant on the premises under this Act the assessment of the premises or the rate of premium on the policy is increased, the tenant shall be liable to pay to the landlord sums equal to the amount by which —

(a) the rates payable by the landlord are increased by reason of the increase of such assessment;

(b) the fire premium payable by the landlord is increased by reason of the increase in the rate of premium;

Appendix A

and the sums so payable by the tenant shall be deemed to be in the nature of rent and shall be recoverable as such from the tenant.

Holdings to which Part I applies
s.17. **1.** The holdings to which this Part of this Act applies are any premises held under a lease, other than a mining lease, made whether before or after the commencement of this Act, and used wholly or partly for carrying on thereat any trade or business, and not being agricultural holdings within the meaning of the Agricultural Holdings Act 1986.

2. This Part of this Act shall not apply to any holding let to a tenant as the holder of any office, appointment or employment, from the landlord, and continuing so long as the tenant holds such office, appointment or employment, but in the case of a tenancy created after the commencement of this Act, only if the contract is in writing and expresses the purpose for which the tenancy is created.

3. For the purposes of this section, premises shall not be deemed to be premises used for carrying on thereat a trade or business –
- (a) by reason of their being used for the purpose of carrying on thereat any profession;
- (b) by reason that the tenant thereof carries on the business of subletting the premises as residential flats, whether or not the provision of meals or any other service for the occupants of the flats is undertaken by the tenant.

Provided that, so far as this Part of this Act relates to improvements, premises regularly used for carrying on a profession shall be deemed to be premises used for carrying on a trade or business.

4. In the case of premises used partly for purposes of a trade or business and partly for other purposes, this Part of this Act shall apply to improvements only if and so far as they are improvements in relation to the trade or business.

© *Crown copyright*

2. Parts II, III and IV Landlord and Tenant Act 1954

PART II
Security of tenure for business, professional and other tenants

Tenancies to which Part II applies
s.23. **1.** Subject to the provisions of this Act, this Part of this Act applies to any tenancy where the property comprised in the tenancy is or includes premises which are occupied by the tenant and are so occupied for the purposes of a business carried on by him or for those and other purposes.

2. In this Part of this Act the expression "business" includes a trade, profession or employment and includes any activity carried on by a body of persons, whether corporate or unincorporate.

3. In the following provisions of this Part of this Act the expression "the holding" in relation to a tenancy to which this Part of the Act applies, means the property comprised in the tenancy, there being excluded any part thereof which is occupied neither by the tenant nor by a person employed by the tenant and so employed for the purposes of a business by reason of which the tenancy is one to which this Part of this Act applies.

4. Where the tenant is carrying on a business, in all or any part of the property comprised in a tenancy, in breach of a prohibition (however expressed) of use for business purposes which subsists under the terms of the tenancy and extends to the whole of that property, this Part of this Act shall not apply to the tenancy unless the immediate landlord or his predecessor in title has consented to the breach or the immediate landlord has acquiesced therein.

In this subsection the reference to a prohibition of use for business purposes does not include a prohibition of use for the purposes of a specified business, or of use for purposes of any but a specified business, but save as aforesaid includes a prohibition of use for the purposes of some one or more only of the classes of business specified in the definition of that expression in subsection (2) of this section.

Continuation of tenancies to which Part II applies and grant of new tenancies.
s.24. **1.** A tenancy to which this Part of this Act applies shall not come to an end unless terminated in accordance with the provisions of this Part of

Appendix A

this Act; and, subject to the provisions of section 29 of this Act, the tenant under such a tenancy may apply to the court for a new tenancy –

(a) if the landlord has given notice under section 25 of this Act to terminate the tenancy, or

(b) if the tenant has made a request for a new tenancy in accordance with section 26 of this Act.

2. The last foregoing subsection shall not prevent the coming to an end of a tenancy by notice to quit given by the tenant, by surrender or forfeiture, or by the forfeiture of a superior tenancy unless –

(a) in the case of a notice to quit, the notice was given before the tenant had been in occupation in right of the tenancy for one month; or

(b) in the case of an instrument of surrender, the instrument was executed before, or was executed in pursuance of an agreement made before, the tenant had been in occupation in right of the tenancy for one month.

3. Notwithstanding anything in subsection (1) of this section –

(a) where a tenancy to which this Part of this Act applies ceases to be such a tenancy, it shall not come to an end by reason only of the cesser, but if it was granted for a term of years certain and has been continued by subsection (1) of this section then (without prejudice to the termination thereof in accordance with any terms of the tenancy) it may be terminated by not less than three nor more than six months' notice in writing given by the landlord to the tenant;

(b) where, at a time when a tenancy is not one to which this Part of the Act applies, the landlord gives notice to quit, the tenancy becomes one to which this Part of this Act applies after the giving of the notice.

Rent while tenancy continues by virtue of s.24
s.24A. 1. The landlord of a tenancy to which this Part of this Act applies may, –

(a) if he has given notice under section 25 of this Act to terminate the tenancy; or

(b) if the tenant has made a request for a new tenancy in accordance with section 26 of this Act;

apply to the court to determine a rent which it would be reasonable for the tenant to pay while the tenancy continues by virtue of section 24 of this Act, and the court may determine a rent accordingly.

2. A rent determined in proceedings under this section shall be deemed to

be the rent payable under the tenancy from the date on which the proceedings were commenced or the date specified in the landlord's notice or the tenant's request, whichever is the later.

3. In determining a rent under this section the court shall have regard to the rent payable under the terms of the tenancy, but otherwise subsections (1) and (2) of section 34 of this Act shall apply to the determination as they would apply to the determination of a rent under that section if a new tenancy from year to year of the whole of the property comprised in the tenancy were granted to the tenant by order of the court.

Termination of tenancy by the landlord
s.25. 1. The landlord may terminate a tenancy to which this Part of this Act applies by a notice given to the tenant in the prescribed form specifying the date at which the tenancy is to come to an end (hereinafter referred to as "the date of termination").

Provided that this subsection has effect subject to the provisions of Part IV of this Act as to the interim continuation of tenancies pending the disposal of applications to the court.

2. Subject to the provisions of the next following subsection, a notice under this section shall not have effect unless it is given not more than twelve nor less than six months before the date of termination specified therein.

3. In the case of a tenancy which apart from this Act could have been brought to an end by notice to quit given by the landlord –

(a) the date of termination specified in a notice under this section shall not be earlier than the earliest date on which apart from this Part of this Act the tenancy could have been brought to an end by notice to quit given by the landlord on the date of the giving of the notice under this section; and

(b) where apart from this Part of this Act more than six months' notice to quit would have been required to bring the tenancy to an end, the last foregoing subsection shall have effect with the substitution for twelve months of a period six months longer than the length of notice to quit which would have been required as aforesaid.

4. In the case of any other tenancy, a notice under this section shall not specify a date of termination earlier than the date on which apart from this Part of this Act the tenancy would have come to an end by effluxion of time.

5. A notice under this section shall not have effect unless it requires the tenant, within two months after the giving of the notice, to notify the landlord in writing whether or not, at the date of termination, the tenant will be willing to give up possession of the property comprised in the tenancy.

6. A notice under this section shall not have effect unless it states whether the landlord would oppose an application to the court under this Part of this Act for the grant of a new tenancy and, if so, also states on which of the grounds mentioned in section 30 of this Act he would do so.

Appendix A

Tenant's request for a new tenancy
s.26. 1. A tenant's request for a new tenancy may be made where the tenancy under which he holds for the time being (hereinafter referred to as "the current tenancy") is a tenancy granted for a term of years certain exceeding one year, whether or not continued by section 24 of this Act, or granted for a term of years certain and thereafter from year to year.

2. A tenant's request for a new tenancy shall be for a tenancy beginning with such date, not more than twelve nor less than six months after the making of the request, as may be specified therein.

Provided that the said date shall not be earlier than the date on which apart from this Act the current tenancy would come to an end by effluxion of time or could be brought to an end by notice to quit by the tenant.

3. A tenant's request for a new tenancy shall not have effect unless it is made by notice in the prescribed form given to the landlord and sets out the tenant's proposals as to the property to be comprised in the new tenancy (being either the whole or part of the property comprised in the current tenancy), as to the rent to be payable under the new tenancy and as to other terms of the new tenancy.

4. A tenant's request for a new tenancy shall not be made if the landlord has already given notice under the last foregoing section to terminate the current tenancy, or if the tenant has already given notice to quit or notice under the next following section; and no such notice shall be given by the landlord or the tenant after the making by the tenant of a request for a new tenancy.

5. Where the tenant makes a request for a new tenancy in accordance with the foregoing provisions of this section, the current tenancy shall, subject to the provisions of subsection (2) of section 36 of this Act and the provisions of Part IV of this Act as to the interim continuation of tenancies, terminate immediately before the date specified in the request for the beginning of the new tenancy.

6. Within two months of the making of a tenant's request for a new tenancy the landlord may give notice to the tenant that he will oppose an application to the court for the grant of a new tenancy, and any such notice shall state on which of the grounds mentioned in section 30 of this Act the landlord will oppose the application.

Termination by the tenant for fixed term
s.27. 1. Where the tenant under a tenancy to which this Part of this Act applies, being a tenancy granted for a term of years certain, gives to the immediate landlord, not later than three months before the date on which apart from this Act the tenancy would come to an end by effluxion of time, a notice in writing that the tenant does not desire the tenancy to be continued, section 24 of this Act shall not have effect in relation to the tenancy unless the notice is given before the tenant has been in occupation in right of the tenancy for one month.

2. A tenancy granted for a term of years certain which is continuing by

virtue of section 24 of this Act may be brought to an end on any quarter day by not less than three months' notice in writing given by the tenant to the immediate landlord, whether the notice is given ... after the date on which apart from this Act the tenancy would have come to an end or before that date, but not before the tenant has been in occupation in right of the tenancy for one month.

Renewal of tenancies by agreement
s.28 Where the landlord and tenant agree for the grant to the tenant of a future tenancy of the holding, or of the holding with other land, on terms and from a date specified in the agreement, the current tenancy shall continue until that date but no longer, and shall not be a tenancy to which this Part of this Act applies.

Order by court for grant of a new tenancy
s.29. **1.** Subject to the provisions of this Act, on an application under subsection (1) of section 24 of this Act for a new tenancy the court shall make an order for the grant of a tenancy comprising such property, at such rent and on such other terms, as are hereinafter provided.

2. Where such an application is made in consequence of a notice given by the landlord under section 25 of this Act, it shall not be entertained unless the tenant has duly notified the landlord that he will not be willing at the date of termination to give up possession of the property comprised in the tenancy.

3. No application under subsection (1) of section 24 of this Act shall be entertained unless it is made not less than two nor more than four months after the giving of the landlord's notice under section 25 of this Act or, as the case may be, after the making of the tenant's request for a new tenancy.

Objections by landlord to application for a new tenancy
s.30. **1.** The grounds on which a landlord may oppose an application under subsection (1) of section 24 of this Act are such of the following grounds as may be stated in the landlord's notice under section 25 of this Act or, as the case may be, under subsection (6) of section 26 thereof, that is to say:

- (a) where under the current tenancy the tenant has any obligations as respects the repair and maintenance of the holding, that the tenant ought not to be granted a new tenancy in view of the state of repair of the holding, being a state resulting from the tenant's failure to comply with the said obligations;
- (b) that the tenant ought not to be granted a new tenancy in view of his persistent delay in paying rent which has become due;
- (c) that the tenant ought not to be granted a new tenancy in view of other substantial breaches by him of his obligations under the current tenancy, or for any other reason connected with the tenant's use or management of the holding;
- (d) that the landlord has offered and is willing to provide or secure the provision of alternative accommodation for the tenant, that the terms

Appendix A

on which the alternative accommodation is available are reasonable having regard to the terms of the current tenancy and to all other relevant circumstances, and that the accommodation and the time at which it will be available are suitable for the tenant's requirements (including the requirement to preserve goodwill) having regard to the nature and class of his business and to the situation and extent of, and facilities afforded by, the holding;

(e) where the current tenancy was created by the sub-letting of part only of the property comprised in a superior tenancy and the landlord is the owner of an interest in reversion expectant on the termination of that superior tenancy, that the aggregate of the rents reasonably obtainable on separate lettings of the holding and the remainder of that property would be substantially less than the rent reasonably obtainable on a letting of that property as a whole, that on the termination of the current tenancy the landlord requires possession of the holding for the purpose of letting or otherwise disposing of the said property as a whole, and that in view thereof the tenant ought not to be granted a new tenancy;

(f) that on the termination of the current tenancy the landlord intends to demolish or reconstruct the premises comprised in the holding or a substantial part of those premises or to carry out substantial work of construction on the holding or part thereof and that he could not reasonably do so without obtaining possession of the holding;

(g) subject as hereinafter provided, that on the termination of the current tenancy the landlord intends to occupy the holding for the purposes, or partly for the purposes, of a business to be carried on by him therein, or as his residence.

2. The landlord shall not be entitled to oppose an application on the ground specified in paragraph (g) of the last foregoing subsection if the interest of the landlord, or an interest which has merged in that interest and but for the merger would be the interest of the landlord, was purchased or created after the beginning of the period of five years which ends with the termination of the current tenancy, and at all times since the purchase or creation thereof the holding has been comprised in a tenancy or successive tenancies of the description specified in subsection (1) of section 23 of this Act.

3. Where the landlord has a controlling interest in a company any business to be carried on by the company shall be treated for the purposes of subsection (1)(g) of this section as a business to be carried on by him.

For the purposes of this subsection, a person has a controlling interest in a company if and only if either –

(a) he is a member of it and able, without the consent of any other person, to appoint or remove the holders of at least a majority of the directorships; or

(b) he holds more than one-half of its equity share capital, there being disregarded any shares held by him in a fiduciary capacity or as nominee for another person;

and in this subsection "company" and "share" have the same meanings assigned to them by section 455(1) of the Companies Act 1948 and "equity share capital" the meaning assigned to it by section 154(5) of that Act.

Dismissal of application for new tenancy where landlord successfully opposes
s.31. **1.** If the landlord opposes an application under subsection (1) of section 24 of this Act on grounds on which he is entitled to oppose it in accordance with the last foregoing section and establishes any of those grounds to the satisfaction of the court, the court shall not make an order for the grant of a new tenancy.

2. Where in a case not falling within the last foregoing subsection the landlord opposes an application under the said subsection (1) on one or more of the grounds specified in paragraphs (d), (e) and (f) of subsection (1) of the last foregoing section but establishes none of those grounds to the satisfaction of the court, then if the court would have been satisfied of any of those grounds if the date of termination specified in the landlord's notice or, as the case may be, the date specified in the tenant's request for a new tenancy as the date from which the new tenancy is to begin, had been such later date as the court may determine, being a date not more than one year later than the date so specified, –

(a) the court shall make a declaration to that effect, stating of which of the said grounds the court would have been satisfied as aforesaid and specifying the date determined by the court as aforesaid, but shall not make an order for the grant of a new tenancy;

(b) if, within fourteen days after the making of the declaration, the tenant so requires the court shall make an order substituting the said date for the date specified in the said landlord's notice or tenant's request, and thereupon that notice or request shall have effect accordingly.

Grant of new tenancy in some cases where s.30(1)(f) applies
s.31A. **1.** Where the landlord opposes an application under section 24(1) of this Act on the ground specified in paragraph (f) of section 30(1) of this Act the court shall not hold that the landlord could not reasonably carry out the demolition, reconstruction or work of construction intended without obtaining possession of the holding if –

(a) the tenant agrees to the inclusion in the terms of the new tenancy of terms giving the landlord access and other facilities for carrying out the work intended and, given that access and those facilities, the landlord could reasonably carry out the work without obtaining possession of the holding and without interfering to a substantial extent or for a substantial time with the use of the holding for the purposes of the business carried on by the tenant; or

(b) the tenant is willing to accept a tenancy of an economically separable part of the holding and either paragraph (a) of this section is satisfied with respect to that part or possession of the remainder of the holding would be reasonably sufficient to enable the landlord to carry out the intended work.

2. For the purposes of subsection (1)(b) of this section a part of a holding shall be deemed to be an economically separable part if, and only if, the aggregate of the rents which, after the completion of the intended work, would be reasonably obtainable on separate lettings of that part and the remainder of the premises affected by or resulting from the work would not be substantially less than the rent which would then be reasonably obtainable on a letting of those premises as a whole.

Property to be comprised in new tenancy
s.32. 1. Subject to the following provisions of this section, an order under section 29 of this Act for the grant of a new tenancy shall be an order for the grant of a new tenancy of the holding; and in the absence of agreement between the landlord and the tenant as to the property which constitutes the holding the court shall in the order designate that property by reference to the circumstances existing at the date of the order.

1A. Where the court, by virtue of paragraph (b) of section 31A(1) of this Act, makes an order under section 29 of this Act for the grant of a new tenancy in a case where the tenant is willing to accept a tenancy of part of the holding, the order shall be an order for the grant of a new tenancy of that part only.

2. The foregoing provisions of this section shall not apply in a case where the property comprised in the current tenancy includes other property besides the holding and the landlord requires any new tenancy ordered to be granted under section 29 of this Act to be a tenancy of the whole of the property comprised in the current tenancy but in any such case –

(a) any order under the said section 29 for the grant of a new tenancy shall be an order for the grant of a new tenancy of the whole of the property comprised in the current tenancy, and

(b) reference in the following provisions of this Part of this Act to the holding shall be construed as references to the whole of that property.

3. Where the current tenancy includes rights enjoyed by the tenant in connection with the holding, those rights shall be included in a tenancy ordered to be granted under section 29 of this Act except as otherwise agreed between the landlord and the tenant or, in default of such agreement, determined by the court.

Duration of new tenancy
s.33. Where on an application under this Part of this Act the court makes an order for the grant of a new tenancy, the new tenancy shall be such tenancy as may be agreed between the landlord and the tenant, or, in default of such an agreement, shall be such a tenancy as may be determined by the court to be reasonable in all the circumstances being, if it is a tenancy for a term of years certain, a tenancy for a term not exceeding fourteen years, and shall begin on the coming to an end of the current tenancy.

Rent under new tenancy
s.34. 1. The rent payable under a tenancy granted by order of the court under this Part of this Act shall be such as may be agreed between the landlord

and the tenant or as, in default of such agreement, may be determined by the court to be that at which, having regard to the terms of the tenancy (other than those relating to rent), the holding might reasonably be expected to be let in the open market by a willing lessor, there being disregarded —

   (a) any effect on rent of the fact that the tenant has or his predecessors in title have been in occupation of the holding,
   (b) any goodwill attached to the holding by reason of the carrying on thereat of the business of the tenant (whether by him or by a predecessor of his in that business),
   (c) any effect on rent of an improvement to which this paragraph applies,
   (d) in the case of a holding comprising licensed premises, any addition to its value attributable to the licence, if it appears to the court that having regard to the terms of the current tenancy and any other relevant circumstances the benefit of the licence belongs to the tenant.

2. Paragraph (c) of the foregoing subsection applies to any improvement carried out by a person who at the time it was carried out was the tenant, but only if it was carried out otherwise than in pursuance of an obligation to his immediate landlord, and either it was carried out during the current tenancy or the following conditions are satisfied, that is to say, —

   (a) that it was completed not more than twenty-one years before the application for the new tenancy was made; and
   (b) that the holding or any part of it affected by the improvement has at all times since the completion of the improvement been comprised in tenancies of the description specified in section 23(1) of this Act; and
   (c) that at the termination of each of those tenancies the tenant did not quit.

3. Where the rent is determined by the court the court may, if it thinks fit, further determine that the terms of the tenancy shall include such provision for varying the rent as may be specified in the determination.

Other terms of the new tenancy
s.35 The terms of a tenancy granted by order of the court under this Part of this Act (other than terms as to the duration thereof and as to the rent payable thereunder) shall be such as may be agreed between the landlord and the tenant or as, in default of such agreement, may be determined by the court; and in determining those terms the court shall have regard to the terms of the current tenancy and to all relevant circumstances.

Carrying out of order for new tenancy
s.36. **1.** Where under this Part of this Act the court makes an order for the grant of a new tenancy, then unless the order is revoked under the next following subsection or the landlord and the tenant agree not to act upon the order, the landlord shall be bound to execute or make in favour of the tenant, and the tenant shall be bound to accept, a lease or agreement for

a tenancy of the holding embodying the terms agreed between the landlord and the tenant or determined by the court in accordance with the foregoing provisions of this Part of this Act; and where the landlord executes or makes such a lease or agreement the tenant shall be bound, if so required by the landlord, to execute a counterpart or duplicate thereof.

2. If the tenant, within fourteen days after the making of an order under this Part of this Act for the grant of a new tenancy, applies to the court for the revocation of the order the court shall revoke the order; and where the order is so revoked, then if it is so agreed between the landlord and the tenant or determined by the court, the current tenancy shall continue, beyond the date at which it would have come to an end apart from this subsection, for such period as may be so agreed or determined to be necessary to afford to the landlord a reasonable opportunity for reletting or otherwise disposing of the premises which would have been comprised in the new tenancy; and while the current tenancy continues by virtue of this subsection it shall not be a tenancy to which this Part of this Act applies.

3. Where an order is revoked under the last foregoing subsection any provision thereof as to payment of costs shall not cease to have effect by reason only of the revocation; but the court may, if it thinks fit, revoke or vary any such provision or, where no costs have been awarded in the proceedings for the revoked order, award such costs.

4. A lease executed or agreement made under this section, in a case where the interest of the lessor is subject to a mortgage, shall be deemed to be one authorised by section 99 of the Law of Property Act 1925 (which confers certain powers of leasing on mortgagors in possession), and subsection (13) of that section (which allows those powers to be restricted or excluded by agreement) shall not have effect in relation to such a lease or agreement.

Compensation where order for new tenancy precluded on certain grounds
s.37. 1. Where on the making of an application under section 24 of this Act the court is precluded (whether by subsection (1) or subsection (2) of section 31 of this Act) from making an order for the grant of a new tenancy by reason of any of the grounds specified in paragraphs (e), (f), and (g) of subsection (1) of section 30 of this Act and not of any grounds specified in any other paragraph of that subsection or where no other ground is specified in the landlord's notice under section 25 of this Act or, as the case may be, under section 26(6) thereof, than those specified in the said paragraphs (e), (f) and (g) and either no application under the said section 24 is made or such an application is withdrawn, then, subject to the provisions of this Act, the tenant shall be entitled on quitting the holding to recover from the landlord by way of compensation an amount determined in accordance with the following provisions of this section.

2. Subject to subsections (5A) to (5D) of this section the said amount shall be as follows, that is to say, –
    (a) where the conditions specified in the next following subsection are satisfied it shall be the product of the appropriate multiplier and twice the rateable value of the holding,

(b) in any other case it shall be the product of the appropriate multiplier and the rateable value of the holding.

3. The said conditions are –

(a) that, during the whole of the fourteen years immediately preceding the termination of the current tenancy, premises being or comprised in the holding have been occupied for the purposes of a business carried on by the occupier or for those and other purposes;

(b) that, if during those fourteen years there was a change in the occupier of the premises, the person who was the occupier immediately after the change was the successor to the business carried on by the person who was the occupier immediately before the change.

4. Where the court is precluded from making an order for the grant of a new tenancy under this Part of this Act in the circumstances mentioned in subsection (1) of this section, the court shall on the application of the tenant certify that fact.

5. For the purposes of subsection (2) of this section the rateable value of the holding shall be determined as follows –

(a) where in the valuation list in force at the date on which the landlord's notice under section 25 or, as the case may be, subsection (6) of section 26 of this Act is given a value is then shown as the annual value (as hereinafter defined) of the holding, the rateable value of the holding shall be taken to be that value;

(b) where no such value is so shown with respect to the holding but such a value or such values is or are so shown with respect to premises comprised in or comprising the holding or part of it, the rateable value of the holding shall be taken to be such value as is found by a proper apportionment or aggregation of the value or values so shown;

(c) where the rateable value of the holding cannot be ascertained in accordance with the foregoing paragraphs of this subsection, it shall be taken to be the value which, apart from any exemption from assessment to rates, would on a proper assessment be the value to be entered in the said valuation list as the annual value of the holding;

and any dispute, arising, whether in proceedings before the court or otherwise, as to the determination for those purposes of the rateable value of the holding shall be referred to the Commissioners of Inland Revenue for decision by a valuation officer.

An appeal shall lie to the Lands Tribunal from any decision of a valuation officer under this subsection, but subject thereto any such decision shall be final.

5A. If part of the holding is domestic property, as defined in section 66 of the Local Government Finance Act 1988, –

(a) the domestic property shall be disregarded in determining the rateable value of the holding under subsection (5) of this section; and

Appendix A

(b) if, on the date specified in subsection (5)(a) of this section, the tenant occupied the whole or any part of the domestic property, the amount of compensation to which he is entitled under subsection (1) of this section shall be increased by the addition of a sum equal to his reasonable expenses in removing from the domestic property.

5B. Any question as to the amount of the sum referred to in paragraph (b) of subsection (5A) of this section shall be determined by agreement between the landlord and the tenant or, in default of agreement, by the court.

5C. If the whole of the holding is domestic property, as defined in section 66 of the Local Government Finance Act 1988, for the purposes of subsection (2) of this section the rateable value of the holding shall be taken to be an amount equal to the rent at which it is estimated the holding might reasonably be expected to let from year to year if the tenant undertook to pay all usual tenant's rates and taxes and to bear the cost of the repairs and insurance and the other expenses (if any) necessary to maintain the holding in a state to command that rent.

5D. The following provisions shall have effect as regards a determination of an amount mentioned in subsection (5C) of this section –

(a) the date by reference to which such a determination is to be made is the date on which the landlord's notice under section 25 or, as the case may be, subsection (6) of section 26 of this Act is given;

(b) any dispute arising, whether in proceedings before the court or otherwise, as to such a determination shall be referred to the Commissioners of Inland Revenue for decision by a valuation officer;

(c) an appeal shall lie to the Lands Tribunal from such a decision but subject to that, such a decision shall be final.

6. The Commissioners of Inland Revenue may by statutory instrument make rules prescribing the procedure in connection with references under this section.

7. In this section –

the reference to the termination of the current tenancy is a reference to the date of termination specified in the landlord's notice under section 25 of this Act or, as the case may be, the date specified in the tenant's request for a new tenancy as the date from which the new tenancy is to begin;

the expression "annual value" means rateable value except that where the rateable value differs from the net annual value the said expression means net annual value;

the expression "valuation officer" means any officer of the Commissioners of Inland Revenue for the time being authorised by a certificate of the Commissioners to act in relation to a valuation list.

8. In subsection (2) of this section "the appropriate multiplier" means such multiplier as the Secretary of State may by order made by statutory instrument prescribe and different multipliers may be so prescribed in relation to different cases.

9. A statutory instrument containing an order under subsection (8) of this section shall be subject to annulment in pursuance of a resolution of either House of Parliament.

Restriction on agreement excluding provisions of Part II
s.38. 1. Any agreement relating to a tenancy to which this Part of this Act applies (whether contained in the instrument creating the tenancy or not) shall be void except as provided by subsection (4) of this section in so far as it purports to preclude the tenant from making an application or request under this Part of this Act or provides for the termination or the surrender of the tenancy in the event of his making such an application or request or for the imposition of any penalty or disability on the tenant in that event.

2. Where —
   (a) during the whole of the five years immediately preceding the date on which the tenant under a tenancy to which this Part of this Act applies is to quit the holding, premises being or comprised in the holding have been occupied for the purposes of a business carried on by the occupier or for those and other purposes, and
   (b) if during those five years there was a change in the occupier of the premises, the person who was the occupier immediately after the change was the successor to the business carried on by the person who was the occupier immediately before the change,
any agreement (whether contained in the instrument creating the tenancy or not and whether made before or after the termination of that tenancy) which purports to exclude or reduce compensation under the last foregoing section shall to that extent be void, so however that this subsection shall not affect any agreement as to the amount of any such compensation which is made after the right to compensation has accrued.

3. In a case not falling within the last foregoing subsection the right to compensation conferred by the last foregoing section may be excluded or modified by agreement.

4. The court may —
   (a) on the joint application of the persons who will be the landlord and the tenant in relation to a tenancy to be granted for a term of years certain which will be a tenancy to which this Part of this Act applies, authorise an agreement excluding in relation to that tenancy the provisions of sections 24 to 28 of this Act; and
   (b) on the joint application of the persons who are the landlord and the tenant in relation to a tenancy to which this Part of this Act applies, authorise an agreement for the surrender of the tenancy on such date or in such circumstances as may be specified in the agreement and on such terms (if any) as may be so specified;
if the agreement is contained in or endorsed on the instrument creating the

tenancy or such other instrument as the court may specify; and an agreement contained in or endorsed on an instrument in pursuance of an authorisation given under the subsection shall be valid notwithstanding anything in the preceding provisions of this section.

Saving for compulsory acquisitions
s.39. **2.** If the amount of the compensation which would have been payable under section 37 of this Act if the tenancy had come to an end in the circumstances giving rise to compensation under that section and the date at which the acquiring authority obtained possession had been the termination of the current tenancy exceeds the amount of the compensation payable under section 121 of the Lands Clauses Consolidation Act 1845 or section 20 of the Compulsory Purchase Act 1965 in the case of a tenancy to which this Part of this Act applies, that compensation shall be increased by the amount of the excess.

3. Nothing in section 24 of this Act shall affect the operation of the said section 121.

Duty of tenants and landlords of premises to give information to each other
s.40. **1.** Where any person having an interest in any business premises, being an interest in reversion expectant (whether immediately or not) on a tenancy of those premises, serves on the tenant a notice in the prescribed form requiring him to do so, it shall be the duty of the tenant to notify that person in writing within one month of the service of the notice –

(a) whether he occupies the premises or any part thereof wholly or partly for the purposes of a business carried on by him, and

(b) whether his tenancy has effect subject to any sub-tenancy on which his tenancy is immediately expectant and, if so, what premises are comprised in the sub-tenancy, for what term it has effect (or, if it is terminable by notice by what notice it can be terminated), what is the rent payable thereunder, who is the sub-tenant, and (to the best of his knowledge and belief) whether the sub-tenant is in occupation of the premises or of part of the premises comprised in the sub-tenancy and, if not, what is the sub-tenant's address.

2. Where the tenant of any business premises, being a tenant under such a tenancy as is mentioned in subsection (1) of section 26 of this Act, serves on any of the persons mentioned in the next following subsection a notice in the prescribed form requiring him to do so, it shall be the duty of that person to notify the tenant in writing within one month after the service of the notice –

(a) whether he is the owner of the fee simple in respect of those premises or any part thereof or the mortgagee in possession of such an owner and, if not,

(b) (to the best of his knowledge and belief) the name and address of the person who is his or, as the case may be, his mortgagor's immediate landlord in respect of those premises or of the part in respect of which he or his mortgagor is not the owner in fee simple, for what term his or his mortgagor's tenancy thereof has effect and what is the earliest date (if any) at which that tenancy is terminable by notice to quit given by the landlord.

3. The persons referred to in the last foregoing subsection are, in relation to the tenant of any business premises, −

(a) any person having an interest in the premises, being an interest in reversion expectant (whether immediately or not) on the tenant's, and

(b) any person being a mortgagee in possession in respect of such an interest in reversion as is mentioned in paragraph (a) of this subsection;

and the information which any such person as is mentioned in paragraph (a) of this subsection is required to give under the last foregoing subsection shall include information whether there is a mortgagee in possession of his interest in the premises and, if so, what is the name and address of the mortgagee.

4. The foregoing provisions of this section shall not apply to a notice served by or on the tenant more than two years before the date on which apart from this Act his tenancy would come to an end by effluxion of time or could be brought to an end by notice to quit given by the landlord.

5. In this section −

the expression "business premises" means premises used wholly or partly for the purposes of a business;

the expression "mortgagee in possession" includes a receiver appointed by the mortgagee or by the court who is in receipt of the rents and profits, and the expression "his mortgagor" shall be construed accordingly;

the expression "sub-tenant" includes a person retaining possession of any premises by virtue of the Rent Act 1977 after the coming to an end of a subtenancy, and the expression "sub-tenancy" includes a right so to retain possession.

Trusts

s.41. **1.** Where a tenancy is held on trust, occupation by all or any of the beneficiaries under the trust, and the carrying on of a business by all or any of the beneficiaries, shall be treated for the purposes of section 23 of this Act as equivalent to occupation or the carrying on of a business by the tenant; and in relation to a tenancy to which this Part of this Act applies by virtue of the foregoing provisions of this subsection −

(a) references (however expressed) in this Part of this Act and in the Ninth Schedule to this Act to the business or, to the carrying on of business, use, occupation or enjoyment by, the tenant shall be construed as including references to the business of, or to carrying on of business, use, occupation or enjoyment by, the beneficiaries or beneficiary;

(b) the reference in paragraph (d) of subsection (1) of section 34 of this Act to the tenant shall be construed as including the beneficiaries or beneficiary; and

Appendix A

(c) a change in the persons of the trustees shall not be treated as a change in the person of the tenant.

2. Where the landlord's interest is held on trust the references in paragraph (g) of subsection (1) of section 30 of this Act to the landlord shall be construed as including references to the beneficiaries under the trust or any of them; but, except in the case of a trust arising under a will or on the intestacy of any person, the reference in subsection (2) of that section to the creation of the interest therein mentioned shall be construed as including the creation of the trust.

Partnerships
s.41A. 1. The following provisions of this section apply where –

(a) a tenancy is held jointly by two or more persons (in this section referred to as the joint tenants); and
(b) the property comprised in the tenancy is or includes premises occupied for the purposes of a business; and
(c) the business (or some other business) was at some time during the existence of the tenancy carried on in partnership by all the persons who were then the joint tenants or by those and other persons and the joint tenants' interest in the premises was then partnership property; and
(d) the business is carried on (whether alone or in partnership with other persons) by one or some only of the joint tenants and no part of the property comprised in the tenancy is occupied, in right of the tenancy, for the purposes of a business carried on (whether alone or in partnership with other persons) by the other or others.

2. In the following provisions of this section those of the joint tenants who for the time being carry on the business are referred to as the business tenants and the others as the other joint tenants.

3. Any notice given by the business tenants which, had it been given by all the joint tenants, would have been –

(a) a tenant's request for a new tenancy made in accordance with section 26 of this Act; or
(b) a notice under subsection (1) or subsection (2) of section 27 of this Act;

shall be treated as such if it states that it is given by virtue of this section and sets out the facts by virtue of which the persons giving it are the business tenants; and references in those sections and in section 24A of this Act to the tenant shall be construed accordingly.

4. A notice given by the landlord to the business tenants which, had it been given to all the joint tenants, would have been a notice under section 25 of this Act shall be treated as such a notice, and references in that section to the tenant shall be construed accordingly.

5. An application under section 24(1) of this Act for a new tenancy may,

193

instead of being made by all the joint tenants, be made by the business tenants alone; and where it is so made –

> (a) this Part of this Act shall have effect, in relation to it, as if the references therein to the tenant included references to the business tenants alone; and
>
> (b) the business tenants shall be liable, to the exclusion of the other joint tenants, for the payment of rent and the discharge of any other obligation under the current tenancy for any rental period beginning after the date specified in the landlord's notice under section 25 of this Act or, as the case may be, beginning on or after the date specified in their request for a new tenancy.

6. Where the court makes an order under section 29(1) of this Act for the grant of a new tenancy on an application made by the business tenants it may order the grant to be made to them or to them jointly with the persons carrying on the business in partnership with them, and may order the grant to be made subject to the satisfaction, within a time specified by the order, of such conditions as to guarantors, sureties or otherwise as appear to the court equitable, having regard to the omission of the other joint tenants from the persons who will be the tenant under the new tenancy.

7. The business tenants shall be entitled to recover any amount payable by way of compensation under section 37 or section 59 of this Act.

Groups of companies
s.42. 1. For the purposes of this section two bodies corporate shall be taken to be members of a group if and only if one is a subsidiary of the other or both are subsidiaries of a third body corporate.

In this subsection "subsidiary" has the same meaning as is assigned to it for the purposes of the Companies Act 1985 by section 736 of that Act.

2. Where a tenancy is held by a member of a group, occupation by another member of the group, and the carrying on of a business by another member of the group, shall be treated for the purposes of section 23 of this Act as equivalent to occupation or the carrying on of a business by the member of the group holding the tenancy; and in relation to a tenancy to which this Part of this Act applies by virtue of the foregoing provisions of this subsection –

> (a) references (however expressed) in this Part of this Act and in the Ninth Schedule to this Act to the business of or to use, occupation or enjoyment by the tenant shall be construed as including references to the business of or to use, occupation or enjoyment as including references to the business of or to use, occupation or enjoyment by the said other member;
>
> (b) the reference in paragraph (d) of subsection (1) of section 34 of this Act to the tenant shall be construed as including the said other member; and
>
> (c) an assignment of the tenancy from one member of the group to another shall not be treated as a change in the person of the tenant.

Appendix A

3. Where the landlord's interest is held by a member of a group –

  (a) the reference in paragraph (g) of subsection (1) of section 30 of this Act to intended occupation by the landlord for the purposes of a business to be carried on by him shall be construed as including intended occupation by any member of the groups for the purposes of a business to be carried on by that member; and

  (b) the reference in subsection (2) of that section to the purchase or creation of an interest shall be construed as a reference to a purchase from or creation by a person other than a member of the group.

Tenancies excluded from Part II
s.43. 1. This Part of this Act does not apply –

  (a) to a tenancy of an agricultural holding or a tenancy which would be a tenancy of an agricultural holding if the proviso to subsection (1) of section 2 of the Agricultural Holdings Act 1986 did not have effect or, in a case where the approval of the Minister of Agriculture, Fisheries and Food was given as mentioned in the said subsection (2) subsection (3) of section 2 of the Agricultural Holdings Act 1986 did not have effect or, in a case where approval was given under subsection (1) of that section, if that approval had not been given;

  (b) to a tenancy created by a mining lease;

  (c) ...

  (d) to a tenancy of premises licensed for the sale of intoxicating liquor for consumption on the premises, other than –
    i) premises which are structurally adapted to be used, and are bona fide used, for a business which comprises one or both of the following, namely, the reception of guests and travellers desiring to sleep on the premises and the carrying on of a restaurant, being a business a substantial proportion of which consists of transactions other than the sale of intoxicating liquor;
    ii) premises adapted to be used, and bona fide used, only for one or more of the following purposes, namely for judicial or public administrative purposes, or as a theatre or place of public or private entertainment, or as public gardens or picture galleries, or for exhibitions, or for any similar purpose to which the holding of the licence is merely ancillary;
    iii) premises adapted to be used, and bona fide used, as refreshment rooms at a railway station. [*NB effect of Landlord and Tenant (Licensed Premises) Act 1990.*]

2. This Part of this Act does not apply to a tenancy granted by reason that the tenant was the holder of an office, appointment or employment from the grantor thereof and continuing only so long as the tenant holds the office, appointment or employment, or terminable by the grantor on the tenant's ceasing to hold it, or coming to an end at a time fixed by reference to the time at which the tenant ceased to hold it.

Provided that this subsection shall not have effect in relation to a tenancy granted after the commencement of this Act unless the tenancy was granted by an instrument in writing which expressed the purpose for which the tenancy was granted.

3. This Part of this Act does not apply to a tenancy granted for a term certain not exceeding six months unless –

(a) the tenancy contains provision for renewing the term or for extending it beyond six months from its beginning; or

(b) the tenant has been in occupation for a period which, together with any period during which any predecessor in the carrying on of the business carried on by the tenant was in occupation, exceeds twelve months.

Jurisdiction of county court to make declaration
s.43A Where the rateable value of the holding is such that the jurisdiction conferred on the court by any other provision of this Part of this Act is, by virtue of section 63 of this Act, exercisable by the county court, the county court shall have jurisdiction (but without prejudice to the jurisdiction of the High Court) to make any declaration as to any matter arising under this Part of this Act, whether or not any other relief is sought in the proceedings.

Meaning of "the landlord" in Part II and provisions as to mesne landlords, etc
s.44. **1.** Subject to the next following subsection, in this Part of this Act the expression "the landlord", in relation to a tenancy (in this section referred to as "the relevant tenancy"), means the person (whether or not he is the immediate landlord) who is the owner of that interest in the property comprised in the relevant tenancy which for the time being fulfils the following conditions, that is to say –

(a) that it is an interest in reversion expectant (whether immediately or not) on the termination of the relevant tenancy, and

(b) that it is either the fee simple or a tenancy which will not come to an end within fourteen months by effluxion of time and, if it is such a tenancy that no notice has been given by virtue of which it will come to an end within fourteen months or any further time by which it may be continued under section 36(2) or section 64 of this Act,

and is not itself in reversion expectant (whether immediately or not) on an interest which fulfils those conditions.

2. References in this Part of this Act to a notice to quit given by the landlord are references to a notice to quit given by the immediate landlord.

3. The provisions of the Sixth Schedule to this Act shall have effect for the application of this Part of this Act to cases where the immediate landlord of the tenant is not the owner of the fee simple in respect of the holding.

Interpretation of Part II
s.46 In this Part of this Act –

"business" has the meaning assigned to it by subsection (2) of section 23 of this Act;

"current tenancy" has the meaning assigned to it by subsection (1) of section 26 of this Act;

Appendix A

"date of termination" has the meaning assigned to it by subsection (1) of section 25 of this Act;

subject to the provisions of section 32 of this Act, "the holding" has the meaning assigned to it by subsection (3) of section 23 of this Act;

"mining lease" has the same meaning as in the Landlord and Tenant Act 1927.

PART III

Time for making claims for compensation for improvements
s.47. **1.** Where a tenancy is terminated by notice to quit, whether given by the landlord or by the tenant, or by a notice given by any person under Part I or Part II of this Act, the time for making a claim for compensation at the termination of the tenancy shall be a time falling within the period of three months beginning on the date on which the notice is given.

Provided that where the tenancy is terminated by a tenant's request for a new tenancy under section 26 of this Act, the said time shall be a time falling within the period of three months beginning on the date on which the landlord gives notice, or (if he has not given such a notice) the latest date on which he could have given notice, under subsection (6) of the said section 26 or, as the case may be, paragraph (a) of subsection (4) of section 57 or paragraph (b) of subsection (1) of section 58 of this Act.

2. Where a tenancy comes to an end by effluxion of time the time for making such a claim shall be a time not earlier than six nor later than three months before the coming to an end of the tenancy.

3. Where a tenancy is terminated by forfeiture or re-entry, the time for making such a claim shall be a time falling within the period of three months beginning with the effective date of the order of the court for the recovery of possession of the land comprised in the tenancy or, if the tenancy is terminated by re-entry without such an order, the period of three months beginning with the date of the re-entry.

4. In the last foregoing subsection the reference to the effective date of an order is a reference to the date on which the order is to take effect according to the terms thereof or the date on which it ceases to be subject to appeal, whichever is the later.

Amendments as to limitations on tenant's right to compensation
s.48. **1.** So much of paragraph (b) of subsection (1) of section 2 of the Act of 1927 as provides that a tenant shall not be entitled to compensation in

respect of any improvement made in pursuance of a statutory obligation shall not apply to any improvement begun after the commencement of this Act, but section 3 of the Act of 1927 (which enables a landlord to object to a proposed improvement) shall not have effect in relation to an improvement made in pursuance of a statutory obligation except so much thereof as —

(a) requires the tenant to serve on the landlord notice of his intention to make the improvement together with such a plan and specification as are mentioned in that section and to supply copies of the plan and specification at the request of any superior landlord; and

(b) enables the tenant to obtain at his expense a certificate from the landlord or the tribunal that the improvement has been duly executed.

2. Paragraph (c) of the said subsection (1) (which provides that a tenant shall not be entitled to compensation in respect of an improvement made less than three years before the termination of the tenancy) shall not apply to any improvement begun after the commencement of this Act.

3. No notice shall be served after the commencement of this Act under paragraph (d) of the said subsection (1) (which excludes rights to compensation where the landlord serves on the tenant notice offering a renewal of the tenancy on reasonable terms).

Restrictions on contracting out
s.49 In section 9 of the Act of 1927 (which provides that Part I of that Act shall apply notwithstanding any contract to the contrary made after the date specified in that section) the proviso (which requires effect to be given to such a contract where it appears to the tribunal that the contract was made for adequate consideration) shall cease to have effect except as respects a contract made before the tenth day of December nineteen hundred and fifty three.

Interpretation of Part III
s.50 In this Part of this Act the expression "Act of 1927" means the Landlord and Tenant Act of 1927, the expression "compensation" means compensation under Part I of that Act in respect of an improvement, and other expressions used in this Part of this Act and in the Act of 1927 have the same meanings in this Part of this Act as in that Act.

PART IV

Compensation for possession obtained by misrepresentation
s.55. 1. Where under Part I of this Act an order is made for possession of the property comprised in a tenancy, or under Part II of this Act the court refuses an order for the grant of a new tenancy, and it is subsequently made to appear to the court that the order was obtained, or the court induced to refuse the grant, by misrepresentation or the concealment of material facts,

the court may order the landlord to pay to the tenant such sum as appears sufficient as compensation for damage or loss sustained by the tenant as the result of the order or refusal.

2. In this section the expression "the landlord" means the person applying for possession or opposing an application for the grant of a new tenancy, and the expression "the tenant" means the person against whom the order for possession was made or to whom the grant of a new tenancy was refused.

Application to Crown
s.56. 1. Subject to the provision of this and the four next following sections, Part II of this Act shall apply where there is an interest belonging to Her Majesty in right of the Crown or the Duchy of Lancaster or belonging to the Duchy of Cornwall, or belonging to a Government department or held on behalf of Her Majesty for the purposes of a Government department, in like manner as if that interest were an interest not so belonging or held.

2. The provisions of the Eighth Schedule to this Act shall have effect as respects the application of Part II of this Act to cases where the interest of the landlord belongs to Her Majesty in right of the Crown or the Duchy of Lancaster or to the Duchy of Cornwall.

3. Where a tenancy is held by or on behalf of a Government department and the property comprised therein is or includes premises occupied for any purposes of a Government department, the tenancy shall be one to which Part II of this Act applies; and for the purposes of any provision of the said Part II or the Ninth Schedule to this Act which is applicable only if either or both of the following conditions are satisfied, that is to say –

(a) that any premises have during any period been occupied for the purposes of the tenant's business;
(b) that on any change of occupier of any premises the new occupier succeeded to the business of the former occupier,

the said conditions shall be deemed to be satisfied respectively, in relation to such a tenancy, if during that period or, as the case may be, immediately before and immediately after the change, the premises were occupied for the purposes of a Government department.

4. The last foregoing subsection shall apply in relation to any premises provided by a Government department without any rent being payable to the department therefor as if the premises were occupied for the purposes of a Government department.

5. The provisions of Parts III and IV of this Act, amending any other enactment which binds the Crown or applies to land belonging to Her Majesty in right of the Crown or the Duchy of Lancaster, or land belonging to the Duchy of Cornwall, or to land belonging to any Government department, shall bind the Crown or apply to such land.

6. Sections 53 and 54 of this Act shall apply where the interest of the landlord, or any other interest in the land in question, belongs to Her Majesty

in right of the Crown or the Duchy of Lancaster or to the Duchy of Cornwall, or belongs to a Government department, in like manner as if that interest were an interest not so belonging or held.

7. Part I of this Act shall apply where —

(a) there is an interest belonging to Her Majesty in right of the Crown and that interest is under the management of the Crown Estate Commissioners; or

(b) there is an interest belonging to Her Majesty in right of the Duchy of Lancaster or belonging to the Duchy of Cornwall;

as if it were an interest not so belonging.

Modification on grounds of public interest of rights under Part II
s.57. **1.** Where the interest of the landlord or any superior landlord in the property comprised in any tenancy belongs to or is held by the purposes of a Government department or is held by a local authority, statutory undertakers or a development corporation, the Minister or Board in charge of any Government department may certify that it is requisite for the purposes of the first-mentioned department, or, as the case may be, of the authority, undertakers or corporation, that the use or occupation of the property or a part thereof shall be changed by a specified date.

2. A certificate under the last foregoing subsection shall not be given unless the owner of the interest belonging or held as mentioned in the last foregoing subsection has given to the tenant a notice stating —

(a) that the question of the giving of such a certificate is under consideration by the Minister or Board specified in the notice, and

(b) that if within twenty-one days of the giving of the notice the tenant makes to that Minister or Board representations in writing with respect to that question, they will be considered before the question is determined.

and if the tenant makes any such representations within the said twenty-one days the Minister or Board shall consider them before determining whether to give the certificate.

3. Where a certificate has been given under subsection (1) of this section in relation to any tenancy, then —

(a) if a notice given under subsection (1) of section 25 of this Act specifies as the date of termination a date not earlier than the date specified in the certificate and contains a copy of the certificate subsections (5) and (6) of that section shall not apply to the notice and no application for a new tenancy shall be made by the tenant under section 24 of this Act;

(b) if such a notice specifies an earlier date as the date of termination and contains a copy of the certificate, then if the court makes an order under Part II of this Act for the grant of a new tenancy the new tenancy shall be for a term expiring not later than the date

Appendix A

specified in the certificate and shall not be a tenancy to which Part II of this Act applies.

4. Where a tenant makes a request for a new tenancy under section 26 of this Act, and the interest of the landlord or any superior landlord in the property comprised in the current tenancy belongs or is held as mentioned in subsection (1) of this section, the following provisions shall have effect:

(a) if a certificate has been given under the said subsection (1) in relation to the current tenancy, and within two months after the making of the request the landlord gives notice to the tenant that the certificate has been given and the notice contains a copy of the certificate, then, −
  (i) if the date specified in the certificate is not later than that specified in the tenant's request for a new tenancy, the tenant shall not make an application under section 24 of this Act for the grant of a new tenancy;
  (ii) if, in any other case, the court makes an order under Part II of this Act for the grant of a new tenancy the new tenancy shall be for a term expiring not later than the date specified in the certificate and shall not be a tenancy to which Part II of this Act applies;
(b) if no such certificate has been given but notice under subsection (2) of this section has been given before the making of the request or within two months thereafter, the request shall not have effect, without prejudice however, to the making of a new request when the Minister or Board has determined whether to give a certificate.

5. Where application is made to the court under Part II of this Act for the grant of a new tenancy and the landlord's interest in the property comprised in the tenancy belongs or is held as mentioned in subsection (1) of this section, the Minister or Board in charge of any Government department may certify that it is necessary in the public interest that if the landlord makes an application in that behalf the court shall determine as a term of the new tenancy that it shall be terminable by six months' notice to quit given by the landlord.

Subsection (2) of this section shall apply in relation to a certificate under this subsection, and if notice under the said subsection (2) has been given to the tenant −

(a) the court shall not determine the application for the grant of a new tenancy until the Minister or Board has determined whether to give a certificate,
(b) if a certificate is given, the court shall on the application of the landlord determine as a term of the new tenancy that it shall be terminable as aforesaid, and section 25 of this Act shall apply accordingly.

6. The foregoing provisions of this section shall apply to an interest held by a Regional Health Authority, Family Practitioner Committee, District Health Authority, Area Health Authority or special health authority as they apply to an interest held by a local authority, but with the substitution, for the reference to the purposes of the authority, of a reference to the purposes of the National Health Service Act 1977.

7. Where the interest of the landlord or any superior landlord in the property comprised in any tenancy belongs to the National Trust the Minister of Works may certify that it is requisite, for the purpose of securing that the property will as from a specified date be used or occupied in a manner better suited to the nature thereof, that the use or occupation of the property should be changed; and subsections (2) to (4) of this section shall apply in relation to certificates under this subsection, and to cases where the interest of the landlord or any superior landlord belongs to the National Trust, as those subsections apply in relation to certificates under subsection (1) of this section and to cases where the interest of the landlord or any superior landlord belongs or is held as mentioned in that subsection.

8. In this and the next following section the expression "Government department" does not include the Commissioners of Crown Lands and the expression "landlord" has the same meaning as in Part II of this Act; and in the last foregoing subsection the expression "National Trust" means the National Trust for Places of Historic Interest or Natural Beauty.

Termination on special grounds of tenancies to which Part II applies
s.58. **1.** Where the landlord's interest in the property comprised in any tenancy belongs to or is held for the purposes of a Government department, and the Minister or Board in charge of any Government department certifies that for reasons of national security it is necessary that the use or occupation of the property should be discontinued or changed, then –

    (a) if the landlord gives a notice under subsection (1) of section 25 of this Act containing a copy of the certificate, subsections (5) and (6) of that section shall not apply to the notice and no application for a new tenancy shall be made by the tenant under section 24 of this Act;

    (b) if (whether before or after the giving of the certificate) the tenant makes a request for a new tenancy under section 26 of this Act, and within two months after the making of the request the landlord gives notice to the tenant that the certificate has been given and the notice contains a copy of the certificate –
        (i) the tenant shall not make an application under section 24 of this Act for the grant of a new tenancy, and
        (ii) if the notice specifies as the date on which the tenancy is to terminate a date earlier than that specified in the tenant's request as the date on which the new tenancy is to begin but neither earlier than six months from the giving of the notice nor earlier than the earliest date at which apart from this Act the tenancy would come to an end or could be brought to an end, the tenancy shall terminate on the date specified in the notice instead of that specified in the request.

2. Where the landlord's interest in the property comprised in any tenancy belongs to or is held for the provision of a Government department, nothing in this Act shall invalidate an agreement to the effect –

Appendix A

(a) that on the giving of such a certificate as is mentioned in the last foregoing subsection the tenancy may be terminated by notice to quit given by the landlord of such length as may be specified in the agreement, if the notice contains a copy of the certificate; and

(b) that after the giving of such a notice containing such a copy the tenancy shall not be one to which Part II of this Act applies.

3. Where the landlord's interest in the property comprised in any tenancy is held by statutory undertakers, nothing in this Act shall invalidate an agreement to the effect –

(a) that where the Minister or Board in charge of a Government department certifies that possession of the property comprised in the tenancy or a part thereof is urgently required for carrying out repairs (whether on that property or elsewhere) which are needed for the proper operation of the landlord's undertaking, the tenancy may be terminated by notice to quit given by the landlord of such length as may be specified in the agreement, if the notice contains a copy of the certificate; and

(b) that after the giving of such a notice containing such a copy, the tenancy shall not be one to which Part II of this Act applies;

4. Where the court makes an order under Part II of this Act for the grant of a new tenancy and the Minister or Board in charge of any Government department certifies that the public interest requires the tenancy to be subject to such a term as is mentioned in paragraph (a) or (b) of this subsection, as the case may be, then –

(a) if the landlord's interest in the property comprised in the tenancy belongs to or is held for the purposes of a Government department, the court shall on the application of the landlord determine as a term of the new tenancy that such an agreement as is mentioned in subsection (2) of this section and specifying such length of notice as is mentioned in the certificate shall be embodied in the new tenancy;

(b) if the landlord's interest in that property is held by statutory undertakers, the court shall on the application of the landlord determine as a term of the new tenancy that such an agreement as is mentioned in subsection (3) of this section and specifying such length of notice as is mentioned in the certificate shall be embodied in the new tenancy.

Compensation for exercise of powers under ss. 57 and 58
s.59. 1. Where by virtue of any certificate given for the purposes of either of the two last foregoing sections or, subject to subsections (1A) or (1B) below the tenant is precluded from obtaining an order for the grant of a new tenancy, or of a new tenancy for a term expiring later than a specified date, the tenant shall be entitled on quitting the premises to recover from the owner of the interest by virtue of which the certificate was given an amount by way of compensation, and subsections (2), (3) and (5) to (7) of section 37

of this Act shall with the necessary modifications apply for the purposes of ascertaining the amount.

1A. No compensation shall be recoverable under subsection (1) above where the certificate was given under section 60A below and either —

- (a) the premises vested in the Welsh Development Agency under section 7 (property of Welsh Industrial Estates Corporation) or 8 (land held under Local Employment Act 1972) of the Welsh Development Agency Act 1975, or
- (b) the tenant was not tenant of the premises when the said Agency acquired the interest by virtue of which the certificate was given.

1B. No compensation shall be recoverable under section (1) above where the certificate was given under section 60B below and either —

- (a) the premises are premises which —
  - (i) were vested in the Welsh Development Agency by section 8 of the Welsh Development Agency Act 1975 or were acquired by the Agency when no tenancy subsisted in the premises; and
  - (ii) vested in the Development Board for Rural Wales under section 24 of the Development of Rural Wales Act 1976; or
- (b) the tenant was not the tenant of the premises when the Board acquired the interest by virtue of which the certificate was given.

2. Subsections (2) and (3) of section 38 of this Act shall apply to compensation under this section as they apply to compensation under section 37 of this Act.

Special provisions as to premises in development or intermediate areas
s.60. **1.** Where the property comprised in a tenancy consists of premises of which the Secretary of State or the English Industrial Estates Corporation is the landlord, being premises situated in a locality which is either —

- (a) a development area; or
- (b) an intermediate area;

and the Secretary of State certifies that it is necessary or expedient for achieving the purpose mentioned in section 2(1) of the Local Employment Act 1972 that the use or occupation of the property should be changed, paragraphs (a) and (b) of subsection (1) of section 58 of this Act shall apply as they apply where such a certificate is given as is mentioned in that subsection.

2. Where the court makes an order under Part II of this Act for the grant of a new tenancy of any such premises as aforesaid, and the Secretary of State certifies that it is necessary or expedient as aforesaid that the tenancy should be subject to a term, specified in the certificate, prohibiting or restricting the tenant from assigning the tenancy or sub-letting, charging or parting with possession of the premises or any part thereof or changing the use of the premises or any part thereof, the court shall determine that the terms of the tenancy shall include the terms specified in the certificate.

3. In this section "development area" and "intermediate area" mean an

Appendix A

area for the time being specified as a development area or, as the case may be, as an intermediate area by an order made, or having effect as if made, under section 1 of the Industrial Development Act 1982.

Welsh Development Agency premises
s.60A. 1. Where the property comprised in a tenancy consists of premises of which the Welsh Development Agency is the landlord, and the Secretary of State certifies that it is necessary or expedient, for the purpose of providing employment appropriate to the needs of the area in which the premises are situated, that the use or occupation of the property should be changed, paragraphs (a) and (b) of section 58(1) above shall apply as they apply where such a certificate is given as is mentioned in that subsection.

2. Where the court makes an order under Part II of this Act for the grant of a new tenancy of any such premises as aforesaid, and the Secretary of State certifies that it is necessary or expedient as aforesaid that the tenancy should be subject to a term, specified in the certificate, prohibiting or restricting the tenant from assigning the tenancy or subletting, charging or parting with possession of the premises or any part of the premises or changing the use of the premises or any part of the premises, the court shall determine that the terms of the tenancy shall include the terms specified in the certificate.

Development Board for Rural Wales premises
s.60B. 1. Where the property comprised in the tenancy consists of premises of which the development Board for Rural Wales is the landlord, and the Secretary of State certifies that it is necessary or expedient, for the purpose of providing employment appropriate to the needs of the area in which the premises are situated, that the use or occupation of the property should be changed, paragraphs (a) and (b) of section 58(1) above shall apply as they apply where such a certificate is given as is mentioned in that subsection.

2. Where the court makes an order under Part II of this Act for the grant of a new tenancy of any such premises as aforesaid, and the Secretary of State certifies that it is necessary or expedient as aforesaid that the tenancy should be subject to a term, specified in the certificate, prohibiting or restricting the tenant from assigning the tenancy or subletting, charging or parting with possession of the premises or any part of the premises or changing the use of the premises or any part of the premises, the court shall determine that the terms of the tenancy shall include the terms specified in the certificate.

Jurisdiction of court for purposes of Part I and II and of Part I of Landlord and Tenant Act 1927 [*NB repealed from 1 July 1991 by Courts and Legal Services Act 1990.*]
s.63. 1. Any jurisdiction conferred on the court by any provision of Part I of this Act shall be exercised by the county court.

2. Any jurisdiction conferred on the court by any provision of Part II of this Act or conferred on the tribunal by Part I of the Landlord and Tenant Act 1927, shall, subject to the provision of this section, be exercised, –
    (a) where the rateable value of the holding is not over the county court limit, by the county court;

(b) where it is over the county court limit, by the High Court.

3. Any jurisdiction exercisable under the last foregoing subsection may by agreement in writing between the parties be transferred from the county court to the High Court or from the High Court to a county court specified in the agreement.

4. The following provisions shall have effect as respects transfer of proceedings from or to the High Court or the county court, that is to say –

- (a) where an application is made to the one but by virtue of subsection (2) of this section cannot be entertained except by the other, the application shall not be treated as improperly made but any proceedings thereon shall be transferred to the other court;
- (b) any proceedings under the provisions of Part II of this Act or of Part I of the Landlord and Tenant Act 1927, which are pending before one of those courts may by order of that court made on the application of any person interested be transferred to the other court, if it appears to the court making the order that it is desirable that the proceedings and any proceedings before the other court should both be entertained by the other court.

5. In any proceedings where in accordance with the foregoing provisions of this section the county court exercises jurisdiction the powers of the judge of summoning one or more assessors under subsection (1) of section 63 of the County Courts Act 1984, may be exercised notwithstanding that no application is made in that behalf by any party to the proceedings.

6. Where in any such proceedings an assessor is summoned by a judge under the said subsection (1), –

- (a) he may, if so directed by the judge, inspect the land to which the proceedings relate without the judge and report to the judge in writing thereon;
- (b) the judge may on consideration of the report and any observations of the parties thereon give such judgment or make such order in the proceedings as may be just;
- (c) the remuneration of the assessor shall be at such rate as may be determined by the Lord Chancellor with the approval of the Treasury and shall be defrayed out of moneys provided by Parliament.

7. In this section the expression "the holding" –

- (a) in relation to proceedings under Part II of this Act, has the meaning assigned to it by subsection (3) of section 23 of this Act.
- (b) in relation to proceedings under Part I of the Landlord and Tenant Act 1927, has the same meaning as in the said Part I.

8. Subsections (5) to (7) of section 37 of this Act shall apply for determining the rateable value of the holding for the purposes of this section as they apply for the purposes of subsection (2) of the said section 37, but with the

Appendix A

substitution in paragraph (a) of the said subsection (5) of a reference to the time at which application is made to the court for the reference to the date mentioned in that subsection.

9. Nothing in this section shall prejudice the operation of section 29 of the Supreme Court Act 1981 (which relates to the removal into the High Court of proceedings commenced in a county court).

Interim continuation of tenancies pending determination by court
s.64. **1.** In any case where –

(a) a notice to terminate a tenancy has been given under Part I or Part II of this Act or a request for a new tenancy has been made under Part II thereof, and

(b) an application to the court has been made under the said Part I or the said Part II, as the case may be, and

(c) apart from this section the effect of the notice or request would be to terminate the tenancy before the expiration of the period of three months beginning with the date on which the application is finally disposed of,

the effect of the notice or request shall be to terminate the tenancy at the expiration of the said period of three months and not at any other time.

2. The reference in paragraph (c) of subsection (1) of this section to the date on which an application is finally disposed of shall be construed as a reference to the earliest date by which the proceedings on the application (including any proceedings on or in consequence of an appeal) have been determined and any time for appealing or further appealing has expired, except that if the application is withdrawn or any appeal is abandoned the reference shall be construed as a reference to the date of the withdrawal or abandonment.

Provisions as to reversions
s.65. **1.** Where by virtue of any provision of this Act a tenancy (in this subsection referred to as "the inferior tenancy") is continued for a period such as to extend to or beyond the end of the term of a superior tenancy, the superior tenancy shall, for the purposes of this Act and of any other enactment and of any rule of law, be deemed so long as it subsists to be an interest in reversion expectant upon the termination of the inferior tenancy and, if there is no intermediate tenancy, to be the interest in reversion immediately expectant upon the termination thereof.

2. In the case of a tenancy continuing by virtue of any provision of this Act after the coming to an end of the interest in reversion immediately expectant upon the termination thereof, subsection (1) of section 139 of the Law of Property Act 1925 (which relates to the effect of the extinguishment of a reversion) shall apply as if references in the said subsection (1) to the surrender or merger of the reversion included references to the coming to an end of the reversion for any reason other than surrender or merger.

3. Where by virtue of any provision of this Act a tenancy (in this subsection referred to as "the continuing tenancy") is continued beyond the beginning of a reversionary tenancy which was granted (whether before or after the commencement of this Act) so as to begin on or after the date on which apart from this Act the continuing tenancy would have come to an end, the reversionary tenancy shall have effect as if it had been granted subject to the continuing tenancy.

4. Where by virtue of any provision of this Act a tenancy (in this subsection referred to as "the new tenancy") is granted for a period beginning on the same date as a reversionary tenancy or for a period such as to extend beyond the beginning of the term of a reversionary tenancy, whether the reversionary tenancy in question was granted before or after the commencement of this Act, the reversionary tenancy shall have effect as if it had been granted subject to the new tenancy.

Provisions as to notices
s.66. 1. Any form of notice required by this Act to be prescribed shall be prescribed by regulations made by the Secretary of State by statutory instrument.

2. Where the form of notice to be served on persons of any description is to be prescribed for any of the purposes of this Act, the form to be prescribed shall include such an explanation of the relevant provisions of this Act as appears to the Secretary of State requisite for informing persons of that description of their rights and obligations under those provisions.

3. Different forms of notice may be prescribed for the purposes of the operation of any provision of this Act in relation to different cases.

4. Section 23 of the Landlord and Tenant Act 1927 (which relates to the service of notices) shall apply for the purposes of this Act.

5. Any statutory instrument under this section shall be subject to annulment in pursuance of a resolution of either House of Parliament.

Provisions as to mortgagees in possession
s.67 Anything authorised or required by the provisions of this Act, other than subsection (2) or (3) of section 40, to be done at any time by, to or with the landlord, or a landlord of a specified description, shall, if at that time the interest of the landlord in question is subject to a mortgage and the mortgagee is in possession or a receiver appointed by the mortgagee or by the court is in receipt of the rents and profits, be deemed to be authorised or required to be done by, to or with the mortgagee instead of that landlord.

Interpretation
s.69. 1. In this Act the following expressions have the meanings hereby assigned to them respectively, that is to say: —
"agricultural holding" has the same meaning as in the Agricultural Holdings Act 1986;
"development corporation" has the same meaning as in the New Towns Act 1946;
"local authority" has the same meaning as in the Town and Country

Appendix A

Planning Act 1947 except that it includes "the Broads Authority", the Inner London Education Authority and a joint authority established by Part IV of the Local Government Act 1985;

"mortgage" includes a charge or lien and "mortgagor" and "mortgagee" shall be construed accordingly;

"notice to quit" means a notice to terminate a tenancy (whether a periodical tenancy or a tenancy for a term of years certain) given in accordance with the provisions (whether express or implied) of that tenancy;

"repairs" includes any work of maintenance, decoration or restoration, and references to repairing, to keeping or yielding up in repair and to state of repair shall be construed accordingly;

"statutory undertakers" has the same meaning as in the Town and Country Planning Act 1947, except that it includes the British Coal Corporation;

"tenancy" means a tenancy created either immediately or derivatively out of the freehold, whether by a lease or underlease, by an agreement for a lease or underlease or by a tenancy agreement or in pursuance of any enactment (including this Act), but does not include a mortgage term or any interest arising in favour of a mortgagor by his attorning tenant to his mortgagee, and references to the granting of a tenancy and to demised property shall be construed accordingly;

"terms", in relation to a tenancy, includes conditions.

2. References in this Act to an agreement between the landlord and the tenant (except in section 17 of subsections (1) and (2) of section 38 thereof) shall be construed as references to an agreement in writing between them.

3. References in this Act to an action for any relief shall be construed as including references to a claim for that relief by way of counterclaim in any proceedings.

Short title and citation, commencement and extent
s.70. **1.** This Act may be cited as the Landlord and Tenant Act 1954, and the Landlord and Tenant Act 1927 and this Act may be cited together as the Landlord and Tenant Acts, 1927 and 1954.

2. This Act shall come into operation on the first day of October, nineteen hundred and fifty-four.

3. This shall not extend to Scotland or to Northern Ireland.

Schedule 6
Provisions for purposes of Part II where immediate landlord is not the freeholder (s.44)

Definitions
1. In this Schedule the following expressions have the meaning hereby assigned to them in relation to a tenancy (in this Schedule referred to as "the relevant tenancy"), that is to say –

"the competent landlord" means the person who in relation to the tenancy is for the time being the landlord (as defined by section 44 of this Act) for the purposes of Part II of this Act;

"mesne landlord" means a tenant whose interest is intermediate between the relevant tenancy and the interest of the competent landlord; and

"superior landlord" means a person (whether the owner of the fee simple or a tenant) whose interest is superior to the interest of the competent landlord.

Power of court to order reversionary tenancies

2. Where the period for which in accordance with the provisions of Part II of this Act it is agreed or determined by the court that a new tenancy should be granted thereunder will extend beyond the date on which the interest of the immediate landlord will come to an end, the power of the court under Part II of this Act to order such a grant shall include power to order the grant of a new tenancy until the expiration of that interest and also to order the grant of such a reversionary tenancy or reversionary tenancies as may be required to secure that the combined effects of those grants will be equivalent to the grant of a tenancy for that period; and the provisions of Part II of this Act shall, subject to the necessary modifications, apply in relation to the grant of a tenancy together with one or more reversionary tenancies as they apply in relation to the grant of one new tenancy.

Acts of competent landlord binding on other landlord

3. (1) Any notice given by the competent landlord under Part II of this Act to terminate the relevant tenancy, and any agreement made between that landlord and the tenant as to the granting, duration, or terms of a future tenancy, being an agreement made for the purposes of the said Part II, shall bind the interest of any mesne landlord notwithstanding that he has not consented to the giving of the notice or was not a party to the agreement.

(2) The competent landlord shall have power for the purposes of Part II of this Act to give effect to any agreement with the tenant for the grant of a new tenancy beginning with the coming to an end of the relevant tenancy notwithstanding that the competent landlord will not be the immediate landlord at the commencement of the new tenancy, and any instrument made in the exercise of the power conferred by this sub-paragraph shall have effect as if the mesne landlord had been a party thereto.

(3) Nothing in the foregoing provisions of this paragraph shall prejudice the provisions of the next following paragraph.

Provisions as to consent of mesne landlord to acts of competent landlord

4. (1) If the competent landlord, not being the immediate landlord, gives any such notice or makes any such agreement as is mentioned in sub-paragraph (1), of the last foregoing paragraph without the consent of every mesne landlord, any mesne landlord whose consent has not been given thereto shall be entitled to compensation from the competent landlord for any loss arising in consequence of the giving of the notice or the making of the agreement.

(2) If the competent landlord applies to any mesne landlord for his consent to such a notice or agreement, that consent shall not be unreasonably withheld, but may be given subject to any conditions which may be reasonable (including

Appendix A

conditions as to the modification of the proposed notice or agreement or as to the payment of compensation by the competent landlord).

(3) Any question arising under this paragraph whether consent has been unreasonably withheld or whether any conditions imposed on the giving of consent are unreasonable shall be determined by the court.

Consent of superior landlord required for agreements affecting his interest
5. An agreement between the competent landlord and the tenant made for the purposes of Part II of this Act in a case where –
    (a) the competent landlord is himself a tenant, and
    (b) the agreement would apart from this paragraph operate as respects any period after the coming to an end of the interest of the competent landlord,

shall not have effect unless every superior landlord who will be the immediate landlord of the tenant during any part of that period is a party to the agreement.

Withdrawal by competent landlord of notice given by mesne landlord
6. Where the competent landlord has given a notice under section 25 of this Act to terminate the relevant tenancy and, within two months after the giving of the notice, a superior landlord –
    (a) becomes the competent landlord; and
    (b) gives to the tenant notice in the prescribed form that he withdraws the notice previously given,

the notice under section 25 of this Act shall cease to have effect, but without prejudice to the giving of a further notice under that section by the competent landlord.

Duty to inform superior landlords
7. If the competent landlord's interest in the property comprised in the relevant tenancy is a tenancy which will come or can be brought to an end within sixteen months (or any further time by which it may be continued under section 36(2) or section 64 of this Act) and he gives to the tenant under the relevant tenancy a notice under section 25 of this Act to terminate the tenancy or is given by him a notice under section 26(3) of this Act –
    (a) the competent landlord shall forthwith send a copy of the notice to his immediate landlord; and
    (b) any superior landlord whose interest in the property is a tenancy shall forthwith send to his immediate landlord any copy which has been sent to him in pursuance of the preceding sub-paragraph or this sub-paragraph.

Schedule 8

Application of Part II to land belonging to Crown and Duchies of Lancaster and Cornwall (s.56)
1. Where an interest in any property comprised in a tenancy belongs to Her Majesty in right of the Duchy of Lancaster, then for the purposes of Part II

of this Act the Chancellor of the Duchy shall represent Her Majesty and shall be deemed to be the owner of the interest.

2. Where an interest in any property comprised in a tenancy belongs to the Duchy of Cornwall, then for the purposes of Part II of this Act such person as the Duke of Cornwall appoints shall represent the Duke of Cornwall or other the possessor aforesaid, and shall be deemed to be the owner of the interest and may do any act or thing under the said Part II which the owner of that interest is authorised or required to do thereunder.

3. ...

4. The amount of any compensation payable under section 37 of this Act by the Chancellor of the Duchy of Lancaster shall be raised and paid as an expense incurred in improvement of land belonging to Her Majesty in right of the Duchy within section 25 of the Act of the fifty-seventh year of King George the Third, Chapter ninety-seven.

5. Any compensation payable under section 37 of this Act by the person representing the Duke of Cornwall or other the possessor for the time being of the Duchy of Cornwall shall be paid, and advances therefor made, in the manner and subject to the provisions of section eight of the Duchy of Cornwall Management Act 1963 with respect to improvements of land mentioned in that section.

© *Crown copyright*

Appendix B

Forms

Contents

		page
1.	Landlord's notice to terminate business tenancy	215
2.	Notification by tenant of business premises or by assured tenant as to giving up of possession	217
3.	Tenant's request for new tenancy of business premises	218
4.	Notice by landlord that he will oppose application for new business tenancy or new assured tenancy	220
5.	Notice by landlord requiring information about occupation and sub-tenancies of business premises	222
6.	Notice by tenant of business premises requiring information from landlord about landlord's interest	224
7.	Notice by tenant of business premises requiring information from mortgagee about landlord's interest	226
8.	Withdrawal of landlord's notice to terminate business tenancy	227
9.	Originating application for new tenancy under Part II of the Landlord and Tenant Act 1954	228
10.	Answer to originating application for new tenancy under Part II of the Landlord and Tenant Act 1954	230
11.	Notice of proceedings	232

Appendix B: Forms

1. Landlord's notice to terminate business tenancy

F815: Landlord's Notice to Terminate Business Tenancy
(The Landlord and Tenant Act 1954 Part II (Notices) Regulations 1989, Form 1)

LANDLORD'S NOTICE TO TERMINATE BUSINESS TENANCY *
(Landlord and Tenant Act 1954, section 25)

To (name of tenant) ....

of (address of tenant)..

....

> IMPORTANT - THIS NOTICE IS INTENDED TO BRING YOUR TENANCY TO AN END. IF YOU WANT TO CONTINUE TO OCCUPY YOUR PROPERTY YOU MUST ACT QUICKLY. READ THE NOTICE AND ALL THE NOTES CAREFULLY. IF YOU ARE IN ANY DOUBT ABOUT THE ACTION YOU SHOULD TAKE, GET ADVICE IMMEDIATELY, eg FROM A SOLICITOR OR SURVEYOR OR A CITIZENS ADVICE BUREAU.

1. This notice is given under section 25 of the Landlord and Tenant Act 1954.

2. It relates to (description of property) ....
....
.... of which you are the tenant.

3. I/We give you notice terminating your tenancy on .... *(See notes 1 and 8)*

4. Within two months after the giving of this notice, you must notify me/us in writing whether or not you are willing to give up possession of the property comprised in the tenancy on the date stated in paragraph 3. *(See notes 2 and 3)*

5. ** If you apply to the court under Part II of the Landlord and Tenant Act 1954 for the grant of a new tenancy, I/we will not oppose your application.
OR
5. ** If you apply to the court under Part II of the Landlord and Tenant Act 1954 for the grant of a new tenancy, I/we will oppose it on the grounds mentioned in paragraph(s) .... of section 30(1) of the Act. *(See notes 4 and 5)*
   ** *The landlord must cross out one version of paragraph 5. If the second version is used, the paragraph letter(s) must be filled in.*

6. All correspondence about this notice should be sent to †[the landlord] [the landlord's agent] at the address given below.

Date ....

Signature of † [landlord] [landlord's agent]...

Name of landlord...

Address of landlord ....

....

†[Address of agent ....

....]

† Cross out words in square brackets if they do not apply

---

* This form must *not* be used if:
(a) no previous notice terminating the tenancy has been given under section 25 of the Act, AND
(b) the tenancy is the tenancy of a house (as defined for the purpose of Part I of the Leasehold Reform Act 1967), AND
(c) the tenancy is a long tenancy at a low rent (within the meaning of that Act of 1967), AND
(d) the tenant is not a company or other artificial person.
If the above apply, use form No 13 instead of this form.

See notes overleaf

BUSINESS LEASES

Reverse side of Form F815: Landlord's notice to terminate business tenancy

NOTES

Termination of tenancy
1. This notice is intended to bring your tenancy to an end. You can apply to the court for a new tenancy under the Landlord and Tenant Act 1954 by following the procedure outlined in notes 2 and 3 below. If you do your tenancy will continue after the date shown in paragraph 3 of this notice while your claim is being considered. The landlord can ask the court to fix the rent which you will have to pay while the tenancy continues. The terms of any new tenancy not agreed between you and the landlord will be settled by the court.

Claiming a new tenancy
2. If you want to apply to the court for a new tenancy you must:
   (1) notify the landlord in writing not later than 2 months after the giving of this notice that you are not willing to give up possession of the property; AND
   (2) apply to the court, not earlier than 2 months nor later than 4 months after the giving of this notice, for a new tenancy. You should apply to the County Court unless the rateable value of the business part of your premises is above the current County Court limit. In that case you should apply to the High Court.
3. The time limits in note 2 run from the giving of the notice. The date of the giving of the notice may not be the date written on the notice or the date on which you actually saw it. It may, for instance, be the date on which the notice was delivered through the post to your last address known to the person giving the notice. If there has been any delay in your seeing this notice you may need to act very quickly. If you are in any doubt get advice immediately.

> **WARNING TO TENANT**
> IF YOU DO NOT KEEP TO THE TIME LIMITS IN NOTE 2, YOU WILL *LOSE* YOUR RIGHT TO APPLY TO THE COURT FOR A NEW TENANCY.

Landlord's opposition to claim for a new tenancy
4. If you apply to the court for a new tenancy, the landlord can only oppose your application on one or more of the grounds set out in section 30(1) of the 1954 Act. These grounds are set out below. The paragraph letters are those given in the Act. The landlord can only use a ground if its paragraph letter is shown in paragraph 5 of the notice.

Grounds
(a) where under the current tenancy the tenant has any obligations as respects the repair and maintenance of the holding, that the tenant ought not to be granted a new tenancy in view of the state of repair of the holding, being a state resulting from the tenant's failure to comply with the said obligations;
(b) that the tenant ought not to be granted a new tenancy in view of his persistent delay in paying rent which has become due;
(c) that the tenant ought not to be granted a new tenancy in view of other substantial breaches by him of his obligations under the current tenancy, or for any other reason connected with the tenant's use or management of the holding;
(d) that the landlord has offered and is willing to provide or secure the provision of alternative accommodation for the tenant, that the terms on which the alternative accommodation is available are reasonable having regard to the terms of the current tenancy and to all other relevant circumstances, and that the accommodation and the time at which it will be available are suitable for the tenant's requirements (including the requirement to preserve goodwill) having regard to the nature and class of his business and to the situation and extent of, and facilities afforded by, the holding;
(e) where the current tenancy was created by the sub-letting of part only of the property comprised in a superior tenancy and the landlord is the owner of an interest in reversion expectant on the termination of that superior tenancy, that the aggregate of the rents reasonably obtainable on separate lettings of the holding and the remainder of that property would be substantially less than the rent reasonably obtainable on a letting of that property as a whole, that on the termination of the current tenancy the landlord requires possession of the holding for the purposes of letting or otherwise disposing of the said property as a whole, and that in view thereof the tenant ought not to be granted a new tenancy;
(f) that on the termination of the current tenancy the landlord intends to demolish or reconstruct the premises comprised in the holding or a substantial part of those premises or to carry out substantial work of construction on the holding or part thereof and that he could not reasonably do so without obtaining possession of the holding;
(If the landlord uses this ground, the court can sometimes still grant a new tenancy if certain conditions set out in section 31A of the Act can be met.)
(g) that on the termination of the current tenancy the landlord intends to occupy the holding for the purposes, or partly for the purposes, of a business to be carried on by him therein, or as his residence.
(The landlord must normally have been the landlord for at least five years to use this ground.)

Compensation
5. If you cannot get a new tenancy solely because grounds (e), (f) or (g) apply, you are entitled to compensation under the 1954 Act. If your landlord has opposed your application on any of the other grounds as well as (e), (f) or (g) you can only get compensation if the Court's refusal to grant a new tenancy is based solely on grounds (e), (f) or (g). In other words you cannot get compensation under the 1954 Act if the Court has refused your tenancy on *other* grounds even if (e), (f) or (g) also apply.
6. If your landlord is an authority possessing compulsory purchase powers (such as a local authority) you may be entitled to a disturbance payment under Part III of the Land Compensation Act 1973.

Negotiating a new tenancy
7. Most leases are renewed by negotiation. If you do try to agree a new tenancy with your landlord, remember -
   (1) that your present tenancy will not be extended after the date in paragraph 3 of this notice unless you *both*:
       (a) give written notice that you will not vacate (note 2(1) above); *and*
       (b) apply to the court for a new tenancy (note 2(2) above);
   (2) that you will lose your right to apply to the court if you do not keep to the time limits in note 2.

Validity of this notice
8. The landlord who has given this notice may not be the landlord to whom you pay your rent. "Business" is given a wide meaning in the 1954 Act and is used in the same sense in this notice. The 1954 Act also has rules about the date which the landlord can put in paragraph 3. This depends on the terms of your tenancy. If you have any doubts about whether this notice is valid, get immediate advice.

Explanatory booklet
9. The Department of the Environment and Welsh Office booklet "Business Leases and Security of Tenure" explains the main provisions of Part II of the 1954 Act. It is available from the Department of the Environment Publications Store, Building No 3, Victoria Road, South Ruislip, Middlesex.

© September 1989 Fourmat Publishing   133 Upper Street London N1 1QP

Appendix B

2. Notification by tenant of business premises or by assured tenant as to giving up of possession

NOTIFICATION BY TENANT OF BUSINESS PREMISES OR BY ASSURED TENANT AS TO GIVING UP OF POSSESSION

Landlord and Tenant Act 1954

To: ....
(name of landlord)

of ....

....
(address of landlord)

This counter-notice relates to ....

....
(description of property)

of which you are landlord.

I/We have, on................................., received your notice under Section 25 of the Landlord and Tenant Act 1954 to terminate my/our tenancy of the above property

on ....

†Cross out words in square brackets if they do not apply

I/We hereby give you notice that I/we [are] [are not]† willing to give up possession of the property comprised in the tenancy.

Date ....

Signature of [tenant] [tenant's agent]† ....

Address of tenant ....

....

[Address of agent ....

....]†

Notification by tenant of business premises or by assured tenant as to giving up of possession.

Form F816
© Fourmat Publishing
27 & 28 St. Albans Place
London N1 0NX
April 1984

Notes: Notification that the tenant is not willing to give up possession to the landlord must be made not later than two months after the giving by the landlord of notice to terminate the tenancy. Application to the court for a new tenancy must be made not earlier than two months nor later than four months after the giving of notice to terminate the tenancy.

BUSINESS LEASES

3. Tenant's request for new tenancy of business premises

TENANT'S REQUEST FOR NEW TENANCY OF BUSINESS PREMISES
Landlord and Tenant Act 1954, Section 26

To: ....
(name of landlord)

of ....

....
(address of landlord)

> IMPORTANT — THIS IS A REQUEST FOR A NEW TENANCY OF YOUR PROPERTY OR PART OF IT. IF YOU WANT TO OPPOSE THIS REQUEST YOU MUST ACT QUICKLY. READ THE REQUEST AND ALL THE NOTES CAREFULLY. IF YOU ARE IN ANY DOUBT ABOUT THE ACTION YOU SHOULD TAKE, GET ADVICE IMMEDIATELY, eg FROM A SOLICITOR OR SURVEYOR OR A CITIZENS ADVICE BUREAU.

1. This request is made under Section 26 of the Landlord and Tenant Act 1954.

2. You are the landlord of ....

   ....
   (description of property)

3. I/We request you to grant a new tenancy beginning on ....

4. I/We propose that:

   (a) the property comprised in the new tenancy should be ....

   ....

   ....

   (b) the rent payable under the new tenancy should be ....

   ....

   (c) the other terms of the new tenancy should be

†Cross out words in square brackets if they do not apply

5. All correspondence about this request should be sent to [the tenant] [the tenant's agent]† at the address given below.

   Date ....

   Signature of [tenant] [tenant's agent]† ....

Tenant's request for new tenancy of business premises

Form F817 (No. 8)
© Fourmat Publishing
133 Upper Street
London N1 1QP
October 1989

   Name of tenant ....

   Address of tenant ....

   ....

   [Address of agent ....

   ....]†
   (See notes overleaf)

218

Appendix B

Reverse side of Form F817: Tenant's request for new tenancy of business premises

NOTES

Request for a new tenancy

1. This request by your tenant for a new tenancy brings his current tenancy to an end on the day before the date mentioned in paragraph 3 above. He can apply to the court under the Landlord and Tenant Act 1954 for a new tenancy. If he does, his current tenancy will continue after the date mentioned in paragraph 3 of this request while his application is being considered by the court. You can ask the court to fix the rent which your tenant will have to pay whilst his tenancy continues. The terms of any *new* tenancy not agreed between you and your tenant will be settled by the court.

Opposing a request for a new tenancy

2. If you do not want to grant a new tenancy, you *must* within two months of the making of this request, give your tenant notice saying that you will oppose any application he makes to the court for a new tenancy. You do not need a special form to do this, but you must state on which of the grounds set out in the 1954 Act you will oppose the application — see note 4.

3. The time limit in note 2 runs from the making of this request. The date of the making of the request may not be the date written on the request or the date on which you actually saw it. It may, for instance, be the date on which the request was delivered through the post to your last address known to the person making the request. If there has been any delay in your seeing this request you may need to act very quickly. If you are in any doubt get advice immediately.

```
                WARNING TO LANDLORD
IF YOU DO NOT KEEP TO THE TIME LIMIT IN NOTE
2, YOU WILL LOSE YOUR RIGHT TO OPPOSE YOUR
TENANT'S APPLICATION TO THE COURT FOR A
NEW TENANCY IF HE MAKES ONE.
```

Grounds for opposing an application

4. If your tenant applies to the court for a new tenancy, you can only oppose the application on one or more of the grounds set out in section 30(1) of the 1954 Act. These grounds are set out below. The paragraph letters are those given in the Act.

Grounds

(a) where under the current tenancy the tenant has any obligations as respects the repair and maintenance of the holding, that the tenant ought not to be granted a new tenancy in view of the state of repair of the holding, being a state resulting from the tenant's failure to comply with the said obligations;

(b) that the tenant ought not to be granted a new tenancy in view of his persistent delay in paying rent which has become due;

(c) that the tenant ought not to be granted a new tenancy in view of other substantial breaches by him of his obligations under the current tenancy, or for any other reason connected with the tenant's use or management of the holding;

(d) that you have offered and are willing to provide or secure the provision of alternative accommodation for the tenant, that the terms on which the alternative accommodation is available are reasonable having regard to the terms of the current tenancy and to all other relevant circumstances, and that the accommodation and the time at which it will be available are suitable for the tenant's requirements (including the requirement to preserve goodwill) having regard to the nature and class of his business and to the situation and extent of, and facilities afforded by, the holding;

(e) where the current tenancy was created by the sub-letting of part only of the property comprised in a superior tenancy and you are the owner of an interest in reversion expectant on the termination of that superior tenancy, that the aggregate of the rents reasonably obtainable on separate lettings of the holding and the remainder of that property would be substantially less than the rent reasonably obtainable on a letting of that property as a whole, that on the termination of the current tenancy you require possession of the holding for the purpose of letting or otherwise disposing of the said property as a whole, and that in view thereof the tenant ought not to be granted a new tenancy;

(f) that on the termination of the current tenancy you intend to demolish or reconstruct the premises comprised in the holding or a substantial part of those premises or to carry out substantial work of construction on the holding or part thereof and that you could not reasonably do so without obtaining possession of the holding;

(If you use this ground, the court can sometimes still grant a new tenancy if certain conditions set out in section 31A of the Act can be met.)

(g) that on the termination of the current tenancy you intend to occupy the holding for the purposes, or partly for the purposes, of a business to be carried on by you therein, or as your residence.

(You must normally have been the landlord for at least five years to use this ground.)

You can only use one or more of the above grounds if you have stated them in the notice referred to in note 2 above.

Compensation

5. If your tenant cannot get a new tenancy solely because grounds *(e), (f)* or *(g)* apply, he is entitled to compensation from you under the 1954 Act. If you have opposed his application on any of the other grounds as well as *(e), (f)* or *(g)* he can only get compensation if the court's refusal to grant a new tenancy is based solely on grounds *(e), (f)* or *(g)*. In other words he cannot get compensation under the 1954 Act if the court has refused his tenancy on *other* grounds even if *(e), (f)* or *(g)* also apply.

6. If you are an authority possessing compulsory purchase powers (such as a local authority) you will be aware that your tenant may be entitled to a disturbance payment under Part III of the Land Compensation Act 1973.

Negotiating a new tenancy

7. Most leases are renewed by negotiation. If you do try to agree a new tenancy with your tenant—

(1) YOU should remember that you will not be able to oppose an application to the court for a new tenancy unless you give the notice mentioned in note 2 above within the time limit in that note;

(2) YOUR TENANT should remember that he will lose his right to apply to the court for a new tenancy unless he makes the application not less than two nor more than four months after the making of this request.

Validity of this notice

8. The landlord to whom this request is made may not be the landlord to whom the tenant pays the rent. "Business" is given a wide meaning in the 1954 Act and is used in the same sense in this request. The 1954 Act also has rules about the date which the tenant can put in paragraph 3. This depends on the terms of the tenancy. If you have any doubts about whether this request is valid, get immediate advice.

Explanatory booklet

9. The Department of the Environment and Welsh Office booklet "Business Leases and Security of Tenure" explains the main provisions of Part II of the 1954 Act. It is available from the Department of the Environment Publications Store, Building No. 3, Victoria Road, South Ruislip, Middlesex.

BUSINESS LEASES

4. Notice by landlord that he will oppose application for new business tenancy or new assured tenancy

NOTICE BY LANDLORD THAT HE WILL OPPOSE TENANT'S APPLICATION FOR NEW TENANCY OF BUSINESS PREMISES OR NEW ASSURED TENANCY

Landlord and Tenant Act 1954, Section 26

To: ....
(name of tenant)

of ....

....
(address of tenant)

This notice relates to ....

....
(description of property)
of which you are the tenant.

I/We have received, on ...., your Request under Part II of the Landlord and Tenant Act 1954 for a new tenancy of the above property.

I/We hereby give you notice that I/we will oppose your application on the following grounds:

State the grounds; see notes overleaf

Date ....

† Cross out words in square brackets if they do not apply

Signature of [landlord] [landlord's agent]† ....

Notice by landlord that he will oppose application for new business tenancy or new assured tenancy

Form F817A
© Fourmat Publishing
27/28 St. Alban's Place
London N1 0NX
April 1983

Address of landlord ....

....

[Address of landlord's agent ....

....]†

Notes: If the landlord wishes to oppose the tenant's application for a new tenancy, he must, within two months of the making of the tenant's request, serve notice on the tenant that he will oppose the application. The notice must state the grounds.

Appendix B

Reverse side of Form F817A: Notice by landlord that he will oppose application for new business tenancy or new assured tenancy

NOTES

The landlord may only oppose the application on one or more of the grounds set out in Section 30(1) of the Landlord and Tenant Act 1954. These grounds are set out below:

(a) where under the current tenancy the tenant has any obligations as respects the repair and maintenance of the holding, that the tenant ought not to be granted a new tenancy in view of the state of repair of the holding, being a state resulting from the tenant's failure to comply with the said obligations;

(b) that the tenant ought not to be granted a new tenancy in view of his persistent delay in paying rent which has become due;

(c) that the tenant ought not to be granted a new tenancy in view of other substantial breaches by him of his obligations under the current tenancy, or for any other reason connected with the tenant's use or management of the holding;

(d) that the landlord has offered and is willing to provide or secure the provision of alternative accommodation for the tenant, that the terms on which the alternative accommodation is available are reasonable having regard to the terms of the current tenancy and to all other relevant circumstances, and that the accommodation and the time at which it will be available are suitable for the tenant's requirements (including the requirement to preserve goodwill) having regard to the nature and class of his business and to the situation and extent of, and facilities afforded by, the holding. In the case of an assured tenancy, the 1954 Act, as applied by the Housing Act 1980, lays down detailed rules about what accommodation is "suitable";

(e) where the current tenancy was created by the sub-letting of part only of the property comprised in a superior tenancy and the landlord is the owner of an interest in reversion expectant on the termination of that superior tenancy, that the aggregate of the rents reasonably obtainable on separate lettings of the holding and the remainder of that property would be substantially less than the rent reasonably obtainable on a letting of that property as a whole, that on the termination of the current tenancy the landlord requires possession of the holding for the purposes of letting or otherwise disposing of the said property as a whole, and that in view thereof the tenant ought not to be granted a new tenancy;

(f) that on the termination of the current tenancy the landlord intends to demolish or reconstruct the premises comprised in the holding or a substantial part of those premises or to carry out substantial work of construction on the holding or part thereof and that he could not reasonably do so without obtaining possession of the holding;
(If the landlord uses this ground, the court can sometimes still grant a new tenancy if certain conditions set out in section 31A of the Act can be met.)

(g) that on the termination of the current tenancy the landlord intends to occupy the holding for the purposes, or partly for the purposes, of a business to be carried on by him therein, or as his residence.
(The landlord must normally have been the landlord for at least five years to use this ground.)

BUSINESS LEASES

5. Notice by landlord requiring information about occupation and sub-tenancies of business premises

LF818: Notice by landlord requiring information about occupation and sub-tenancies of business premises
(The Landlord and Tenant Act 1954 Part II (Notices) Regulations 1983, Form 9)

NOTICE BY LANDLORD REQUIRING INFORMATION ABOUT OCCUPATION AND SUB-TENANCIES OF BUSINESS PREMISES
(Landlord and Tenant Act 1954, section 40(1))

To (name of tenant) ....
Of (address of tenant) ....
....

IMPORTANT - THIS NOTICE REQUIRES YOU TO GIVE YOUR LANDLORD CERTAIN INFORMATION. YOU MUST ACT QUICKLY. READ THE NOTICE AND ALL THE NOTES CAREFULLY. IF YOU ARE IN ANY DOUBT ABOUT THE ACTION YOU SHOULD TAKE, GET ADVICE IMMEDIATELY, EG FROM A SOLICITOR OR SURVEYOR OR A CITIZENS ADVICE BUREAU.

1. This notice is given under section 40(1) of the Landlord and Tenant Act 1954.

2. It relates to (description of business premises) ....
   ....
   of which you are the tenant.

3. I/We require you to notify me/us in writing, within one month of the service of this notice on you:
   (a) whether you occupy the premises or any part of them wholly or partly for business purposes; and
   (b) whether you have a sub-tenant.

4. If you have a sub-tenant, I/we also require you to state:
   (a) what premises are comprised in the sub-tenancy;
   (b) if the sub-tenancy is for a fixed term, what the term is, or, if the sub-tenancy is terminable by notice, by what notice it can be terminated;
   (c) what rent the sub-tenant pays;
   (d) the sub-tenant's full name;
   (e) whether, to the best of your knowledge and belief, the sub-tenant occupies either the whole or part of the premises sub-let to him and, if not, what is his address.

5. All correspondence about this notice should be sent to [†][the landlord] [the landlord's agent] at the address given below.

Date ....

Signature of † [landlord] [landlord's agent] ....

Name of landlord ....

Address of landlord ....
....
†[Address of agent ....
....]

† Cross out words in square brackets if they do not apply

See notes overleaf

Appendix B

Reverse side of Form LF818: Notice by landlord requiring information about occupation and sub-tenancies of business premises

Notes

Purpose of this notice
1. Your landlord (or if he is a tenant himself, possibly his landlord) has served this notice on you to obtain the information he needs in order to find out his position under Part II of the Landlord and Tenant Act 1954 in relation to your tenancy. He will then know, for example, whether, when your tenancy expires, you will be entitled to apply to the court for a new tenancy of the whole of the premises comprised in your present tenancy; you may not be entitled to a new tenancy of any part of the premises which you have sub-let. (In certain circumstances, a sub-tenant may become a direct tenant of the landlord.)

Replying to this notice
2. Section 40 of the 1954 Act says that you *must* answer the questions asked in the notice and you *must* let the landlord have your answers in writing within one month of the service of the notice. You do not need a special form for this. If you don't answer these questions or give the landlord incorrect information he might suffer a loss for which, in certain circumstances, you could be held liable.

3. If you have let to more than one sub-tenant you should give the information required in respect of each sub-letting.

Validity of this notice
4. The landlord who has given this notice may not be the landlord to whom you pay your rent. "Business" is given a wide meaning in the 1954 Act and is used in the same sense in this notice. The landlord cannot ask for this information earlier than two years before your tenancy is due to expire or could be brought to an end by notice given by him. If you have any doubts about whether this notice is valid get immediate advice.

Explanatory booklet
5. The Department of the Environment and Welsh Office booklet "Business Leases and Security of Tenure" explains the main provisions of Part II of the 1954 Act. It is available from the Department of the Environment Publications Store, Building No. 3, Victoria Road, South Ruislip, Middlesex.

© September 1989   Fourmat Publishing 133 Upper Street London N1 1QP

BUSINESS LEASES

6. Notice by tenant of business premises requiring information from landlord about landlord's interest

NOTICE BY TENANT OF BUSINESS PREMISES REQUIRING INFORMATION FROM LANDLORD ABOUT LANDLORD'S INTEREST

Landlord and Tenant Act 1954 Section 40(2)

To: ....
(name of landlord)

of ....

....
(address of landlord)

> IMPORTANT — THIS NOTICE REQUIRES YOU TO GIVE YOUR TENANT CERTAIN INFORMATION. YOU MUST ACT QUICKLY. READ THE NOTICE AND ALL THE NOTES CAREFULLY. IF YOU ARE IN ANY DOUBT ABOUT THE ACTION YOU SHOULD TAKE, GET ADVICE IMMEDIATELY, eg FROM A SOLICITOR OR SURVEYOR OR A CITIZENS ADVICE BUREAU.

1. This notice is given under Section 40(2) of the Landlord and Tenant Act 1954.

2. It relates to ....

....
(description of business premises)

   of which you are the landlord.

3. I/We give you notice requiring you to notify me/us in writing, within one month of the service of this notice on you:

   (a) whether you are the freeholder of the whole or part of the premises.
   If you are *not* the freeholder:
   (b) I/We also require you to state, to the best of your knowledge and belief:
      (i) the name and address of the person who is your immediate landlord in respect of the premises or the part of which you are not the freeholder;
      (ii) the length of your tenancy; and
      (iii) the earliest date (if any) at which your tenancy can be terminated by notice to quit given by your immediate landlord.

4. I/We also require you to notify me/us:
   (a) whether there is a mortgagee in possession of your interest in the property and, if so, his name and address; and
   (b) if there is a receiver appointed by the mortgagee or by the court, his name and address also.

5. All correspondence about this notice should be sent to [the tenant] [the tenant's agent]† at the address given below.

†Cross out words in square brackets if they do not apply

Date ....

Signature of [tenant] [tenant's agent]† ....

Notice by tenant of business premises requiring information from landlord about landlord's interest

Name of tenant ....

Address of tenant ....

....

Form F822 (No. 10)
© Fourmat Publishing
27/28 St. Alban's Place
London N1 0NX
April 1983

[Address of agent ....

....]†
(See notes overleaf)

Appendix B

Reverse side of Form F822: Notice by tenant of business premises requiring information from landlord about landlord's interest

NOTES

Purpose of this notice

1. Your tenant has served this notice on you to obtain the information he needs in order to find out who is his landlord for the purposes of Part II of the Landlord and Tenant Act 1954. The Act in certain circumstances enables a tenant of business premises to obtain a new tenancy from that landlord.

Replying to this notice

2. Section 40 of the 1954 Act says that you *must* answer the questions asked in the notice and you *must* let your tenant have your answers in writing within one month of the service of this notice. You do not need a special form for this. If you do not answer these questions or give your tenant incorrect information he might suffer a loss for which, in certain circumstances, you could be held liable.

Validity of this notice

3. "Business" is given a wide meaning in the 1954 Act and is used in the same sense in this notice. Your tenant cannot ask for this information earlier than two years before his current tenancy is due to expire or could be brought to an end by notice to quit given by you. If you have any doubts about whether this notice is valid, get immediate advice.

Explanatory booklet

4. The Department of the Environment booklet "Business Tenancies" explains the provisions of Part II of the 1954 Act in more detail than these notes. It is available from Her Majesty's Stationery Office or through booksellers.

BUSINESS LEASES

7. Notice by tenant of business premises requiring information from mortgagee about landlord's interest

LF 880: Landlord & Tenant Act 1954 Part II (Notices) Regulations 1983 Form 11

NOTICE BY TENANT OF BUSINESS PREMISES REQUIRING INFORMATION FROM MORTGAGEE ABOUT LANDLORD'S INTEREST
(Landlord & Tenant Act 1954, s.40(2))

To: (Name of mortgagee)

of (Address of mortgagee)

IMPORTANT - THIS NOTICE REQUIRES YOU TO GIVE THE TENANT OF PREMISES OF WHICH YOU ARE THE MORTGAGEE IN POSSESSION, CERTAIN INFORMATION. YOU MUST ACT QUICKLY. READ THE NOTICE AND ALL THE NOTES CAREFULLY. IF YOU ARE IN DOUBT ABOUT THE ACTION YOU SHOULD TAKE GET ADVICE IMMEDIATELY eg FROM A SOLICITOR OR SURVEYOR OR A CITIZENS ADVICE BUREAU.

1. This notice is given under section 40(2) of the Landlord and Tenant Act 1954.

2. It relates to (Description of business premises)

   which [I] [we] believe to be in mortgage to you.

3. [I][We] give you notice requiring you to notify [me] [us] in writing, within one month of the service of this notice on you:
   (a) whether the mortgagor is the freeholder of the whole or part of the premises;
   If he is not the freeholder:
   (b) [I][we] also require you to state, to the best of your knowledge and belief:
      (i) the name and address of the person who is your mortgagor's immediate landlord in respect of the premises or part of which he is not the freeholder;
      (ii) the length of your mortgagor's tenancy; and
      (iii) the earliest date (if any) at which his tenancy can be terminated by notice to quit given by his immediate landlord.

4. All correspondence about this notice should be sent to †[the tenant] [the tenant's agent] at the address given below.

Date:

Signature of †[tenant] [tenant's agent]

Name of tenant:
Address of tenant:

[Address of agent:

† Cross out words in square brackets if they do not apply]†

Notes
Purpose of this notice
1. You are either the mortgagee in possession of business premises or a receiver appointed by the mortgagee or by the court. A tenant of the whole or part of the premises has served this notice on you to obtain the information he needs in order to find out who is his landlord for the purposes of Part II of the Landlord and Tenant Act 1954. The Act in certain circumstances enables a tenant of business premises to obtain a new tenancy from that landlord.
Replying to this notice
2. Section 40 of the 1954 Act says that you <u>must</u> answer the questions asked in this notice and you <u>must</u> let the tenant have your answers in writing within one month of the service of this notice. You do not need a special form for this. If you do not answer these questions or give the tenant incorrect information he might suffer a loss for which in certain circumstances, you could be held liable.
Validity of this notice
3. "Business" is given a wide meaning in the 1954 Act and is used in the same sense in this notice. The tenant cannot ask for this information earlier than two years before his current tenancy is due to expire or could be brought to an end by notice to quit given by his landlord. If you have any doubts about whether this notice is valid, get immediate advice.
Explanatory booklet
4. The Department of the Environment and Welsh Office booklet "Business Leases and Security of Tenure" explains the main provisions of Part II of the 1954 Act. It is available from the Department of the Environment Publications Store, Building No. 3, Victoria Road, South Ruislip, Middlesex.

© September 1989   Fourmat Publishing 133 Upper Street London N1 1QP

Appendix B

8. Withdrawal of landlord's notice to terminate business tenancy

LF 881: Landlord & Tenant Act 1954, Part II (Notices) Regulations 1983, Form 12

WITHDRAWAL OF LANDLORD'S NOTICE TO TERMINATE BUSINESS TENANCY
(Landlord & Tenant Act 1954, s.44 & para. 6 of Sched. 6)

To (name of tenant)

of (address of tenant)

IMPORTANT- THIS NOTICE IS INTENDED TO WITHDRAW A PREVIOUS NOTICE TO TERMINATE YOUR TENANCY. READ THIS NOTICE AND ALL THE NOTES CAREFULLY. IF YOU ARE IN ANY DOUBT ABOUT YOUR POSITION, GET ADVICE IMMEDIATELY, eg FROM A SOLICITOR OR SURVEYOR OR A CITIZENS' ADVICE BUREAU.

1. This notice is given under section 44 of, and paragraph 6 of Schedule 6 to, the Landlord and Tenant Act 1954.

2. It relates to (description of property)

    of which you are the tenant.

3. [I] [We] have become your landlord for the purposes of the Act.

4. [I] [We] withdraw the notice given to you by (name of former landlord)

    of (address of former landlord)

    terminating your tenancy on

5. Any correspondence about this notice should be sent to †[the landlord] [the landlord's agent] at the address given below.

Date:
Signature of †[landlord] [landlord's agent] ....

Name of landlord:

Address of landlord:

[Address of agent:]

†Cross out words in square brackets if they do not apply

Notes
Purpose of this notice
1. You were earlier given a notice bringing your tenancy to an end, but there has now been a change of landlord for the purposes of the 1954 Act. This new notice has been given to you by your new landlord and withdraws the earlier notice, which now has no effect. However, the new landlord can, if he wishes, give you a fresh notice with the intention of bringing your tenancy to an end.
Validity of this notice
2. The landlord who has given notice may not be the landlord to whom you pay your rent. "Business" is given a wide meaning in the 1954 Act and is used in the same sense in this notice. This notice can only be given within two months after the giving of the earlier notice. If you have any doubts about whether this notice is valid, get immediate advice. If it is *not* valid you may have to act quickly to preserve your position under the earlier notice.
Explanatory booklet
3. The Department of the Environment and Welsh Office booklet "Business Leases and Security of Tenure" explains the main provisions of Part II of the 1954 Act. It is available from the Department of the Environment Publications Store, Building No. 3, Victoria Road, South Ruislip, Middlesex.

© September 1989   Fourmat Publishing 133 Upper Street London N1 1QP

BUSINESS LEASES

9. Originating application for new tenancy under Part II of the Landlord and Tenant Act 1954

IN THE   COUNTY COURT

Case no:

In the matter of the Landlord and Tenant Act 1954

Between

and

Applicant

Respondent

1   I,
      of

apply to the Court for the grant of a new tenancy pursuant to Part II of the Landlord and Tenant Act 1954.

2   The premises to which this application relates are *(address of premises)*:

3   The rateable value of the premises is

4   The nature of the business carried on at the premises is

5   The following are particulars of my current tenancy of the premises:

     (a) *(Date of lease or agreement for a lease or tenancy agreement)*

     (b) *(Names of parties to lease or agreement)*

     (c) *(Term granted by lease or agreement)*

     (d) *(Rent reserved by lease or agreement)*

     (e) *(Terms as to date and mode of termination of tenancy)*

     (f) *(Whether any and, if so, what part of the property comprised in the tenancy is occupied neither by the tenant, nor by a person employed by the tenant for the purposes of the business carried on by the tenant in the premises)*

6   On   19   the Respondent served on me a notice to terminate dated in accordance with the provisions of Section 25 of the Act giving   19   as the date for termination and stating that the Respondent would [not] oppose an application to this Court for a new tenancy.

[On   19   I served on the Respondent a counter notice dated   19   stating that I would not be willing to give up possession of the premises on the date of termination] *or*

P.T.O.

Originating application for new tenancy under Part II of the Landlord and Tenant Act 1954
(O.43, r.6(1))

Form F819 (N397)
© Fourmat Publishing
27/28 St. Albans Place
London N1 0NX
December 1984

Appendix B

Reverse side of Form F819: Originating application for new tenancy under Part II of the Landlord and Tenant Act 1954

[On   19   I served on the Respondent a request
dated   19   for a new tenancy in accordance with
the provisions of Section 26 of the Act specifying

19   as the date for the commencement of the new tenancy.] [The Respondent has not served on me any counter notice] *or* [On

19   the Respondent served on me a counter notice dated

19   stating that he would oppose an application to the Court for the grant of a new tenancy.]

7   The following are my proposals as to the period, rent and other terms of the new tenancy for which I am applying:

8   The following persons are to my knowledge interested in reversion in the premises on the termination of my current tenancy:*   * Names and addresses and nature of interest in the premises (whether immediately or in not more than 14 years) of persons other than the Respondent

9   The following other persons have to my knowledge an interest in the premises other than a freehold interest and are likely to be affected by the grant of a new tenancy:†   † Names and addresses and nature of interest

10 The names and address of the Respondent on whom this application is intended to be served:

11 My address for service is:

Dated this   day of   19

Solicitor for the Applicant

229

BUSINESS LEASES

10. Answer to originating application for new tenancy under Part II of the Landlord and Tenant Act 1954

IN THE   COUNTY COURT

Case no:

In the matter of the Landlord and Tenant Act 1954

Between

                                    Applicant

and

                                      Respondent

I,
of

the respondent in this matter, in answer to the application of

for a new tenancy of the premises known as

say that

Strike out the statements which do not apply

(1) Here set out the grounds

1 *[I do not oppose the grant of a new tenancy]
   [I oppose the grant of a new tenancy on the following grounds stated in my notice under section [25] [26(6)] of the Act, namely (1)

]

(2) Here set out the terms to which you object

2 If a new tenancy is granted, *[I do not object to its being granted on the terms proposed by the applicant] *[I object to its being granted on the following terms proposed by the applicant namely(2)

Answer to originating
application for new
tenancy under Part II
of The Landlord
and Tenant Act 1954
(O.43, r.7)

Form F820 (N400)
© Fourmat Publishing
27/28 St. Albans Place
London N1 0NX
September 1983

PTO

Appendix B

Reverse side of Form F820: Answer to originating application for new tenancy under Part II of the Landlord and Tenant Act 1954

and the following are my counterproposals as to the period, rent and other terms of such a new tenancy:

]

3 *[I am not a tenant under a lease having less than 14 years unexpired at the date of the termination of the applicant's current tenancy.]
*[I am a tenant under a lease having less than 14 years unexpired at the date of the termination of the applicant's current tenancy and the name and address of the person[s] having an interest in the reversion expectant on the termination of the respondent's tenancy immediately or within not more than 14 years of the date of such termination [is] [are]: (3)

(3) Here set out the names and addresses of any reversioners

4 The following persons are to my knowledge likely to be affected by the grant of a new tenancy: (4)

(4) Here set out the names, addresses and nature of the interests in the premises of all persons, other than a freeholder or a tenant, who are likely to be affected

[5 I require that any new tenancy ordered to be granted shall be a tenancy of the whole of the property comprised in the applicant's current tenancy.] (5)

[6 I hereby apply to the court under Section 24A of the Act to determine a rent which it would be reasonable for the applicant to pay while the tenancy continues by virtue of Section 24 of the Act.] (6)

(5) If the applicant's current tenancy is one to which section 32(2) of the Act applies, include this paragraph if required

(6) Include this paragraph if required

Dated this   day of   19

Solicitor for the Respondent

231

BUSINESS LEASES

11. Notice of proceedings

<table>
<tr><td>IN THE</td><td>COUNTY COURT</td></tr>
</table>

Case no:

In the matter of the Landlord and Tenant Act 1954

Between

and

Applicant

Respondent

To
of

TAKE NOTICE that

* Delete as appropriate

the landlord/tenant* of the premises known as

† Here state shortly the nature of the relief claimed

has made an application to the   County Court
under the Landlord and Tenant Act 1954 for†

and that the application has been fixed for hearing/pre-trial review* at

on   day, the   day of   19
at   o'clock

Notice of proceedings
(O.43, r.14)

Your attention is drawn to the Note below

Form F821 (N405)
© Fourmat Publishing
27 & 28 St Albans Place
London N1 0NX
November 1987

Note: The County Court Rules provide that any person served with a notice in this form who wishes to be made a party to the proceedings must within 8 days from receipt of the notice apply to the court for directions *(O.43, r.14(1))*.

Index

Agreement to grant of a new lease 61, 76, 82
    application to court, after .... 89 – 90
    registration of 82
Agreement to terms of a new lease 131
Agricultural tenancies .... 44 – 46, 149
Application for new tenancy following landlord's notice
    or tenant's request .... 80 – 81
    costs of .... 86, 131 – 132
    jurisdiction to hear .... 82 – 83
    number of properties covered by 84
    opposition to, landlord's grounds of .... 98 – 118
    parties to .... 83 – 84
    procedural rules governing:
        county court proceedings .... 84 – 85
        High Court proceedings .... 85 – 86
    registration of .... 86 – 87
    rejection of .... 119 – 130
        compensation for disturbance, and .... 121 – 127, 128 – 129
        compensation for misrepresentation, and .... 129 – 130
    time limits for .... 87 – 89
    withdrawal of .... 89 – 90
Avoidance measures – see *Contracting out*

Break clauses .... 134 – 135
"Business":
    definitions of .... 151 – 152
    occupation for the purposes of a .... 39 – 44
        ancillary user .... 41 – 42
        mixed user, and .... 42 – 43
        unauthorised user, and .... 43 – 44
    use for the purposes of a .... 150 – 151
"Business tenants", special provision relating to 23

Common law methods of termination of lease 10
Compensation:
    disturbance, for .... 121 – 124
        amount of .... 124 – 126, 126 – 127
        exclusion of right to .... 128 – 129
        right to renew is excluded, where .... 28, 123 – 124

improvements, for .... 144 – 168
misrepresentation, for .... 129 – 130
Continuation tenancy .... 10, 11, 55 – 57, 134
   determination by court, pending .... 120 – 121
   interim rent during .... 91 – 97
     application for .... 92 – 94
     calculation of .... 95 – 97
   termination of by landlord .... 59 – 60
   termination of by tenant .... 57 – 59
Contracting out .... 27 – 28, 49 – 54, 152
   compensation, exclusion of the right to .... 28, 128 – 129
   tenant's improvements, in relation to .... 165 – 166
Costs:
   tenant's application for new tenancy, and .... 86, 131 – 132
   tenant's application for revocation, and .... 131 – 132
Counternotice:
   landlord, by 12, 80, 81
     grounds of opposition .... 98 – 118
   tenant, by .... 73 – 75
Covenant, breach of – see *Forfeiture*
Crown, the:
   landlord, as .... 23 – 24, 49
   tenant, as 24
   See also *Government departments*

Ecclesiastical property, special provisions relating to .... 28 – 29
Excluded tenancies .... 44 – 49, 52 – 53
   agricultural tenancies .... 44 – 46
   avoidance measures designed to create .... 51 – 54
   contract out, agreements to .... 49 – 51
   Crown as landlord .... 23 – 24, 49
   government department as landlord 49
   mining leases 46
   on-licensed premises .... 46 – 48
   residential user 46
   service tenancies 48
   short tenancies 48
   surrender, tenancies terminated by .... 52 – 53
   tenancies at will 49
Exclusive possession .... 31, 32 – 33, 34

Forfeiture .... 10, 59 – 60, 98

Government departments:
   landlord, as .... 24 – 27
     contracting out of statutory provisions, and .... 27 – 28

Index

```
    national security, tenant's right to renew refused on
        grounds of  ..................................... 26 – 27
    public interest, tenant's right to renew refused on
        grounds of  ..................................... 25 – 26
    tenant, as  ........................................... 24
Grounds of opposition to new lease, landlord's  ............ 98 – 118
    ground A: breach of repair  ............................. 99
    ground B: rent arrears  ............................. 99 – 100
    ground C: breaches of other obligations  ............... 100 – 102
    ground D: alternative accommodation  ................ 102 – 103
    ground E: uneconomic subletting  ..................... 103 – 104
    ground F: demolition and reconstruction  ............. 104 – 113
        intention  ..................................... 104 – 109
        landlord's need for possession  ................. 111 – 113
        nature of intended works  ....................... 109 – 111
    ground G: own occupation  ............................ 113 – 118
        business or residential purposes  ................... 116
        five years as landlord  ......................... 116 – 118
        intention  ......................................... 114
        occupation  .................................... 114 – 116
    misrepresentation in  ......................... 81 – 82, 129 – 130

Holding over by tenant – see *Continuation tenancy*

Improvements, compensation for  ....................... 144 – 168
    avoidance by landlord of statutory provisions
        relating to  ................................... 165 – 166
    "improvement", classification of work as  ............ 152 – 154
        qualifying conditions  ......................... 154 – 156
    procedural steps for obtaining  ...................... 156 – 166
        certificate of due execution  .................. 160 – 161
        certificate of "proper improvement"  ............ 159 – 160
        notice of claim for compensation  ............... 161 – 162
        objection by landlord  ......................... 158 – 159
        preliminary notice of intention  ................ 157 – 158
        right to payment  .............................. 161 – 162
        time limits for notice of claim  ............... 162 – 163
    quantum  ............................................ 163 – 164
    reclaiming from a superior landlord  ................. 164 – 165
    tenancies falling outside scope of statutory provsions
        relating to  ................................... 148 – 150
    tenancies falling within scope of statutory provisions
        relating to  ................................... 146 – 147
        "lease", definition of  ............................ 148
        "premises", definition of  ..................... 147 – 148
        "trade or business", definition of  ............. 151 – 152
```

"used wholly or partly" for a trade or business,
    definition of 150–151
  tenant's statutory rights in relation to 145–146
Information gathering, by service of a s 40 notice 17–18, 38
Interim tenancy – see *Continuation tenancy*

Joint tenancy 22–23, 38, 83
Jurisdiction of courts to determine applications 82–83

Landlord:
  competent 14–16, 63–64
    relationship of with mesne and superior landlord 18–20
  Crown, as 23–24, 49
  government department, as 24–27
  immediate 14, 16
  mesne 18, 19–20, 164–165
  superior 18, 84, 164–165
Landlord and Tenant Act 1927:
  compensation for tenant's improvements, provisions
    relating to 144–151, 152–162
    comparison with 1954 Act 151–152
  effect of 2–3
  Part I 6, 171–177
  service of notices, provisions relating to modes of 21–22
Landlord and Tenant Act 1954, Part II 178–197
  avoidance measures, and 51–54
    offer back clauses 53–54
    surrenders 52–53
  comparison with 1927 Act 151–152
  contracting out of provisions of 27–28, 49–54
    compensation, and 28, 128–129
  excluded tenancies 44–49, 52–53
    agricultural tenancies 44–46
    Crown as landlord 49
    government department as landlord 49
    mining leases 46
    on-licensed premises 46–48
    residential user 46
    service tenancies 48
    short tenancies 48
    tenancies at will 49
    tenancies terminated by surrender 52–53
  interplay of provisions of 12–14
  landlord's notice under s 25 .... 11, 12, 21, 56, 59, 63–73
    tenant's counternotice 73–75
  operation of provisions of, in outline 10–12
  pre-requisites for application of provisions of 30–44

Index

    authorised business use .... 43 – 44
    business, for purposes of a .... 39 – 44
    lease, as opposed to a licence .... 30 – 35
    occupation by tenant .... 36 – 39
    premises, tenancy of .... 35 – 36
  security of tenure provisions of, in outline .... 9 – 14
  tenant's request under s 26 for new tenancy .... 76 – 81
    landlord's counternotice .... 81 – 82
    tenant's application to court for new tenancy .... 82 – 90
Law of Property Act 1969 .... 5 – 6, 9, 49 – 50, 122
Licence, as opposed to a lease .... 30 – 35, 148
Licensed premises .... 46 – 48, 141

Mesne landlords .... 18, 19 – 20, 164 – 165
Mining leases .... 46, 148 – 149
Misrepresentation in landlord's grounds of opposition .... 81 – 82
  compensation for .... 129 – 130
Mixed user .... 42 – 43, 150 – 151

National security, as ground for refusal of tenant's
  right to renew .... 26 – 27
New lease granted by court .... 131 – 143
  agreement to 61, 76, 82
  application for revocation of .... 131 – 132
  terms of .... 131 – 143
    change of .... 141 – 143
    commencement date .... 135 – 136
    duration .... 133 – 136
    property comprised in the holding .... 132 – 133
    rent, assessment of .... 137 – 141
    rent review clause, incorporation of into 141
New lease, statutory provisions for – see *Renewal procedure, statutory*
Notice, landlord's (s 25) .... 11, 12, 21, 56, 59, 63 – 73
  competent landlord, and .... 63 – 64
  counternotice by tenant .... 73 – 75
  form and content .... 65 – 68
    defects and omissions in .... 68 – 71
  government department as landlord, and .... 25 – 26, 27
  grounds of opposition contained in .... 98 – 118
    misrepresentation, and .... 81 – 82, 129 – 130
  "pre-emptive strike" by tenant .... 76 – 78
  split reversions, and .... 71 – 73
  sub-tenants, and 64
  superior landlord, and 20
  timing of service of 65

Notice, service under s 40 .... 17–18, 38
Notice to quit, tenant's (s 27) 10–11, 12, 56, 58–59

"Occupation" by tenant, meaning of 36–39
   beneficiaries, partnerships and companies, in relation to ... 38–39
   "use" by tenant, as compared with 150
Offer back clauses 53–54

Parties to court proceedings, to determine tenant's
   application 83–84
Partnerships 22–23, 38
"Pre-emptive strike" by tenant (s 26) 76–78
"Premises" meaning of 35–36
Proceedings, court, in relation to application for lease
   renewal 82–89
   costs 86
   county court, in 84–85
   High Court, in 85–86
   parties 83
   registration of tenant's application 86–87
   time limits, and 87–89
   withdrawal of application, and 89–90
Public interest, as ground for refusal of tenant's right
   to renew 25–26

Registration:
   agreement to new lease, of 82
   tenant's application to court, of 86–87
Rejection of a new tenancy by the court 11
Renewal procedure, statutory 63–90
   diagrammatic form, in 13
   landlord, by 63–75
   tenant, by 76–87
   time limits relating to 87–89
   See also *Notice, landlord's (s 25); Request for new tenancy,
   tenant's (s 26)*
Rent:
   interim 91–97
     application for 92–94
     commencement of 94–95
     quantum 95–97
   new lease, and 137–141
Request for new tenancy, tenant's (s 26) 12, 57, 59, 76–90
   availability of the right 78–79
   counternotice, landlord's 12, 80, 81
   effect of 80–81
   form and content 79–80
     defects in 79, 81

Index

government department as landlord, and 24–27
    compensation payable to tenant 123–124
Reversionary leases 18–20, 84
    compensation for improvements, and 165
Revocation, tenant's application for 131–132
    costs, and 131–132

Service of notices, modes of 21–22
    partnerships and joint tenancies 22–23
Service tenancies 48
Short tenancies 48
Statutory protection:
    development of 1–8
    leases qualifying for 30–44
        contracting out and avoidance of statutory rights 49–54
        excluded tenancies 44–49
Statutory undertakers as landlord 25, 28, 51
Sub-tenants, statutory protection of 18–20
    compensation for improvements, and 164–165
Superior landlords 18, 84, 164–165
Surrender 10, 52–53, 61–62
    agreements to 52–53, 61–62

Tenancies at will 49
Tenant's application for new tenancy – see *Application for new tenancy following landlord's notice or tenant's request*
Tenant's request for new tenancy – see *Request for new tenancy, tenant's (s 26)*
Termination, means of 10–11
    agreement, by 52–53, 61–62, 76, 82
        grant new lease, to 61, 76, 82
        surrender lease, to 52–53, 61–62
    landlord, by 59–61
    tenant, by 57–59
Time limits for applications to court 87–89
Trustee tenants 38, 83, 164

Unauthorised business use 43–44, 152